MW01243413

Platonic Myth and Platonic Writing

A Philosophico-Literary Exploration

revised edition

by

Dr. Robert Zaslavsky

ISBN-10: 1532906838
ISBN-13: 978-1532906831

To my daughter

CORDELIA

"So young my lord, and true."
—*King Lear* I. i. 106

TABLE OF CONTENTS

	Acknowledgements	vii
	Note On Translations	vii
I.	Introduction	1
II.	Λόγος and Μῦθος	5
III.	Platonic Writing	9
IV.	The Platonic Myth: *The Seventh Epistle* 341b7-345c3	13
V.	The Socratic Myth: *Phaedrus*	25
VI.	The *Republic* Tetralogy: *Republic*, *Timaeus*, *Critias*, [*Hermocrates*]	63
VII.	A Non-Myth and Myths: *Gorgias*, *Protagoras*, *Phaedo*, *Theaetetus*	87
VIII.	Paramyths: *Republic*, *Laws*, *Phaedo*	97
IX	Conclusion	101
	Appendix I: ΜΥΘΟΣ and its derivatives in the Platonic corpus	105
	Appendix II: *Epistles* 7. 341b7-345c3	113
	Bibliography	117
	Index	123
	English	123
	Greek	129

All yet seems well, and if it end so meet,
The bitter past, more welcome is the sweet
—*All's Well That Ends Well*, V. iii. 327-328

ACKNOWLEDGEMENTS

Although I owe far too much to far too many others ever to repay them properly, yet insofar as the acknowledgement of a felt debt is a repayment in however small a measure, the acknowledgement must be made—

To my parents, Harry and Sally Zaslavsky, against whose better judgment I decided to study philosophy, but through whose rearing I had the tenacity to do so anyway, for good or for ill.

To my first teachers at Temple University: Robert Anderson, later of Chestertown College, who taught me that in the reading of philosophical texts less could be more and the canon of philosophers as circumscribed by philosophy departments is far too small; Victor Gourevitch, later of Wesleyan, who taught me how to read a philosophical text word by word and who introduced me to the writings of Leo Strauss; William Rossky, now deceased, whose pedagogy demonstrated to me that a person formally untrained in philosophy could still be philosophical.

To my teachers in the graduate department of English Literature at New York University, who showed me that academically I belonged—if anywhere—in philosophy.

To my teachers (now all deceased) in the Philosophy Department of the Graduate Faculty of the New School for Social Research: Hans Jonas, whose lecturing showed me the power of philosophy and whose breadth showed me that philosophy need not be a narrow cell; Aron Gurwitsch, whose lectures and counsel (especially in the year during which I was his teaching assistant) opened up to me the tradition of modern rationalism and whose classes were like cathedrals of clarity; Howard White, whose seminars were exhilarating journeys through the great texts in political philosophy, from Plato and Aristotle to Shakespeare, from Jefferson to Melville, and who taught me that philosophy is always a journey without an end; Seth Benardete, whose command of ancient languages made them seem new and inspired many to learn them, whose lectures on ancient texts were models of thoroughness, whose mesmeric διδασκαλία drew from his students work far beyond that of which they believed themselves capable, and whose person demonstrated that brilliance and scholarly competence could be combined. Anyone who studied at the Graduate Faculty in the middle of the last century realizes what a privileged place it was for the study of philosophy.

To my daughter, Cordelia, now fully grown with a family of her own, who as a child bore all the irascibilities that attended the writing of the initial version of this manuscript and who forbore scorning me or it; to her this book is dedicated—I would that if she reads in it now, so many years from its initial composition, she is not embarrassed for her father on account of it.

NOTE ON TRANSLATIONS

Unless otherwise specified, all translations are mine.

Having a Desire to see those Antients, who were most renowned for Wit and Learning, I set apart one Day on purpose. I proposed that *Homer* and *Aristotle* might appear at the Head of all their Commentators; but these were so numerous, that some Hundreds were forced to attend in the Court and outward Rooms of the Palace. I knew and could distinguish those two Heroes at first Sight, not only from the Croud, but from each other. *Homer* was the taller and comelier Person of the two, walked very erect for one of his Age, and his Eyes were the most quick and piercing I ever beheld. *Aristotle* stooped much, and made use of a Staff. His Visage was meager, his Hair lank and thin, and his Voice hollow. I soon discovered that both of them were perfect Strangers to the rest of the Company, and had never seen or heard of them before. And I had a Whisper from a Ghost, who shall be nameless, that these Commentators always kept in the most distant Quarters from their Principals in the lower World, through a Consciousness of Shame and Guilt, because they had so horribly misrepresented the Meaning of those Authors to Posterity. I introduced *Didymus* and *Eustathius* to *Homer*, and prevailed on him to treat them better than perhaps they deserved; for he soon found they wanted a Genius to enter into the Spirit of a Poet. But *Aristotle* was out of all Patience with the Account I gave him of *Scotus* and *Ramus*, as I presented them to him; and he asked them whether the rest of the Tribe were as great Dunces as themselves.

—Lemuel Gulliver, in *Gulliver's Travels*,
Part III, Chapter VIII,
in *The Writings of Jonathan Swift*,
edd. Robert A. Greenberg and William B. Piper
(NY, Norton Critical Edition, 1973), pp. 168-169

I. INTRODUCTION

If one assumes, as many do,[1] that philosophy is something that asserts the supremacy of reason or logos, one wonders how to explain its use of the non-rational or mythos. Perhaps it uses the non-rational as the sweet outer covering of the bitter pill of rationality, i. e., as a window dressing (an allurement, a charm, an incantation) enticing non-philosophers toward the pursuit and/or acquisition and/or acceptance of the rational (i. e., philosophically achieved) truth.[2] There would be two possible justifications for this usage: (1) the justification grounded in the notion that although all humans are capable of achieving philosophical insight, not all are capable of achieving it philosophically; (2) the justification grounded in the notion that although not all humans are capable of achieving philosophical insight, they all are capable of non-philosophically accepting philosophical insight that has been achieved philosophically by others. There are difficulties that beset both these approaches.

To the first justification, one would object that the only meaningful way in which one is able to speak of the achieving of philosophical insight is in terms of its philosophical achievement. After all, philosophy is not simply truth achieved, but it is first and foremost a way to achieve truth. Even more, philosophy seems to require a *way-to* the way-to-achieve-truth (e.g., a qualified acceptance of all human opinions and sensings, the meta-way for Socratic philosophy, or a methodical doubt with respect to all human opinions and sensings and knowledges, the meta-way for Cartesian philosophy). Hence, it would seem self-violating and self-contradictory for philosophy to assume that it can bestow the fruits of its labors upon, and that these fruits can be assimilated by, those who are incapable of laboring to produce those fruits themselves. Such an assumption would be tantamount to asserting that the mere eating of an apple makes one a farmer, a patently false assertion.

---

1 In this introductory discussion, I have not cited in each instance the specific works that explicitly or implicitly employ the arguments that I formulate. Instead, I have placed all the works that I have consulted in the bibliography. Since I have formulated the arguments out of my impressions from the literature on Greek 'myth' generally and on Platonic 'myth' specifically, and since I have not wished to engage in individual polemics, I have let the arguments stand as impressions. I only hope that, whether I am correct or incorrect in my criticism, I have at least fairly stated the positions that I have criticized. To give the reader the opportunity to judge this, in the bibliography, after each work that pertains to this discussion, I have placed in brackets the relevant chapters and/or page references.

2 This view would be particularly congenial to the classical modern philosophers. Cf. Leibniz, *Discours de métaphysique*, section 26: "And nothing could be taught us of which we do not already have in the spirit [i. e., the mind] the idea which is as the matter of which this thought forms itself. This is that which Plato has very excellently considered when he has put forward his [teaching of] reminiscence which has much solidity, provided that one grasps it well, one purges it of the error of pre-existence, and one does not imagine that the soul ought already to have known and thought distinctly at another time what it learns and thinks now. Also [in the *Meno*] Plato has confirmed his sentiment by a beautiful experiment, introducing a little boy whom he leads insensibly to some very difficult truths of geometry touching incommensurables, without teaching him anything, only by making ordered and relevant demands. Which makes [one] see that the soul knows all that virtually and needs only *mental-steering* (*animadversion*) in order to cognize the truths, and, consequently, it has at the least its ideas on which these truths depend. One even is able to say that it already possesses these truths, when one grasps them for the relations of the ideas." (Et rien ne nous saurait être appris, dont nous n'ayons déjà dans l'esprit l'idée qui est comme la matière dont cette pensée se forme. C'est ce que Platon a excellemment bien considéré, quand il a mis en avant sa réminiscence qui a beaucoup de solidité, pourvu qu'on la prenne bien, qu'on la purge de l'erreur de la préexistence, et qu'on ne s'imagine point que l'âme doit déjà avoir su et pensé distinctement autrefois ce qu'elle apprend et pense maintenant. Aussi a-t-il confirmé son sentiment par une belle expérience, introduisant un petit garçon qu'il mène insensiblement à des vérités très difficiles de la géométrie touchant les incommensurables, sans lui rien apprendre, en faisant seulement des demandes par ordre et à propos. Ce qui fait voir que notre âme sait tout cela virtuellement, et n'a besoin que d'*animadversion* pour connaître les vérités, et, par conséquent, qu'elle a au moins ses idées dont ces vérités dépendent. On peut même dire qu'elle possède déjà ces vérités, quand on les prend pour les rapports des idées. —Leibniz, *Discours de métaphysique et correspondance avec Arnaud*, intr., texte et comm. par George Le Roy, deuxieme éd. (Paris, 1966), p. 64.)

One is forced, it would seem, to fall back upon the second justification, namely that although not all humans are capable of becoming, say, farmers, they all are capable of discerning the quality of apples. The difficulty here, however, is that the promulgation of philosophical insight would depend upon a catering, as it were, to the taste of the non-philosophical multitude based upon the assumption that non-philosophical taste is, or can be consonant with, philosophical nourishment that—because simply philosophical nourishment is unpalatable to non-philosophical taste—is non-philosophically prepared.

If such a consonance is possible, how can it be achieved? Presumably by the education of non-philosophical taste. But on the level of taste itself, taste is multifarious. How, then, can one guarantee the *proper* consonance? Presumably either by persuasion or by force, either of which would have to be limitless in its power, just as the material on which each works would have to be limitless in its malleability. In either case, one would have to rely on the wisdom of the persuaders or forcers and on their justice, an apparently utopian demand. Besides, even if the proper consonance could be brought about in either of these ways, one would have to ask whether this is the proper means of effecting the already agreed proper end or whether the employment of such a means necessitates paying the price of vitiating the end.[1]

In addition, what if the possessors of philosophical insight are by this very insight rendered powerless to effect changes in the non-philosophical multitude? How, then, can the multitude be protected from domination by powerful purveyors of an improper consonance?[2] In any case, if it should turn out that the proper means of effecting the proper consonance is myth (by which typically is meant some form of persuasive non-rational speech), then one would have to create a speech that is both rationally composed and non-rationally intelligible to, acceptable to, and capable of compelling assent from all humans, a decidedly utopian requirement.

In short, these justifications for the use of myth by the philosopher founder on the respective rocks of self-contradiction and utopianism. And as a set, they assume that although myth is essential to the dissemination of philosophical insight, it is somehow extrinsic to philosophy itself, i. e., to the philosophical practice of philosophy.

Perhaps, then, although myth is somehow not intrinsic to philosophy itself, somehow it is not extrinsic to it either. In other words, perhaps the non-rational is the complement to the rational, i. e., perhaps the non-rational expresses what is beyond and/or below reason, namely it expresses that which reason only divines and hence must articulate oracularly (mythically).[3] The difficulty that besets this view of myth is that its own justification cannot be a rational one, for by definition myth is a representation of that which is intractable or inaccessible to, and unrepresentable by, reason. In addition, this extra-rational realm is the realm of those things without which reason becomes contextless, so that consequently reason becomes dependent for its meaning and value upon things with respect to the validity of which it is criterionless, at least rationalistically criterionless. In other words, the pursuit of philosophical insight is deprived of the legitimacy of its claim to self-validation, to self-reflexiveness, on the very level that is most damaging to itself, namely on the level of its claim, as distinguished from that of the other knowledges, to be able to justify not only the grounds of the other knowledges but especially the ground of itself.[4] Hence, the relegation of philosophy to the position of handmaiden to an

---

1 This problem is treated by—among others—Plato in *The Republic* and Hegel in *The Philosophy of History*.

2 Cf. Leo Strauss, *Natural Right and History* (Chicago, 1953), p. 141: "The few wise cannot rule the many unwise by force. The unwise multitude must recognize the wise as wise and obey them freely because of their wisdom. But the ability of the wise to persuade the unwise is extremely limited . . . . Therefore, it is extremely unlikely that the conditions required for the rule of the wise will ever be met. What is more likely to happen is that an unwise man, appealing to the natural right of wisdom and catering to the lowest desires of the many, will persuade the multitude of his right: the prospects for tyranny are brighter than those for rule of the wise."

3 This is a view with which it is difficult to deal because of its eminent respectability, and even justifiability, from the points of view of both its non-rationalistic adherents and its rationalistic critics who are sympathetic to its non-rationalistic adherents, i. e., from the points of view of both theists and sympathetic non-theists.

4 Cf. *Charmides* 166c2-3 et passim.

extra-philosophical authority de-philosophizes philosophy to such an extent that it would be virtually impossible for philosophy to retain its identity, and philosophy would then become, like a slavish dog, little more than a mirror-image of its extra-philosophical master.[1]

In short, this justification for the philosopher's use of myth, i. e., its use of the non- or extra-rational, founders on the rock of self-dissolution.

Therefore, if the apparent result of philosophy's entering into a relationship with what is today called myth is to vitiate, in one way or another, the philosophical enterprise itself, how is one to explain the use of myth, even the preeminent place of myth, in the work of someone who is acknowledged to be a philosopher par excellence, namely Plato? One must, it seems, at least to begin with, entertain the notion that Plato's understanding of myth differs considerably from our own. Or, to put the matter more neutrally, one must ask the question of what a mythos is from Plato's point of view.

Before one tries to answer this question, it is desirable briefly to survey the fundamental terms, μῦθος and λόγος, as they were used by the Greeks in general and by Plato (and Plato's dramatic interlocutors) in particular.

---

1 I should perhaps add that if philosophy tries to free itself from this subjugation and remembers the 'mythical' attachment that apparently led to it, it may then abjure altogether what it regards as myth and restrict itself of its own volition to a realm that is free from the uncertainty of the mythically represented realm, i. e., it may restrict itself to a realm of unitary structure to which a universal method is to be applied. In other words, philosophy may autonomize itself by scientizing itself and its objects, an avenue of liberation that yields philosophy an enormous power, an enormous ability to create. However, here again philosophy becomes a slave, not to an extra-philosophical authority, but to an intra-philosophical methodology and its creations. When philosophy tries to free itself from this slavishmess, it does not turn back to its origins, because that is seen as a return to the source of the enslavement, but instead it turns forward and away from its current situation. The result is that philosophy, having rejected the certainty to which it has become enslaved, becomes a cosmic alien, rootless and homeless, atomistic and nihilistic. Cf. Leo Strauss, *Liberalism, Ancient and Modern* (NY, 1968), pp. 26-27: "Classical political philosophy . . . is today generally rejected as obsolete. The difference between, not to say the mutual incompatibility of, the two grounds on which it is rejected corresponds to the difference between the two schools of thought which predominate in our age, namely positivism and existentialism. Positivism rejects classical political philosophy with a view to its mode as unscientific and with a view to its substance as undemocratic. There is a tension between these grounds, for, according to positivism, science is incapable of validating any value judgment . . . . But 'the heart has its reasons which reason does not know,' . . . . Moreover there is an affinity between present-day positivism and sympathy for a certain kind of democracy; that affinity is due to the broad, not merely methodological, context out of which positivism emerged or to the hidden premises of positivism which positivism is unable to articulate because it is constitutionally unable to conceive of itself as a problem. Positivism may be said to be more dogmatic than any other position of which we have records. Positivism can achieve this triumph because it is able to present itself as very skeptical.... It is the latest form and it may very well be the last form in which modern rationalism appears; it is that form in which the crisis of modern thought becomes almost obvious to everyone. Once it becomes obvious to a man, he has already abandoned positivism, and if he adheres to the modern premises, he has no choice but to turn to existentialism.

"Existentialism faces the situation with which positivism is confronted but does not grasp the fact that reason has become radically problematic. According to positivism, the first premises are not evident and necessary, but either purely factual or else conventional. According to existentialism, they are in a sense necessary, but they are certainly not evident; all thinking rests on unevident but nonarbitrary premises. Man is in the grip of powers which he cannot master or comprehend . . . ."

Also cf. Hans Jonas, *The Phenomenon of Life* (NY, 1966), p. 234: "The disruption between man and total reality is at the bottom of nihilism. The illogicality of the rupture, that is, of a dualism without metaphysics, makes its fact no less real, nor its seeming alternative any more acceptable: the stare at isolated selfhood, to which it condemns man, may wish to exchange itself for a monistic naturalism which, along with the rupture, would abolish also the idea of man as man. Between that Scylla and this her twin Charybdis, the modern mind hovers. Whether a third road is open to it—one by which the dualistic rift can be avoided and yet enough of the dualistic insight saved to uphold the humanity of man—philosophy must find out." In addition, cf. Jonas, pp. 213-215, 233.

This story, my dear young folks, seems to be false, but it really is true, for my grandfather, from whom I have it, used always, when relating it, to say: "It must be true, my son, or else no one could tell it to you."
—"The Hare and the Hedgehog," in *The Complete Grimm's Fairy Tales*, tr. Margaret Hunt, rev. James Stern (NY, Pantheon, 1944), p. 760.

II. ΛΟΓΟΣ AND ΜΥΘΟΣ

When one surveys the meanings of λόγος and μῦθος and their derivatives, one is met by an apparently bewildering variety of shades of meaning, in particular of λόγος. The Liddell-Scott Lexicon (LSJ), for example, lists altogether fifty-four different but related renderings of λόγος.[1] However, the two fundamental renderings seem to be 'speech' and 'account,' initially without any distinction of true or false, but later with an apparent restriction to 'true account.' One would expect the case of μῦθος to be radically different, but that is not so. Out of twelve different but related renderings, μῦθος too receives the two fundamental renderings 'speech' and 'account.' How, then, is one genuinely to distinguish the meanings of the two terms without artificially imposing upon them a construction that their origins will not bear? The root of the answer lies in the senses in which each of these is an account. Λόγος is an account more in the sense of 'a reckoning,' i. e., it is more closely connected with the here and now, with the domain in which one is 'called to account' for one's present actions (hence the renderings 'plea,' 'law,' 'rule of conduct,' 'command,' 'reputation,' 'worth,' 'enumeration'). Μῦθος, on the other hand, is an account more in the sense of 'une histoire,' i. e., it is more closely connected with the there and then, with the domain in which one is inclined 'to recount' one's motives (hence the renderings 'unspoken word,' 'design,' 'tale,' 'narrative'). Yet even this distinction is not hard and fast, for a μῦθος can be a 'public speech,' and a λόγος can be a 'story.'[2]

Hence, any distinction that one attempts to draw between the two terms is blurred at some point in their origin and/or in their later usages. The Greek language preserves this blurring not only in such words as μυθέομαι ('I speak,' 'I give an account'), μυθολόγος ('storyteller,' 'pertaining to storytelling') and its corresponding denominative μυθολογέω ('I am μυθολόγος,' 'I tell a story'), παραμυθέομαι ('I chat someone beside/beyond himself/herself,' 'I console'),[3] and λογοποιέω ('I make up a story'), but also in the words λόγος and μῦθος themselves. In other words, if it is possible to give a 'μύθιος' λόγος (cf. τὸ λογομύθιον), then the distinction between λόγος and μῦθος seems to be sufficiently blurred as to cast a shadow of doubt over any ostensibly non-ambiguous usage of the terms. Therefore, one should never, even if only in the interest of pedantic precision, presuppose that an ostensibly non-ambiguous usage is only that.[4]

---

1 Cf. LSJ; W. K. C. Guthrie, *History of Greek Philosophy* (Cambridge, Eng., 1962-), vol. 1, pp. 419-424; Heribert Boeder, "Der frügriechische Wort gebrauch von Logos und Aletheia," *Archiv für begriffsgeschichte*, vol. 4, 1959, pp. 82-91 and 101-111.

2 And if one returns to Homer, one finds that the generic verb for speech (which is λέγω in later Attic) is μυθέομαι, and that the noun λόγος appears only twice (*Iliad* 15.393 and *Odyssey* 1.56), both times without an article in the dative plural and in contexts where we would uncritically expect μῦθος.

3 See chapter VIII. PARAMYTHS.

4 Cf. *Laws* 9.872c7-873b1.

What, then, is a myth in Plato? More precisely, by what criterion is one entitled to call a given account in Plato's writings a myth? It would seem that the only safe and unprejudicial operating criterion is the simple principle that one is entitled to call a myth in Plato's writings only what is explicitly so called, and that one is not entitled to call a myth anything that is not explicitly so called. In other words, one must not allow oneself to designate as a myth what modern opinions would lead one to take for granted as a myth. As Socrates, in the *Gorgias*, warns Callicles:

> Indeed hear, [as] they assert, a very beautiful logos, which you will regard
> [to be] a mythos, as I believe, but I a logos.[1]

Despite this warning, preconceptions run so deep and so silent that in commentaries on the *Gorgias*, the account that follows this warning is universally regarded as a myth. Therefore, it is worth emphasizing that even when such a warning is not explicitly stated, one must state it to oneself, and one must be ready to accept the possibility that an ostensible mythos is actually a logos or that an ostensible logos is actually a mythos.

What, then, are the explicitly designated myths in Plato's writings? Perhaps a list (with thematic foci) will be useful:

(1) *Phaedrus*: Socrates's Lysian speech and palinode: the genesis of eros and knowledge.

(2) *Republic* 2.359c6 ff.: Gyges's ancestor and the ring of invisibility: the genesis of justice.

(3) *Republic* 2.376d9 ff.: the entire education of the guardians (a myth about the first myths): the genesis of habitual virtue.

(4) *Republic* 2-7: the genesis of the best regime.[2]

(5) *Republic* 3.414b8-415d8: the gennaic falsehood, *the* political lie: the genesis of the best regime.

(6) *Republic* 8.565d4-566a5: the genesis of the tyrant.

(7) *Republic* 8-9: the de-generating regimes/souls.[3]

(8) *Republic* 9.588b1 ff.: the genesis of the human soul.

(9) *Republic* 10.613e6-621d3: the myth of Er: the genesis of the kind of lifetime that one leads.

(10) *Phaedo* 60b1-c7: the genesis of pleasure and pain.

(11) *Phaedo* 110a8 ff.: the genesis of our knowledge of earth/body.

(12) *Theaetetus* 155e3 ff.: all is motion: the genesis of the assertion that episteme is sensing.

(13) *Gorgias* 492e7-493d4: the soul as a wine jar: the genesis of a name.

(14) *Minos* 318c4-321b5: the genesis of an impious genetic account.

(15) *Laws* 1.636b7-e4: the genesis of homosexuality.

(16) *Laws* 1.644b6-645c3: the account of animals, especially humans, as divine puppets: the genesis of law-abidingness.

(17) *Laws* 4.711d6-712a7: the genesis of the best regime.

(18) *Laws* 4.712e9-714b2: the genesis of (less than the best) cities.

(19) *Laws* 4.719a7-720a2: the genesis of poetic irony.[4]

(20) *Laws* 6.773b4 ff.: the genesis of marriage.

(21) *Laws* 7.790b8-d2 & ff.: the prenatal gymnastic rearing of the body: the genesis of habits.

(22) *Laws* 7.809b3-812b1: the rearing and education of the body in children: the genesis of habits.

---

1 *Gorgias* 523a1-2: Ἄκουε δή, φασί, μάλα καλοῦ λόγου, ὃν σὺ μὲν ἡγήσῃ μῦθον, ὡς ἐγὼ οἶμαι, ἐγὼ δὲ λόγον.
2 Cf. *Republic* 6.501e2; *Timaeus* 25d7 ff.
3 See chapter VI. THE *REPUBLIC* TETRALOGY.
4 Cf. *Laws* 10.908e2.

(23) *Laws* 9.865d3-866a2 & ff.: involuntary homicide: the genesis of guilt.
(24) *Laws* 12.943d4-944c4: loss of arms: the genesis of improper blame.
(25) *Statesman* 268d5 ff.: the cosmic pathos: the genesis of the king.
(26) *Timaeus* 22b3 ff.: the genesis of periodic destructions by cosmic forces.
(27) *Timaeus* 27b7-end: the genesis of the cosmos.
(28) *Protagoras* 320b8-324d1: the account of the apportionment of powers by Prometheus, Epimetheus, and Zeus: the genesis of the universality of justice and modesty and political virtue in general.

Before trying to characterize the myths, it would be useful to cite some of the non-mythical Platonic writings, namely writings in which neither the word μῦθος nor any of its derivatives occurs: (1) *Symposium*, (2) *Parmenides*, (3) *Euthyphro*, (4) *Meno*.[1] The most striking cases here are the *Symposium*, which is virtually universally regarded by commentators as a dialogue filled with myths but which in actuality has none, and the *Meno*, which contains an account that is virtually universally designated as the myth of recollection but is in actuality not a myth at all.

What, then, are the characteristics that the various interlocutors in the Platonic dialogues attribute to myths?[2] They are: epideixeis of true beings,[3] pleasant and playful,[4] perishable and salutary,[5] sometimes imprecise,[6] paradigms,[7] productive of soul growth,[8] persuasive,[9] and partially true and partially false.[10] In addition, myth is variously described as lacking a logos,[11] opposed to logos,[12] the same as logos,[13] and the genus of which logos is a species.[14] Furthermore, it is asserted of myth that the test of its truth is its translatability into deed[15] and that it is the product of the activity of mythologizing.[16] Finally, and most pervasively, myths are said to be accounts of beginnings, of origins, of geneseis.[17]

Of these characteristics, while all the others are equally applicable to logoi, what most clearly marks off a mythos from a logos is that a mythos is first and foremost an account of the genesis of a phenomenon. This would imply that a λόγος in the narrow sense is a non-genetic or descriptive account of a phenomenon. Λόγος, then, would have two senses, a generic and a specific one, i. e., it would refer at times to speech καθόλου and at times to non-myth speech, descriptive speech. This would mean, for example, with respect to the brief account of recollection in the *Meno*,[18] which is not called a myth, but simply something spoken and

1 Except in a quotation at *Meno* 95e4-96a4.
2 For a complete list of occurrences of the word μῦθος and its derivatives in the Platonic corpus, see Appendix I.
3 Cf. *Laws* 6.771a5-d1.
4 Cf. *Timaeus* 59c5-d3; *Phaedo* 108d3, 110b3-4; *Republic* 10.614b1; *Hippias maior* 285d286a2, 297e3-298b1; *Phaedrus* 276e1-7.
5 Cf. *Philebus* 13e4-14a9; also *Republic* 2.380c1-3, 3.392a8-c5, 398a1-b4.
6 Cf. *Timaeus* 22b3-24a2, 29c4-d6.
7 Cf. *Laws* 2.663e5-664a1.
8 Cf. *Republic* 2.377b11-c5.
9 Cf. *Laws* 2.663d2-664e2; also cf. *Laws* 8.840b5-c10, 12.941b2-c4. In addition, consider *Hippias maior* 285d3-286a2; *Epistles* 8. 352c8-353a2. But cf. *Laws* 8.841b5-c8.
10 Cf. *Laws* 1.636b7-e4, 644b6-645c3; *Republic* 1.330d1-e5, 2.377a4-7 (cf. d4-6), 2.382c10-d3, 7.522a3-b4.
11 Cf. *Philebus* 13e4-14a9.
12 Cf. *Gorgias* 523a1-2; *Timaeus* 22a4-b3.
13 Cf. *Epinomis* 979d7-980a6; *Laws* 3.680c2-d6; also *Republic* 3.392d1-3. In addition, consider *Republic* 1.350d9-e10.
14 Cf. *Philebus* 13e4-14a9.
15 Cf. *Timaeus* 25d7-26e5.
16 Cf. *Laws* 6.751d7-752b2.
17 Cf. *Republic* 2.382c10-d3, 8.588b1-e2 (cf. *Phaedo* 60b1-c7); *Critias* 110a3-7; *Laws* 2.663e5-664a1, 3.680c2-d6, 3.682a1-683d5; *Epinomis* 974d3-975a7; *Timaeus* 22a4-24a2, 59c5-d3; *Sophist* 242c4-243a4.
18 *Meno* 81a5-e2.

heard,[1] that the account is not a genetic account of the origin of learning but rather a descriptive account of the experience of having learned, of learning as experienced.[2]

To this procedure someone might object that it is merely a crazy quilt of remarks from the Platonic writings, and it is surely not what Plato means. To this person onee could reply that, at the very least, such a patchwork procedure provides one with the range of the possible characteristics of myth for the Greeks who populate the cosmos of the Platonic corpus. However, the question remains, how does one read off from that range the characteristic or characteristics that Plato himself would delimit? In a simple way, one cannot, unless one brings to the dialogues a preconceived formulation of Plato's doctrine either independent of the testimony of the dialogues themselves or derived from a composite picture of the various interlocutors whom one designates as Plato's thinly disguised spokespersons. Neither of these alternatives is satisfactory: the former, namely the importing of a criterion extrinsic to the Platonic writings, runs the risk of blinding one to their intrinsic criterion or criteria; the latter is, so to speak, a sane quilt of remarks from the Platonic writings that, by virtue of its sanity, begs the decisive question as to whether one is entitled at all to speak of a Platonic spokesperson. The choice boils down to that between the crazy quilt and the sane quilt. And if one considers Plato's own remark that he says nothing in his own voice,[3] together with Socrates's account of philosophy as the highest kind of craziness,[4] one must opt for the crazy quilt,[5] i. e., one must assume that Plato is somehow in all the interlocutors of the dialogues. Does this make sense? To show that it does, one must briefly consider Platonic writing.

---

1 Cf. ἀκήκοα at *Meno* 81a5; Τίνα λόγον λεγόντων at 81a7; οἱ λέγοντες at 81a9 and 10; λέγει at 81b1; λέγουσιν at 81b2; φᾶσι at 81b3; τῷ . . . λόγῳ at 81d5-6.

2 And this is described by Socrates as not only a beautiful account, but also a true one: 'Αληθῆ . . . καὶ καλόν (*Meno* 81a8).

3 Cf. *Epistles* 2.314c1-3.

4 Cf. *Phaedrus* 243e9-257b6; *Sophist* 216c8-d2.

5 Cf. Melville, *Moby Dick*, ch. 82 beginning: "There are some enterprises in which a careful disorderliness is the true method."

III. PLATONIC WRITING

When one reads Plato, one always has to face the unavoidable—but all too often avoided—realization that when one inquires into any particular question raised in the dialogues, one is driven back necessarily into a consideration of Plato's manner of writing, namely a consideration of the dialogue form. If one takes Plato seriously as a philosopher, then one must take him seriously as a writer, and one must assume that the dialogue form is philosophically motivated. Hence, one cannot simply dismiss the dialogic character of the Platonic writings as somehow extraneous to the acknowledged philosophical substance that it encapsulates before one considers its possible philosophical importance for Plato. However, this 'Plato' to whom one seems forced constantly to make reference appears nowhere in the dialogues.[1] To repeat, Plato says nothing in his own voice, but rather he speaks through the interlocutors whom he presents to us.

What it means for a poet to speak through interlocutors is discussed by Socrates in a very neglected passage of the *Republic* (3.392c6-394c6). There, in conversation with Adeimantus, Socrates belabors the obvious distinction between narrating and imitating. Whenever Socrates belabors the obvious, one must scrutinize his assertions very carefully. This is what he says:

> Therefore, have you envisioned [i.e., understood] that up to these verses . . . the poet himself speaks and does not take it in hand to turn our thinking elsewhere as though the person speaking were someone other than himself; but he speaks the things after these as though he himself is Chryses, and he attempts as much as possible with respect to us to make the person speaking to seem to be not Homer but the priest who is old.[2]

If one applies this to Plato's dialogues, in which there is not one utterance by Plato himself, one can see that Plato has effaced himself virtually totally and has spoken through a variety of persons, speaking as much as possible as though each speaker as such were speaking. The more that Plato has effaced himself, the more successful is his method of writing.

Therefore, what any of Plato's persons says is not simply, in any given instance, what Plato says, but instead is what the speaker says:

> But when [the poet] speaks some uttering as though he is someone other, then will we not assert him to be similar as much as possible, with respect to his speaking, to each person whom he bespeaks beforehand as the person uttering?
>
> We shall assert [so].[3]

---

1 Plato himself invites one to consider this question through his making no attempt to conceal his authorship and through the only two mentions of himself in the dialogues, the one in the *Apology of Socrates* (34a1, 38b6), where he is said by Socrates to be present, and the one in the *Phaedo* (59b10), where he is said by Phaedo to have been absent. Thus, he himself indirectly suggests that his presence or absence in the dialogues is a question of some importance.

2 *Republic* 3. 393a3, 6-b2: Οἶσθ' οὖν ὅτι μέχρι μὲν τούτων τῶν ἐπῶν . . . λέγει τε αὐτὸς ὁ ποιητὴς καὶ οὐδὲ ἐπιχειρεῖ ἡμῶν τὴν διάνοιαν ἄλλοσε τρέπειν ὡς ἄλλος τις ὁ λέγων ἢ αὐτός· τὰ δὲ μετὰ ταῦτα ὥσπερ αὐτὸς ὢν ὁ Χρύσης λέγει καὶ πειρᾶται ἡμᾶς ὅτι μάλιστα ποιῆσαι μὴ Ὅμηρον δοκεῖν εἶναι τὸν λέγοντα ἀλλὰ τὸν ἱερέα, πρεσβύτην ὄντα.

3 *Republic* 3. 393c1-4: 'Αλλ' ὅταν γέ τινα λέγῃ ῥῆσιν ὥς τις ἄλλος ὤν, ἆρ' οὐ τότε ὁμοιοῦν αὐτὸν φήσομεν ὅτι μάλιστα τὴν αὐτοῦ λέξιν ἑκάστῳ ὃν ἂν προείπῃ ὡς ἐροῦντα; φήσομεν.

The poet, then, when he or she imitates a person, assimilates himself or herself to that person. That is, the poet does not efface himself or herself, but rather de-faces himself or herself into another person. The reader must deassimilate the poet. In other words, every imitation is like a force vector that the interpreter must resolve into its component forces:

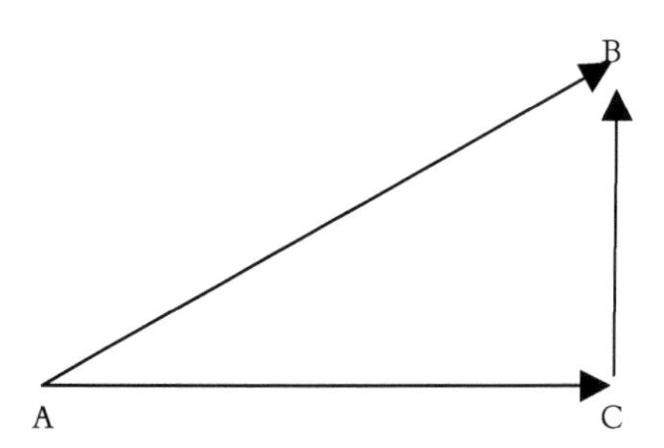

Thus if the diagonal arrow from A to B is the utterance of a person in a dialogue, Plato's view would be the horizontall arrow from A to C, and the vertical arrow from B to C woud be the adjustment to Plato's view that is made with an eye to dramatic context and dramatic interlocutors. The utterer's utterance (AB) would be the sum of the horizontal Plato arrow (AC) and the vertical (*homo ad hominem*) contextual arrow (BC). One can see from this schema how enormously difficult is the task of understanding Plato, because one must engage in this procedure for every remark in a dialogue, however trivial it may seem. That is, one must deassimilate even a "Ναί" and an "Οὐ γὰρ, οὖν," not to mention an "Εἰκός" or an "'Ανάγκη" or an "'Ορθῶς λέγεις," "Καλῶς λέγεις," and "'Αληθῆ λέγεις."

> And if then the poet should hide himself nowhere, both the poeting and narrating would have come to be for him without imitating.[1]

So, in narrating without imitating, the poet hides nowhere, does not hide at all. In other words, even when the poet indirectly narrates what another person speaks and does, the poet is peripherally visible as the one determining (selecting and ordering) for the reader what is spoken and done. By implication, a poet who should narrate through imitating alone, would hide everywhere, i. e., would be, insofar as the imitating is perfect, completely invisible.

> Then learn . . . that the contrary of this [i. e., of simple narrating without imitating] in turn comes to be whenever anyone, taking out the things of the poet between the utterings, leaves behind the interchanges.[2]

Socrates's use here of the imperative Μάνθανε (Learn)[3] focuses especial attention on what he says, and surely this is one of the most important passages in the dialogues for understanding the

1 *Republic* 3. 393c11-d2: Εἰ δέ γε μηδαμοῦ ἑαυτὸν ἀποκρύπτοιτο ὁ ποιητής, πᾶσα αὐτῷ ἄνευ μιμήσεως ἡ ποίησίς τε καὶ διήγησις γεγονυῖα εἴη.

2 *Republic* 3. 394b3-6: Μάνθανε τοίνυν . . . ὅτι ταύτης αὖ ἐναντία γίγνεται, ὅταν τις τὰ τοῦ ποιητοῦ τὰ μεταξὺ τῶν ῥήσεων ἐξαιρῶν τὰ ἀμοιβαῖα καταλείπῃ.

3 In this section as a whole, there is a striking density of forms of the verb μανθάνω (to learn) [see 392c9, d7, 393d2, 394b2, 3, 6, c5; also cf. διδάσκαλος at 392d8]. Hence, this section is also a paradigm of teaching and learning.

dialogue form. Socrates says that even in a purely imitative or dramatic writing, there are intercalary remarks by the poet, but these intercalary remarks have been rendered, as it were, invisible. Clearly, then, the task of interpreting involves restoring to visibility, on the basis of the interchanges that have been left behind, the utterances that have been taken out, erased, rendered invisible. In other words, to understand is to recover the poet's own utterances-between on the basis of the utterances between which those utterances would have been had they not been removed. Therefore, to write a commentary on a Platonic diaogue is to rewrite the dialogue in narrative form, and the model for such an enterprise is provided here by Socrates's re-rendering of the beginning of the *Iliad* as simple narration.[1]

What Plato says, then, is what *all* the interlocutors say, not simply, but rather as metamorphosed Platoes. That is, every interlocutor in a Platonic dialogue is a monster, composed of the speaker in front and Plato behind.[2] One must do with a Platonic dialogue what Socrates asserts that one must do when one rationalizes any so-called myth:

> There is a compulsion for one after this to correct [i.e., explain away] the look of the Centaurs, and in turn the [look] of the Chimaira, but [then] of suchlike Gorgons and Pegasuses and other uncontrivable things, a mob and multitude and eccentricities of certain monstrous natures flow over one, the which if someone distrusting [i.e., being skeptical] will approach [i.e., try to understand] each in accordance with what is likely, since he or she uses a certain boorish wisdom, he or she will need much leisure.[3]

So, if one is going to penetrate to the core of a Platonic dialogue, one must, at least provisionally, use the crazy quilt, or monster, methodology.

The first tentative product of this methodology for the present inquiry is that myths are speeches about genesis.[4]

---

1 *Republic* 3. 392e2-393a2, 393d3-394d7. Here one might add that on this basis, one cannot, strictly speaking, divide the Platonic dialogues into narrated and imitated, but rather they must all—even those 'narrated' by a Platonic dramatic persona—be classified as purely imitative, since there is no 'Plato' narrating the so-called narrated dialogues, as there is a Homer narrating the *Iliad* and *Odyssey*.

2 Cf. *Iliad* 6. 180-181: "And the [Chimaira] then was divine with respect to its race and not of humans, / in front a lion, and in back a snake, and in the middle a she-goat" (ἡ δ' ἄρ' ἔην θεῖον γένος οὐδ' ἀνθρώπων, / πρόσθε λέων, ὄπιθεν δὲ δράκων, μέσση δὲ χίμαιρα). Cf. Nietzsche, Beyond good and evil, tr. Walter Kaufmann (NY, 1966), Part Five, section 190, p. 103: "He [i. e., Plato] was the most audacious of all interpreters and took the whole Socrates only the way one picks a popular tune and folk song from the streets in order to vary it into the infinite and impossible—namely, into all of his own masks and multiplicities. In a jest, Homeric at that: what is the Platonic Socrates after all if not *prosthe Platōn opithen te Platōn messē Chimaira*."

3 *Phaedrus* 229d5-e4: αὐτῷ ἀνάγκη μετὰ τοῦτο τὸ τῶν Ἱπποκενταύρων εἶδος ἐπανορθοῦσθαι, καὶ αὖθις τὸ τῆς Χιμαίρας, καὶ ἐπιρρεῖ δὲ ὄχλος τοιούτων Γοργόνων καὶ Πηγάσων καὶ ἄλλων ἀμηχάνων πλήθη τε καὶ ἀτοπίαι τερατολόγων τινῶν φυσέων· αἷς εἴ τις ἀπιστῶν προσβιβᾷ κατὰ τὸ εἰκος ἕκαστον, ἅτε ἀγροίκῳ τινὶ σοφίᾳ χρώμενος, πολλῆς αὐτῷ σχολῆς δεήσει.

4 In the usage of the dialogues, Λόγος is used both as the generic name for any articulated utterance and as the specific name for simple articulated utterances (i. e., for descriptive accounts) that are not μῦθοι. This is parallel to the way in which, in the discussion of διήγησις, διήγησις is used as both the generic name for any continuous statement of a sequence of events and/or thoughts and as the specific name for simple continuous statements that are not imitated or 'dramatic.' The fundamental instance (cf. *Epinomis* 978b7 ff.) of this pervasive characteristic of human διαίρεσις is the ἡμέρα (i. e., the twenty-four hour day) that is the genus of the two species ἡμέρα (i.e., the daylight day) and νύξ (i. e., the nighttime day). This is one aspect of what is called the problem of the indeterminate dyad (δυὰς ἀόριστος) in the Platonic writings. Cf. Jacob Klein, *Greek mathematical thought and the origin of algebra*, tr. Eva Brann (Cambridge, MA, 1968), p. 98.

> In fact, genesis is the very soul of any myth. To understand the world, the story of its genesis has to be told. To understand the gods, the story of their genesis has to be told. Cosmogony and theogony are the primary subjects of any myth. In order properly to understand any event in human life or the character of a people or a city, the event and the character have always to be related, it seems, to their mythical origins. To tell the myth of something means to tell how this something came to be. An enterprise of this kind does not make much sense unless one relates everything ultimately to beginnings which make any genesis possible.[1]

One might add that the myths in the Platonic dialogues are not chronogenetic, but rather are eidogenetic or ontogenetic.

1 Jacob Klein, "Aristotle, an introduction," in *Ancients and moderns: essays on the tradition of political philosophy in honor of Leo Strauss*, ed. Joseph Cropsey (NY, 1964), p. 58. In addition, consider the following remarks by Leo Strauss, *NRH*: "Philosophy is the quest for the 'principles' of all things, and this means primarily the quest for the 'beginnings' of all things or for the 'first things.' In this, philosophy is at one with myth." (p. 82) [It shold be noted that here, when Strauss is speaking generally of philosophy and not specifically of Plato, he uses the term 'myth' rather in its common signification. That he does not simply regard Platonic myth in this way can be seen from his analysis (p. 117) of the *Protagoras* myth.] "With a view to the connection between right and civil society, the question of the origin of right transforms itself into the question of the origin of civil society or of society in general. This question leads to the question of what man's original condition was like." (p. 95) "And the question of the 'essential' origin of civil society and of right or wrong cannot be answered without consideration of what is known about the beginnings or the 'historical' origins." (p. 96)

IV. THE PLATONIC MYTH: *The Seventh Epistle* 341b7-345c3

Is there anything that Plato himself says about myths? There is, and there is not. Although Plato never discussed myth in his own voice, he did compose an account that he himself explicitly calls a myth, namely the discussion of writings in his own seventh epistle. Perhaps if one examines this closely, one will be able to re-discern the Platonic definition of myth.

The passage may be outlined thus:[1]

Foreword (341b7-342a6)
- I (341b7-d2): writers and non-writers
- II (341d2-e1): possible purposes of writings
- III (341e1-342a1): the audience
- IV (342a1-6): introduction to the myth (= something true)

The Myth (342a7-344d2)
- I (342a7-e2): genesis of exact-knowledge
  - A (342a7-b3): the three/four/five things for each of the beings
  - B (342b3-d8): the explanation
  - C (342d8-e2): conclusion
- II (342e2-344c1): defects of speeches
  - A (342e2-343a4): weakness of speeches
  - B (343a4-344c1): the explanation
- III (344c1-d2): conclusion

Afterword (344d3-345c3)
- I (344d3-9): writers and non-writers
- II (344d9-345a1): possible purposes of writings
- III (345a1-c3): the hearers and repeatability

Plato begins (341b7-c4) by classifying past and future writers who understand nothing about Plato's business (περὶ τοῦ πράγματος),[2] i. e., who understand nothing about philosophy:

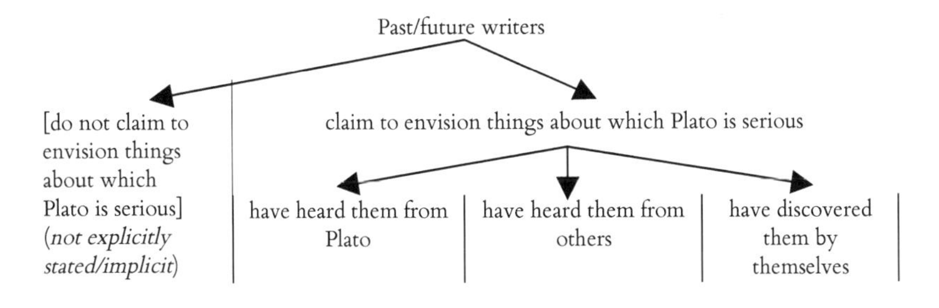

1 For a literal translation of the passage, see Appendix II.
2 Cf. *Apol. Socr.* 20c5; *Phaedo* 61c8; *Theaetetus* 168a8.

By restricting his classification to past and future writers, Plato exempts himself as a present writer. This might be meant to suggest that Plato as a writer is somehow immune to his own charges against writers. In addition, these charges are directed only against writers who claim to be cognizant of Plato's serious concerns, not against writers who do not claim such cognizance. Furthermore, Plato admits that there are things about which he is serious, although—one should recall—this same Plato refers to the childish-playfulness that is the sibling of seriousness.[1]

According to Plato (341c4-6), although learning about the serious things is possible, no writing down about the serious things is permissible and/or possible. However, other learnings, i. e., learnings about non-serious things, may be spoken or written. Plato is a writer. What does he write, and in what way?

That he condemns the serious and/or direct writing *about* the serious things, but not the playful and/or indirect writing *of* them, suggests a tentative definition of Platonic writing: it is playful writing of the serious things.[2] Thus, if learnings about non-serious things may be written, and if it is possible by writing about the non-serious things to write of the serious things, then writing of—although not about—the serious things is possible.

In order to write in this way, one must first learn the serious things. Learning the serious things (341c5-d2) comes from συνουσία (being-together) and συζῆν (living-together), from a togetherness presumably either with the non-serious things, so that one is led to a self-discovery of the serious things, or a togetherness with persons who have learned the serious things, so that one is led by a teacher to the serious things. Learning the serious things must be the result of a continuous process, such as a burning fire undergoes, and it comes as a sudden leap of light. The burning is the συνουσία or συζῆν, the fire is learning the non-serious things, and the flare is learning the serious things.

What is the burnable? On the one hand, it is the kindling, and the kindling would seem to represent the non-serious things that are turned in burning (in being learned) into ashes (stripped of non-essentials). On the other hand, it is the coal that becomes the embers, which would seem to represent the soul, for if the fire nurtures itself in the soul, the soul—or something in the soul—must be burnable. If the possibility of learning is ever-present to the soul, the soul must be—at least in principle—pure burnability, inexhaustible.[3] Not only must the soul be pure burnability, but also, once it catches fire, it always must be burning (which one could call ἡ πρώτη ἐντελέχεια of soul):[4] the flare of light is the effluence of a fire that has been burning. In addition, the structure (burnability) of the soul and the structure (burnability) of its objects are similar to each other, so that the requirement that similar be known by similar is satisfied.[5] However, in the soul—as apparently not in its objects—the persistence of the fire is precarious, because the soul (ἡ ψυχή) is cool (ψυχρά) or a cooling (κατάψυξις).[6]

Plato shifts (341d2) to the question of the possible purposes of writings, and he does so from the point of view of his own interests: the Platonic things would best be spoken by Plato (ὑπ' ἐμοῦ), but written badly they would pain Plato (ἐμὲ). This is an implicit hierarchy:

best:	spoken by Plato
second best:	written by Plato (i. e., written well)
second worst:	spoken by someone else
worst:	written by someone else (i. e., written badly)

1 Cf. *Epistles* 6.323d2; also cf. *Epinomis* 992b3, *Phaedrus* 234d8.

2 Cf. Friedrich Nietzsche, *Beyond Good and Evil*, Part Four, section 94, p. 83: "A man's maturity—consists in having found again the seriousness one had as a child, at play." (Tr. Walter Kaufmann)

3 Cf. Aristotle, *De Anima* B. 4. 416a15-16: "For the fire's increasing is unto the unlimited, so long as there be something burnable" (ἡ μὲν γὰρ τοῦ πυρὸς αὔξησις εἰς ἄπειρον, ἕως ἂν ᾖ τὸ καυστόν).

4 Cf. Aristotle, *De Anima* B. 1. 412a27-28 and context.

5 Cf. Aristotle, *De Anima* A. 2. 404b16-18; Plato, *Timaeus* 452b2 ff.

6 Cf. Aristotle, *De Anima* A. 2. 405b23-29.

Plato is in a dilemma: even though it is certain that at least some of those to whom Plato speaks will speak and write the Platonic things to others, there is no guarantee that those to whom he speaks will speak and write them properly.[1] In the repetition of the Platonic things by another whose understanding is incomplete, there is pain for Plato, both the pain of physical abuse (or potential physical abuse) and the pain of seeing the serious things contorted, incorrectly falsified, and dishonored, a pain that seems unSocratic, because Socrates appeared to be indifferent to the career of his speeches as disseminated by others.[2]

It seems that this twofold pain can be eliminated only by writing anonymously and/or correctly of the serious things. Plato's choice of the dialogue form achieves both these goals. On the one hand, since the dialogues present the conversations of others (i. e., *ad hominem* remarks by a variety of interlocutors, none of which remarks may be attributed simply to Plato), they preserve Plato's anonymity. On the other hand, if the dialogues falsify the serious things, they do so in a noble, not a shameful, way. In addition, the dialogue form invites repeated συνουσίαι and συζῆν with the dialogues, since one cannot simply read off from them a Platonic teaching.

Then Plato indicates (341d2-e1) why he would write if he felt compelled to convey his position sufficiently and to convey it to the many, i. e., why he would write if writing were a beautiful action. He would write, he says, to benefit humans bigly and to bring nature to light for everyone. Plato phrases his remark conditionally and interrogatively. He seems to answer it negatively i.e., he seems to deny that he would write. Yet, there is the massive evidence of the Platonic corpus: Plato *did* write. Why?

In what follows, Plato denies that one can write to benefit all humans, because only a few actually would be benefited. However, he does not deny that one should write to bring nature to light for everyone. In addition, it is implicit that writing should harm no one.

On this basis, then, a second definition of Platonic writing emerges: it is writing for the purpose of bringing nature to light so as to benefit a few and to harm no one.[3]

Furthermore, the repetition of the word "light" (φῶς: d7) recalls its use a few lines above (d1), so that perhaps one could further conclude that the light that flares from the fire, namely that about which Plato is serious, is nature. Therefore, Plato suggests that he is a true φυσιολόγος in his writing and that anyone who writes correctly φυσιολογεῖ.

Next (341e1-342a1), after Plato denies that taking the serious things in hand is good for all humans, he classifies humans according to their capacity with respect to the serious things:

the few:
capable of finding out the serious things themselves with little ἐπίδειξις.

the many:
some: taking the serious things in hand fills them with an incorrect contempt;
others: taking the serious things in hand fills them with a lofty and spongy hope,
based on their assumption that they have learned significant things.

Therefore, writings are not good or beneficial for the many for two reasons: (α) they breed an incorrect contempt; (β) they breed the conceit of believing oneself to know when one does not know. Writings, however, may be good or beneficial for the few.

---

1 In other words, the situation of Socrates, who produces such a bewildering variety of reporters (including persons such as Apollodorus, Phaedo, Plato, Euclides, Terpsion, and so on), is repeated in the case of Plato, who produces Dionysius, Aristotle, and so on.
2 Cf. *Symposium* 173b4-8.
3 Cf. *Republic* 1. 335d11-336a10.

Is it possible to write writings that are beneficial to the few (to one's 'friends') and harmful to no one? That is, is it possible to write a just writing? What would a just writing be? For the few, a just writing would seem to serve a twofold purpose: (α) it would give them the little ἐπίδειξις that they need; (β) it would give them a paradigm for any writings that they themselves may take in hand.[1] For the many, it would prevent them from becoming incorrectly contemptuous, and it would safeguard them from conceit, i. e., it would—if it fulfilled both these requirements—have to be ostensibly both supportive of convention and aporetic or inconclusive. The Platonic dialogues satisfy both requirements.[2]

In his conclusion to the foreword (342a1-3), Plato alludes to another purpose for writing, namely the clarifying what one has already said and/or written, and its corollary, the clarifying what someone else has said and/or written about what oneself has said and/or written. This is one purpose of the seventh epistle itself.

Then (342a3-6) Plato refers to a certain true speech (τις λόγος ἀληθής) that must be spoken to anyone—and that would include both the competent and the others—who dares to write of the serious things, i. e., what follows is written for all writers of the serious things, and it is written—one must assume—with the above considerations in mind. That is, since the true speech is written against writings, it itself must be written in such a way as to correct for all the defects of writings that have been and will be mentioned, because "a precept we cannot suppose to have been consciously violated by its author in the very [writing] in which it occurs."[3] What is here called "a certain true speech" later is called "a myth" (344d3).

Now we come to the myth itself (342a7-344d2). The myth falls into two major parts, the first of which (342a7-e2) takes up the theme of the genesis of ἐπιστήμη (exact-knowledge) and the second of which (342e2-344c1) takes up again the theme of the genesis of writings, after which there is appended a brief conclusion (344c1-d2). This is written to clarify what has already been said about writings. Thus, the discussion of exact knowledge provides the basis for clarifying Plato's view of writing. It is not surprising that this discussion of exact knowledge is one of the most obscure in the Platonic corpus.

However, this much can be asserted: the discussion of exact knowledge provides not only an account of exact knowledge in general, but also a methodological paradigm for the exact knowledge of anything in particular, a paradigm that then is employed in the account of writings that follows it.

Still one must ask, why does Plato insert an account of exact knowledge? The reason seems to be that the writers whom Plato is accusing are persons who claim that they know the Platonically serious, i. e., persons who claim that they *know*.[4]

Plato begins (342a7-b3) by saying that there are three things to each being, out of which, by compulsion, exact knowledge arises as the fourth. The fifth, which must be posited, is the being itself, and this being itself both is knowable and truly is. So, we have the following five things: (1) name (ὄνομα), (2) speech (λόγος), (3) look-alike (εἴδωλον), (4) exact-knowledge (ἐπιστήμη), and (5) the being itself (αὐτὸ . . . ὄν).[5]

1 In addition, perhaps it would fill them with a correct contempt and a solid hope without conceit.

2 Cf. *Crito*, on the one hand, and *Meno*, on the other.

3 Plato, *The Phaedrus of Plato*, ed. W.H. Thompson (NY, 1973), p. xiv.

4 One might add that the Platonically serious so far has been called 'nature' (341d7-e1) and is about to be called 'being itself' (342a8-b1). Being, then, is nature, and nature is being, according to Plato, a formulation that is echoed in the *Republic*, where the Platonic looks (εἴδη) are called 'natures' by Socrates. See *Republic* 10.597b5-e5, where *the* couch is said to be in nature; cf. also 6.501b2, where reference is made to the just and beautiful as by nature. Finally, cf. Aristotle, *Metaphysics* A. 9. 991b7 ff., M. 5. 1080a5 ff.; cf. Plato *Epistles* 7.342c6.

5 Cf. *Laws* 10.895d1-9 & ff.; *Epistles* 2.312d5-e6.

First, it is odd that what one unthinkingly would call the being itself is here called a look-alike, and it looks like something of which apparently one cannot have exact knowledge, although one must posit that it is, presumably as the ground of both the look of the look-alike and the intellectual apprehension of what the look-alike looks like, namely the assumed, but indemonstrable, being itself.

Second, according to what Plato says, if we have the awareness of the look-alike, its name, and its speech, we have exact knowledge, which apparently is not an independent fourth, but rather is the unified view of the three. In most cases, since we have the look-alike and the name, what we lack for exact knowledge primarily and for the most part is the speech, although initially it is not clear precisely what a speech is.

Plato's statement unleashes more perplexities than it dissolves, as Plato himself seems to recognize when he says (342b3-4) that to learn what he means a paradigmatic instance is needed, i. e., one must grasp what Plato says in regard to one thing, and then apply it to all things. The paradigmatic instance here is circle (342b4-d3), a mathematical into which, as such, simplicity and precision come built.

What new light does the instance of the circle shed on the initial perplexities? It specifies, first of all, that a speech is composed of names and verbs,[1] i. e., what is distinctive about a speech is that it contains the actings (the verbs) of that which it bespeaks. In the case of the circle, of which the speech is "that which holds itself everywhere equal from its extremities to its middle," its acting is its holding (ἀπέχον). In other words, the circle itself, i. e., the circle that one means when one draws the circle that one draws, is the inner area, and hence the name "line" does not appear in the speech of circle.[2] Therefore, the line by which one draws the look-alike circle, the line by which one renders the circle visible for oneself, is merely the visible encapsulation of the invisible inner area that is the circle itself. This is why, when the name "circle" is expanded, one finds "rounded and circumferent and circle" but not "round and circumference and circle." As if to give a small example of how what is applicable to circle must be taken as applicable to all things, when the name "circle" becomes triple, so too does exact knowledge become triple (and true opinion is its rounded, and intellectual intuition is its circumferent).

What is applicable to circle and exact knowledge must *mutatis mutandis* be applicable to a writing. If one applies it to a writing, one sees that the speech by which one composes the look-alike writing, the speech by which one renders the writing itself visible for oneself, is merely the visible encapsulation of the invisible inner character of the writing itself. If from a circle full of defects (cf. 343a5-7), one can achieve exact knowledge of the circle itself, then however weak or defective a writing may be, i. e., even if it is thoroughly defective or weak, one still can achieve exact knowledge of the writing itself.

---

1 Cf. *Sophist* 261e4 ff.

2 The same definition appears as the definition of 'rounded' in the *Parmenides* 137e1-3: "And the rounded then somehow is this whose extremities everywhere hold themselves equal from the middle" (Στρογγύλον γέ πού ἐστι τοῦτο οὗ ἂν τὰ ἔσχατα πανταχῇ ἀπὸ τοῦ μέσου ἴσον ἀπέχῃ: cf. 145a8-b3). Also cf. *Timaeus* 33b1-7, 36d8-e5. The Euclidean definitions of circle (Book 1, def. 15 & 16), which do contain the word "line," have the same import: "A circle is the plane shaped-surface which is embraced by one line which is called the circumference, in regard to which all the straight [lines] falling on the circumference of the circle from one point of those lying within the shaped-surface—and the point is called the center of the circle—are equal to each other" (ιε'. Κύκλος ἐστὶ σχῆμα ἐπίπεδον ὑπὸ μιᾶς γραμμῆς περιεχόμενον ἣ καλεῖται περιφέρεια, πρὸς ἣν ἀφ' ἑνὸς σημείου τῶν ἐντὸς τοῦ σχήματος κειμένων πᾶσαι αἱ προσπίπτουσαι εὐθεῖαι πρὸς τὴν τοῦ κύκλου περιφέρειαν ἴσαι ἀλλήλαις εἰσίν. ιζ'. Κέντρον δὲ τοῦ κύκλου τὸ σημεῖον καλεῖται): Euclidis *Elementa*, text of I.L. Heiberg, ed. E.S. Stamatis (Leipzig, Teubner, 1969), vol. 1, liber 1, def. 15 & 16, p. 2. I have kept the full manuscript reading and not the text as emended by Heath [Euclidis, *The Thirteen Books of Euclid's Elements*, tr. with intro. and commentary by Sir Thomas L. Heath, 2nd ed. Rev. (NY, 1956), vol. 1, pp. 153-154, 183-185], and in my rendering I have inserted definition 16 into definition 15 at the proper explanatory place. With regard to my interpretation of both the Platonic and Euclidean definitions, cf. Heath's unapproving summary (p. 184) of an-Nairizi's commentary: "an-Nairizī points to this as the explanation of Euclid's definition of a circle as a *plane figure*, meaning the whole surface bounded by the circumference, and not the circumference itself."

With this in mind, one is ready to embark on—and in a way has been made immune to—Plato's discussion of the defects of writings (342e2-344c1) or, more precisely, the weakness of λόγοι.

Plato presupposes (342e2-343a1) that λόγοι are weak. Even so, they are not simply weak, because they are—it is implied—less weak with respect to each thing's ποῖόν τι (certain sort) than with respect to each thing's ὄν (being), and hence a λόγος must articulate the certain sort with at least as much clarity as the being. In terms of—and in support of—the earlier discussion of writings, λόγοι are more capable for the non-serious things, the ποῖόν τι, than the serious thing, the ὄν, that they look like but are not.

Nonetheless, λόγοι are assumed to be weak. Their weakness leads to two consequences for a person with intellect (343a1-4): (1) that person will not dare to put intellectual intuitions into λόγοι; and (2) that person will not dare to put intellectual intuitions into what is untransmovable. Plato does not say that a person of intellect will not write or speak, but only that such a person will not write or speak intellectual intuitions. With respect to writings in particular, the fundamental defect is untransmovability. One might conjecture, then, that if one could devise a form of writing that possesses transmovability, a living speech, as it were, one could compose a writing without the usual defects of writings. As Socrates says:

> But I believe you would assert this, namely for it to be obligatory for every speech to be composed as a living thing having its own certain body, so as to be neither headless nor footless, but to have both middles and extremities which have been written [so as to be] proper to each other and to the whole.[1]

That is, if a writing could be devised to operate analogously to a living thing by "a certain logographic compulsion,"[2] perhaps a person of intellect would then dare to write.

Then (343a5-e1) Plato uses the instance of the defective look-alike circle to elucidate his meaning. What Plato does not say here is that surely one must know the look-alike circle *as defective*, precisely because one knows the non-defective fifth thing, the circle itself.

Next (343a9-b3) Plato turns to the name, and he gives the speech of name (cf. b4). Since names are not stable, since they are arbitrary, the speech of name seems to be that names, i. e., the particular sound and letter configurations that have been designated as accepted signifiers of certain objects, are purely conventional. He does not say that the things named by those names are conventional, but only that whether one calls object X a table or a krell is a customarily established practice by which all X's are called, say, table, and although the name 'krell' could have been established, X would still be X, but it would be called 'krell.'[3]

Plato proceeds after name to discuss speech, i. e., he gives the speech of the speech (343b4-6), which is the same as the speech of the name. He says that *if* a speech is composed from names and verbs, *then* the speech of the speech is that the speech is in no way sufficiently stable to be stable.

Apparently, verbs are so insignificant a part of the speech that the dominant part of the speech, namely the name, infects the whole speech. This presupposes that, in effect, all speeches are purely nominal, i. e., that they are composed of mere rootless names. This is put conditionally: *if* speeches are from and of names, *then* speeches are intrinsically unstable.

---

1 *Phaedrus* 264c2-5: Ἀλλὰ τόδε γε οἶμαί σε φάναι ἄν, δεῖν πάντα λόγον ὥσπερ ζῷον συνεστάναι σῶμά τι ἔχοντα αὐτὸν αὑτοῦ, ὥστε μήτε ἀκέφαλον εἶναι μήτε ἄπουν, ἀλλὰ μέσα τε ἔχειν καὶ ἄκρα, πρέποντα ἀλλήλοις καὶ τῷ ὅλῳ γεγραμμένα. Cf. *Philebus* 64b6-8, *Statesman* 277b7-c1, *Parmenides* 145a5-b1.

2 *Phaedrus* 264b7: τινὰ ἀνάγκην λογογραφικὴν.

3 Cf. *Cratylus* 433d7-e8 and context.

However, if names were *stable*,[1] and if speeches were from and of names, then speeches would be stable. Or, even if names were intrinsically unstable,[2] then if speeches were not from and of names primarily,[3] speeches might be stable, i. e., perhaps a speech could be composed only from verbs.[4]

In addition, the description of something as unstable is not meant in terms of motion. Recall that one of the defects of a written speech is that it is untransmovable. Perhaps inanimate, i. e., non-living, writings are both untransmovable and unstable, while one should, and could, devise a writing that is both transmovable and stable, a writing such as a dialogue.

Plato returns (343b6-c5) to the distinction between the ποῖόν τι and the ὄν, and remarks that when there are these two, if the soul seeks the ὄν—which is the soul's ultimate goal—i. e., if the soul seeks what it ultimately desires to seek, it finds what it is not seeking and becomes filled with perplexity and indistinctness. It is implicit that in order for the soul to find what it seeks, it must first seek what it does not seek.

What is the consequence of this? First, it follows that the ὄν is not directly accessible to humans, and that any attempt to gain direct access to it is destined to be frustrated. Second, it follows that if the ὄν constitutes the core of the serious things, any writing[5] that should be written so as to provide direct access to the serious things will fail, precisely by virtue of that, to provide access to the serious things. Therefore, if one wants to write so as to provide some access to the serious things, one must do so by providing an access mediated through the non-serious things.

In short, as seen above, proper writing would be playful writing of—but not about—the serious things. More precisely (343c5-d2), proper writing is directed to those who are habituated by a virtuous nurture *not* to seek the true, and it presents them with look-alikes from which extrapolations may be made. Such writing is not laughable to one's companions, although it may be to non-companions. The laughter of non-companions is just as clearly not an important consideration here, even if the trial and death of Socrates were a consequence of such laughter.[6]

What would happen if one should be *compelled* to speak about the fifth thing, about the ὄν itself, something that one would do presumably only under compulsion? This is the question with which Plato deals next (343d2-e1), as he must, because he himself is writing the seventh epistle under such a compulsion, a compulsion that, in a way, is reflected in the darkness and obscurity and indirection with which he writes.

What, then, would result? Of those persons who are capable of turning things upside down, the person who wants to turn things upside down overpowers us. Why? The situation seems to be this. Not everyone who is capable of turning things upside down wants to do so. Surely the person who answers and clarifies the fifth thing would be one of those who possess, but do not wish to employ, this capability. Those who wish to, and do, employ it seem to be

---

1 Cf. *Parmenides* 147d1-6, *Laches* 194c3-6, *Timaeus* 49e7-50a2.

2 Cf. *Timaeus* 49d3-50a4.

3 Cf. *Cratylus* 438e2-3: "Then, o Cratylus, as is likely, it is possible to have learned the beings without names" ("Εστιν ἄρα, ὡς ἔοικεν, ὦ Κρατύλε, δυνατὸν μαθεῖν ἄνευ ὀνομάτων τὰ ὄντα).

4 Cf. *Cratylus* 421a7-b1: "*Socrates.* Then 'name' is like a name which is wrought from a speech which bespeaks that this is a being of which what is sought chances to be. And you would recognize it more [easily] in that by which we bespeak the namable; for herein it distinctly bespeaks this [i. e., the namable] to be the being of which the search is" (ΣΩ. Ἔοικε τοίνυν ἐκ λόγου ὀνόματι συγκεκροτημένῳ, λέγοντος ὅτι τοῦτ' ἔστιν ὄν, οὗ τυγχάνει ζήτημα ὄν, τὸ ὄνομα. μᾶλλον δὲ ἂν αὐτὸ γνοίης ἐν ᾧ λέγομεν τὸ ὀνομαστόν· ἐνταῦθα γὰρ σαφῶς λέγει τοῦτο εἶναι ὂν οὗ μάσμα ἐστίν). I. e., τὸ ὂν οὗ μάσμα becomes τὸ ὀνομαστόν.

5 Although the instance here is about speaking, it seems justified to extrapolate it to writings, in accordance with the principle that what is applicable to one is applicable to all (see above).

6 Cf. *Apol. Socr.* 18c8-d2, 19c2-5; *Euthyphro* 3b9-e3; *Republic* 7. 516e8-517a7, 517d4-e3; *Theaetetus* 173c6-175d7; *Phaedo* 64a10-b1.

interested in victory, not in being. They overpower their interlocutors, it would seem, not because those interlocutors are incapable of overpowering them in turn, if they wished to do so, but because they do not wish either to turn things upside down or merely to be victorious.

Therefore (343d4-6), the person who wishes to win by turning things upside down makes the person giving an exegesis of the fifth, whether in speeches or in writings or in answerings, seem to many of the hearers (readers) to know nothing of things that he takes it in hand to write or to speak. The overturner, then, succeeds in making the exegete seem foolish to the many hearers (readers), but not to all, i.e, some do understand what the exegete presents.

Finally (343d6-e1), the hearers—presumably the many of them—sometimes (but not all the time) fail to recognize two corollary things: (1) that the speaker's or writer's soul is not refuted; (2) that the meanly natured nature of each of the four is refuted. It is understandable that the many do not recognize that the soul is not refuted, for no one can see into another's soul. On the other hand, if a person could recognize what *is* refuted, then the question of soul would be irrelevant. The hearers, then, take a refutation of what is said for a refutation of its ground, either in the sayer's soul or in being itself.

Why does Plato introduce the soul here at all? One could suggest that just as no direct access to being itself is available to humans, similarly no direct access to the soul is available. Therefore, with respect to both the soul and the ὄν, we must extrapolate not only from the look-alike, but also from the name, the speech, and the exact knowledge, even though all these possess a defective, i. e., a meanly natured, nature.

There are two surprises here.

First, there is the somewhat unexpected assertion of the defectiveness of exact knowledge. This is somewhat unexpected because earlier (342c4-5, d1-3), when exact knowledge was expanded by the addition of intellect and true opinion, intellect was said to be the nearest of the three to the fifth thing, while exact knowledge and true opinion were said to be farther, apparently equally far. The suggestion there was that exact knowledge and true opinion are identical, an apparent demotion of exact knowledge that could perhaps be explained perspectivally by the appearance of intellect, i. e., perhaps from the vantage point of ignorance exact knowledge seems very high, while from the vantage point of intellect it seems quite low.

Second, there is the surprise that now name and speech are regarded as natures. Perhaps this too can be explained perspectivally: from the vantage point of the ὄν itself they seem conventional, while from the vantage point of the upside down world of the overturner they seem to be natures.[1]

Plato widens the discussion of the natures of the four by adding a discussion of the natures of human knowers (343e1-344b1).

First, there is the person of good nature, in whom exact knowledge of that which is good natured is brought to birth with difficulty, even if that person is led repeatedly to and through it. Thus, even if the conditions for the birth of exact knowledge are good, still it is produced with difficulty, and there is no guarantee of success. In addition, we see that each of the four, which just had been described as meanly natured, is susceptible of being well natured too.

---

1 Cf. Aristotle, *Generation of Animals* A.23. 731a33-b4: "For [the animals] have sensing, and sensing is a certain knowing. And there is much difference between one who considers its honorableness and dishonorableness in regard to [i.e., compared to] prudence and one who considers it in regard to [i.e., compared to] the class of the unsouled things. For in regard to [i.e., compared to] being prudent, communing with only touch and tasting seems to be as nothing, but in regard to [i.e., compared to] a plant or a stone [it seems to be] wondrous; for [from the point of view of a plant or a stone] the having chanced even upon this [kind of] knowing [i. e., upon touch and tasting] would seem to be cherishable [i.e., desirable], but lying-dead and not-being would not." (αἴσθησιν γὰρ ἔχουσιν, ἡ δ' αἴσθησις γνῶσίς τις. ταύτης δὲ τὸ τιμίον καὶ ἄτιμον πολὺ διαφέρει σκοποῦσι πρὸς φρόνησιν καὶ πρὸς τὸ τῶν ἀψύχων γένος. πρὸς μὲν γὰρ τὸ φρονεῖν ὥσπερ οὐδὲν εἶναι δοκεῖ τὸ κοινωνεῖν ἁφῆς καὶ γεύσεως μόνον, πρὸς δὲ φυτὸν ἢ λίθον θαυμάσιον· ἀγαπητὸν γὰρ ἂν δόξειε καὶ ταύτης τυχεῖν τῆς γνώσεως ἀλλὰ μὴ κεῖσθαι τεθνεὸς καὶ μὴ ὄν.)

Next is the person of bad nature, the person whose soul's attitude or aptitude (ἕξις) has the same nature as the many's soul attitude or aptitude with regard to learning and so-called habits. When habits are corrupted, as they are in the many, the incapacity with regard to knowing is incorrigible. Apparently, learning ability and habituatability are in humans as sight is, and the keen-sighted (Lynceus) may try to make the dull-sighted humans see what he sees by pointing and talking, but the condition of the many cannot be ameliorated.

To clarify this, Plato classifies humans according as they are or are not cogeneric of the just and beautiful things, i. e., of the truth of virtue and badness:

(1) the non-cogeneric (regardless of learning ability): ineducable;

(2) the cogeneric:
(a) learning-resistant and unmemoried: ineducable,
(b) facile-at-learning and memoried: educable.

The emphasis again is on the educability of only the few, namely those of good nature who are cogeneric of the just and beautiful things and who are good learners with good memories. If even a single one of these characteristics is missing in a person, that person is ineducable in the ὄν itself.

Plato returns (344b1-c1) to the theme of learning with which he started (cf. 341c4-d2), but with a significant shift of emphasis. What were initially called the serious things are now specified as the whole beingness (τῆς ὅλης οὐσίας). Where initially he discussed the burning allure of learning by συνουσία and συζῆν, now the emphasis is on the effort involved in igniting the fire of learning, namely diligence (b2, τριβῆς, literally 'rubbing;' cf. b4, τριβόμενα).[1] In addition, there is a revision of the four things: although name and speech remain, the look-alike has been replaced by seeings and sensings (a moving back to the by which, as in the case of learning), and exact knowledge and true opinion have been replaced by prudence (a moving back from the more inflexible to the more flexible, as befits a backward deepening of the genetic movement).

Now one comes to the conclusion (344c1-d2) of what Plato here will call a myth.

The conclusion to be drawn is that all who are serious about serious things need a great deal before they write anything down and publish it amidst the envy and perplexity of humans. The lesson is not that one should not write, but rather that before one risks writing, one should be as non-needy as possible, i. e., one should be as wise as possible,[2] as free as possible from the envy and perplexity that characterize the human condition.

Finally, if someone sees anyone's writings, whether a legislator's laws or anything else, then if the writer is serious, that writer regards the writings in one or the other of two ways. On the one hand, the writer may regard them as non-serious things, in which instance the writer's serious things are in the writer's most beautiful spot, namely the writer's intellect. On the other hand, the writer may regard them as genuinely serious, in which instance mortals have destroyed that writer's senses.

1 This method is applied by Socrates at *Republic* 4.434e4-435a4.
2 Cf. *Symposium* 200a5-201c5, 203d8-204b5.

Why are the laws and the legislator singled out? Plato seems to want to single out either laws as non-serious or legislators as senseless,[1] perhaps because laws and legislators make humans what they are, as a result of which humans are filled with envy and perplexity, and so long as they are—which means always—the position of philosophy or philosophers is extremely precarious. The nature that the philosopher brings to light may be a threat to the prevailing νόμος. This is why a philosopher who seriously presented the serious things would have to be demented, because from the vantage point of philosophy, there will be no cessation of evils for humans until philosophers become rulers. The example of Socrates as the only human who is truly capable with respect to the political things[2] is instructive. The truth is subversive of the city and dangerous to the truth teller, as Antenor found in the Trojan assembly.[3]

Nonetheless, a serious person may be a writer, so long as the writings are non-serious, i. e., as seen before, so long as the serious person writes playfully.

This is the myth, which also is called a wandering, i. e., a digression.

In the afterword (344d3-345c3), Plato spells out the three lessons that the myth teaches.

First, if Dionysius, or his inferior or his superior or anyone else, wrote any of the highest and first things about nature, then he did not hear or learn anything healthy about them from Plato, or his inferior or his superior or anyone else. On the other hand, anyone who did not write unharmoniously and improperly any of the highest and first things about nature, i. e., who did not simply throw the writings together and out, but rather had the reverence for them that Plato does, did hear or learn something healthy about them from someone. In other words, the possibility is left open that there may be a healthy knower aboout the highest and first things about nature who writes or speaks about the lowest and n^{th} things about nature, either for the purpose of simply presenting them in themselves or for the purpose of revealing through them indirectly the highest and first things. One may, then, be a Platonic dialogue writer or a Socratic speaker.

In addition, someone who has learned or heard something healthy about the highest and first things will not simply write and throw writings to the many, and such a person will not write unharmoniously and improperly.

How would such a person write?

First, such a writer would carefully consider the audience and not simply exile (ἐκβάλλω) writings among them without regard either to the exile (the writings) or to the strangers among whom the exile finds itself (an audience for the most part incapable of discerning and/or understanding the highest and first things that the exile adumbrates). The writing is an exile or a stranger in its own land. The suggested paradigm for a writing is Odysseus returned to Ithaca in disguise.[4] In other words, the writings must be disguised not as a god,[5] i. e., not as the highest and first things, but rather as a beggar.[6] So, if one writes, on the one hand, one must write writings that are impoverished, i. e., writings that are, in philosophic terms, aporetic. On the other hand, just as Odysseus, the writings must be many-minded and many-mannered and wandering. They must have an exoteric surface that is unthreatening to conventional opinion and an esoteric philosophic core. In addition, they must wander or be transmovable (cf. 343a3), i. e., they must be living speech, they must be truly conversational, truly dialogic.

---

1 Cf. *Laws* 6.769a1-3 & ff.; *Statesman* 294a6-d2; *Gorgias* passim.

2 Cf. *Republic* 5.473c11-e2; *Gorgias* 521d6-8.

3 See *Iliad* 7.348-364 and context.

4 Cf. Xenophon, *Memorabilia* IV.6.1 & 13-15.

5 Cf. *Sophist* beginning.

6 Cf. *Symposium* 203c5 ff., the description of eros.

Yet the truly dialogic writing, insofar as it is the product of a self-consciously polydianoetic and polytropic writer, must be an artfully dialogic writing, i. e., chance must be eliminated, so that the presented conversation, although mimetic of ordinary conversation, is constructed in such a way that the careful, persistent, and suitably natured reader may see through to the golden core that its surface hides.[1]

The second lesson of the myth (344d9-345a1) is concerned with the possible purposes of writings, of which there are two, as reminders (344d9-e2) and from ambition (344e2-345a1).

The composing of writings as reminders is an acceptable purpose for writing when forgetting presents a genuine problem. In the case of the highest and first things, however, forgetting is no problem, because once the soul grasps them, they can be recalled among the briefest things of all. Once consciousness has memorialized the highest and first things, then, even if they recede into the unthematized margins of consciousness, they can virtually instantaneously be brought back again. Hence, for the knower, for the wise person, writings as reminders are superfluous.

What about the potential knower? For such a person, speeches, whether spoken or written, are means of leading that person to knowledge of the highest and first things.[2] Even Plato made an attempt to lead Dionysius through to them, to narrate them to Dionysius. Apparently, then, there is a place for speeches, and for speeches that can be repeated more than once, a circumstance that can be fulfilled either by the physical presence of a knower (e.g., Plato) verbally repeating the lessons or by a properly constructed writing that can be read and re-read until the teaching becomes assimilated, at which point—and only at which point—the speeches become superfluous.

The second purpose that a writer may have for writing is personal glorification, i.e., the writings are reminders, not of the highest and first things, but of the writer. In this case, the writer writes from shameful φιλοτιμία (love of honor, ambition) in two senses: (1) the writer may claim that the teaching is his or her own; (2) the writer may claim to have partaken of an education in the highest and first things and consequently to have understood them.

Therefore, someone who writes must write out of the opposite of shameful φιλοτιμία.[3] The writer must write, not with desire for self-glory, but so as to preserve anonymity as much as possible. Certainly, this criterion is satisfied by the form of the Platonic dialogue, in which Plato is an invisible and virtually anonymous presence. Whether this kind of absent presence would classify as noble φιλοτιμία is unclear, but it depends upon whether any writing as such involves φιλοτιμία, and whether, in writing, nobility and anonymity are directly proportional to each other,[4] and whether φιλοσοφία is consonant even with noble φιλοτιμία. In addition, the claim that the teaching is one's own would seem to be base or shameful, because the teaching can be no one's own.

With regard to partaking of an education in the highest and first things, one συνουσία or narration is insufficient (345a1-4). How it could be sufficient, "Zeus [alone] kens."[5] This applies only to someone who needs to be educated by another, not to someone who is capable of autodidacticism. The reference to the *Phaedo* points to the evidence for the insufficiency of only one συνουσία or narration: Socrates's attempt to free Phaedo and his friends from the fear of death is a complete failure, and when Socrates is dying, they behave as disgracefully as the women at the beginning of the dialogue.[6]

---

1 Cf. *Symposium* 216d2-217a2, Socrates as Silenus.

2 Cf. *Phaedo* 99c9-d1, Socrates's δεύτερος πλοῦς or second sailing, and context.

3 Whether all φιλοτιμία is shameful is unclear.

4 Cf. *Phaedrus* 257c7.

5 Cf. *Phaedo* 62a8.

6 *Phaedo* 117c3-4; cf. 59e8-60b1.

The teacher (345a4-7) must know who it is that is concerned to find out about the highest and first things, in order to determine the need for repeating the education. It is possible, then, that the person who is concerned to find out could envision [i.e., understand] sufficiently after only one hearing, but the person who is not genuinely concerned to find out is immune even to many hearings.

There is an unmentioned intermediate person, namely a person who is potentially capable of finding out alone, but who needs a repeated narration of them to activate the power to do so.

Finally, even with respect to those who believe that they know the highest and first things sufficiently, for whatever reason, their dishonoring the leader and authority in these things is inexplicable. This indicates one of the problems of φιλοτιμία, or at least of shameful φιλοτιμία: the seeking of honor for oneself necessarily involves the dishonoring of someone else. Hence, by honoring himself, Dionysius de-honored Plato. However, then Plato must de-honor Dionysius and re-honor himself. So, in order to defend the honor of the highest and first things, Plato too must practice φιλοτιμία. Is this noble φιλοτιμία? That is, if the assertion of the false prophet to be a true prophet is base φιλοτιμία, is the discrediting of that claim, the assertion of the true prophet to be the true prophet—is that noble φιλοτιμία? If it is, still how is the audience to distinguish the two competing claims of true prophethood?[1]

This, then, is *the* Platonic myth. What is a Platonic myth? It is a speech, and as such it must be read the way that any speech in a Platonic dialogue is read. What kind of speech is it? It is a speech about genesis, in this case the genesis of exact knowledge and of writing.

---

1 See CHAPTER I. INTRODUCTION.

V. THE SOCRATIC MYTH: *Phaedrus*

It is appropriate to turn now to the *Phaedrus*, because its mythical content is closest to the mythical content of the seventh epistle, and because it is the most originally mythical of the purely Socratic dialogues.[1]

Perceval Frutiger has stressed the originally mythical character of the *Phaedrus* in his survey of the sources of what he considered myths in the Platonic dialogues, and he singles out the fable of the cicadas and the story of Theuth as the only two entirely original myths in Plato's works.[2] Although Frutiger is correct to stress the originality of the *Phaedrus*, he does so for the wrong reasons, because the brief account of the cicadas (258e6-259d9; cf. 230c2-3) and the account of Theuth (274c5-275b2) are not myths, i. e., they are not called myths explicitly either by Socrates or by Phaedrus. To demonstrate the originality of the accounts in the *Phaedrus*, one does not need to select any specified accounts, but only to cite Phaedrus's remark to Socrates:

> Oh Socrates, you easily make[3] speeches [that are] Egyptian and of whatever country, if you will.[4]

In addition, approximately half the dialogue is either mythic or a myth, as the following brief summary will indicate:

> (227a1-230e5) The setting is mythic insofar as it is pervaded by the μυθολόγημα (229c5) of Boreas and Oreithyia, an account of the genesis in eros of the overcoming of death.
>
> (230e6-234c5) Lysias's speech is neither mythic nor a myth. It is described exclusively as a λόγος,[5] i. e., it is regarded as a set of prescriptions for behavior rooted in utility and a low desire for gratification.[6]
>
> (234c6-237a6) This interlude culminates in a reemphasis on the setting of the dialogue.
>
> (237a7-242a1) Socrates's Lysian speech is explicitly called a myth,[7] i.e., it describes the genesis in certain low natural compulsions[8] of the perspective that Lysias adopted in his speech. In other words, the ground of Lysias's speech is the shameful assumption that ἔρως is the vigorous unspeakable natural desire to prey upon beautiful bodies.[9]

---

1 A purely Socratic dialogue is a dialogue in which Socrates is the primary speaker. The remaining dialogues are either mixed dialogues, i. e., dialogues in which Socrates is present but not the primary speaker (*Sophist, Statesman, Parmenides, Symposium, Timaeus, Critias*), or purely non-Socratic dialogues i. e., dialogues in which Socrates is totally absent (*Laws, Epinomis*). For discussions of other legitimate divisions of the dialogues, see Leo Strauss, *The City and Man* (Chicago, 1964), pp. 55-58, and Diogenes Laertius III. 49-51, 56-62.

2 Perceval Frutiger, *Les mythes de Platon; etude philosophique et littéraire* (Paris, 1930), p. 233.

3 Here, this suggests "make up."

4 *Phaedrus* 275b3-4: Ὦ Σώκρατες, ῥᾳδίως σὺ Αἰγυπτίους καὶ ὁποδαποὺς ἂν ἐθέλῃς λόγους ποιεῖς.

5 See *Phaedrus* 227b6, c4, d2, 228a7, b4-5, 6, c1, d7, 230d8, 234c6, d3, e5-6, 235b2, e6, 236e2.

6 Cf. χρὴ . . . ἀστεῖοι καὶ δημοφελεῖς at 227c9-d2, συμφέρειν at 230e7, ὑπολογίζεσθαι at 231b4 (cf. Thompson note ad 231b), περὶ πλείονος ποιήσονται at 231c5, ὠφελεῖσθαι at 232d7, ὠφελίαν at 233c1 and 234c3; also cf. χάριν at 231b1, 233d8, e4, 7, χάριτος at 234c1, χαριεῖσθαι at 231b7, χαρίζεσθαι at 231c4, 233d5, e6, 234b7.

7 τοῦ μύθου at 237a9, ὁ μῦθος at 241e8; also cf. μυθολογίαν at 243a4.

8 Cf. ἔμφυτος at 237d7-8, φύσει at 239a6, and ἡ φύσις at 240b2. Also cf. ἀναγκάζει at 237a9, ἀναγκάζεται at 241b5, ἀνάγκη at 237c2, 238e3, 239a5, 7, b5, 240a4, ἀνάγκης at 240d1, e1, 241b4, 7, ἀναγκαῖον at 240c4, 241c2. In addition, consider οἴστρου at 240d1, and the conclusion that ὡς λύκοι ἄρνας ἀγαπῶσιν, ὣς παῖδα φιλοῦσιν ἐρασταί at 241d1.

9 Cf. 238b7-c4, 236e7-8, 241d1; for the shame attached to it, see 237a4-4, 243b4-7, d3.

(242a1-243e8) In this interlude, Socrates expresses his awareness that he needs to compose a purificatory palinode in the manner of Stesichorus.

(243e9-257b6) Socrates's Stesichorean palinode is a purification of Socrates's shameful Lysian account of nature, i.e., it rhetorically elaborates the genesis of erotic ἔργα in the nature of the whole and the nature of the soul, in the latter case by integrating the low natural desires (the hybristic horse) into a more complete psychic schema, by giving them their due without giving short shrift to the high natural desires (the tractable horse and the reins-holder). The palinode is referred to as a myth[1] and as "some mythic hymn,"[2] and as such it is the ἐρωτικὸς μῦθος that has as its counterpart the ἐρωτικοὶ λόγοι of the *Symposium*.[3] In other words, the palinode is the μῦθος περὶ φιλοσοφίας that has as its counterpart the λόγοι περὶ φιλοσοφίας of the *Symposium*.[4]

(257b7-278b6) This is a lengthy discussion of the characteristics that good writing must have. It seems to form a long gloss on the dense and elliptical discussion of writing in the seventh epistle. This is not a myth, i.e., it is a non-genetic account.

(278b7-279c8) The conclusion culminates in a prayer to Pan.

In accordance with the principle enunciated earlier,[5] those sections of the *Phaedrus* that are routinely called myths in the literature are not myths, whereas sections of the dialogue that are not ever characterized as myths are myths indeed.

In addition, the connection of the *Phaedrus* with the seventh epistle and the setting of the dialogue suggest that the explicit content of the *Phaedrus* is, to an unusually large extent for a Platonic dialogue, the teaching of Plato himself.[6] In particular, when Socrates and Phaedrus decide to talk in the shade of a plane tree, ἡ πλάτανος,[7] the pun on Plato's name (ὁ Πλάτων)—which is not surprising in a dialogue that is full of playful punning—makes the suggestion very strong that the entire discussion of the *Phaedrus* is carried on ὑπὸ τῇ τοῦ Πλάτωνος σκιᾷ.

One may begin the discussion of the *Phaedrus* itself[8] with the interlude following Socrates's palinode, an interlude that justly has been called "le pivot du *Phèdre*."[9]

---

1 253c7: τοῦδε τοῦ μύθου.

2 265c1: μυθικόν τινα ὕμνον; cf. 247c3-4.

3 Cf. *Symposium* 172b2.

4 Cf. *Symposium* 173c3.

5 See Chapter II beginning.

6 See my article, "A Hitherto Unremarked Pun in the *Phaedrus*," *Apeiron*, vol. 15, no. 2, 1981, pp. 115-116.

7 Of the five occurrences of πλάτανος in Plato's works, four are in the *Phaedrus* (229a8, 230b1-2, 6, 236e1). The fifth is at *Laws* 4. 705c4, where it is listed as absent from the site of the colony that is being founded by the interlocutors there.

8 One of the most penetrating analyses of the whole *Phaedrus* is John Sallis, *Being and Logos: the way of Platonic dialogue* (Pittsburgh, 1975), ch. III, which consistently takes into account the arguments as dramatic elements of the dialogue. [cited as Sallis.] An incisive analysis of sections of the *Phaedrus* may be found in Jacob Klein, *A Commentary on Plato's* Meno (Chapel Hill, 1965), pp. 10-16, 20-22, 151-152, 169-171. [cited as Klein, *Meno*.] Also helpful is Herman L. Sinaiko, *Love, Knowledge and Discourse in Plato* (Chicago, 1965), ch. 2. One should also consult: Plato, *Plato's* Phaedrus, tr. with intro. and comm. by R. Hackforth (Indianapolis, 1952) [cited as Hackforth]; Plato, *Oeuvres complètes* (Paris, 1920-1964), tome IV, part 3, *Phèdre*, tr. L. Robin [Robin's introduction to this edition will be cited as Robin, "Notice"]; G.J. de Vries, *Commentary on the* Phaedrus *of Plato* (Amsterdam, 1969) [cited as Vries]; M.J. Verdenius, "Notes on Plato's *Phaedrus*," *Mnemosyne*, ser. 4, vol. 8, 1955; Eric Voegelin, *Order and History*, vol. 3, *Plato and Aristotle* (Baton Rouge, 1957); R.S. Bluck, "The Second Platonic Epistle," *Phronesis*, vol. 5, 1960, pp. 140-151; Plato, *Phaedrus and the Seventh and Eighth Letters*, tr. Walter Hamilton (Penguin Classics); Plato, *Plato's Epistles*, tr. with critical essays and notes by Glenn R. Morrow (Indianapolis, 1962); Josef Pieper, *Enthusiasm and Divine Madness*, tr. Richard and Clara Winston (NY, 1964).

9 Robin, "Notice," p. xxxvii.

Phaedrus's first remark (257b7-c7) after Socrates completes his grand palinode is somewhat puzzling. After little more than a perfunctory response to the palinode and a brief hierarchical ranking of the three preceding speeches in terms of beauty (the most beautiful being Socrates's palinode, the next in beauty Socrates's Lysian speech, the ugliest Lysias's own speech), he fears that Lysias's reputation would be diminished if he should try to compete with Socrates's palinode.[1] The puzzling aspects of Phaedrus's remark are, on the one hand, his apparent immunity—in any affective way—to the power and beauty of Socrates's palinode, so that his wonder leads to nothing more than a low concern for Lysias's honor, and on the other hand, his apparent assumption that speechwriting is fundamentally an activity of the political arena, an assumption that is puzzling coming as it does after such a patently transpolitical paean to erotic craziness as Socrates's mythic hymn is.

The political emphasis here is revealing in several ways. First, it suggests that even though Phaedrus goes outside the city in his valetudinarian quest for bodily health and vigor,[2] psychically he is in and of the city in some decisive sense. Socrates, however, virtually never goes bodily outside the city,[3] and yet in some decisive sense, of all humans he is the least in and of the city,[4] which is an aspect of his being the most erotic.[5] Phaedrus, then, is fundamentally non-erotic by nature, which explains why Lysias's speech extolling the non-lover appeals so strongly to him.

Second, it gives an important clue to understanding Lysias's speech, because it suggests that one must read the erotic argument also as a political argument. Indeed, the 'historical' Lysias was first and foremost a writer of δικανικοὶ λόγοι δημόσιοι.[6] Although he was capable of writing a λόγος ἁπλῶς ἐπιδεικτικός, and although the private setting in which the speech was delivered suggests such a composition, Phaedrus's concern suggests that what we have here is an ἐπιδεικτικός λόγος τε καὶ δικανικός[7] or, in other terms, an ἐρωτικὸς λόγος τε καὶ πολιτικός. Socrates himself had intimated as much even before he heard the speech itself:

> *Phaedrus.* For [Lysias] speaks how one must gratify a non-lover rather than a lover.
> *Socrates.* What noblesse oblige! Would that he would write how it is useful [to gratify] the poor rather than the rich, and the older than the younger, and as many other things as there are [that apply] both to me and to the many of us; for then his speeches would be urbane and beneficial to the populace.[8]

---

1 Consider on this Klein, *Meno*, p. 14: "Phaedrus, who before the Palinode was quite certain (243d8-e1) that he could prevail upon Lysias to write another speech competing with the one Socrates was about to deliver, is very doubtful now (257c) whether Lysias would consent to join the contest. Has he not already been abusively called a mere 'speechwriter'?" What should be added here is that Phaedrus has been aware of the 'abuse' hurled at Lysias for some time, but it had not shaken his confidence in Lysias even through Socrates's first speech. The Socratic palinode has shaken that confidence, but whether the root of the change is a burgeoning conversion to philosophy on Phaedrus's part (cf. Klein, *Meno*, p. 14, n. 34; Hackforth, pp. 13, 111-112, 169) or something else is unclear here.

2 Cf. *Phaedrus* 227a4-b1, and Robin's description of Phaedrus, cited by Hackforth, p. 13.

3 Cf. *Phaedrus* 230c5-e4.

4 The Aristophanean portrait of Socrates hanging from the sky in a basket is the most graphic representation of this.

5 Cf. *Symposium* 177d7-8; also see Sallis, p. 111. There seems to be a fundamental tension between νόμος and ἔρως.

6 Cf. Lysias, *Selected Speeches*, ed. C. D.Adams (Norman, OK, 1970), intro., p. 24.

7 Cf. Socrates's use of ἐπιδεικνύμενος at 258a7, and Vries, note ad loc.; also cf. Hackforth, p. 115.

8 *Phaedrus* 227c7-d2: [ΦΑΙ.] λέγει γὰρ ὡς χαριστέον μὴ ἐρῶντι μᾶλλον ἢ ἐρῶντι. ΣΩ. Ὦ γενναῖος. εἴθε γράψειεν ὡς χρὴ πένητι μᾶλλον ἢ πλουσίῳ, καὶ πρεσβυτέρῳ ἢ νεωτέρῳ, καὶ ὅσα ἄλλα ἐμοί τε πρόσεστι καὶ τοῖς πολλοῖς ἡμῶν· ἦ γὰρ ἂν ἀστεῖοι καὶ δημωφελεῖς εἶεν οἱ λόγοι. Hackforth's rendering of the last phrase ("What an attractive democratic theory that would be!") suggests the political reference but makes the mistake of prejudging that the reference is to democracy rather than, say, to oligarchy or something else. Cf. Stanley Rosen, "The Non-lover in Plato's *Phaedrus*," *Man and World*, vol. 2, no. 3, August 1969, pp. 434-435.

Therefore, any analysis of Lysias's speech that does not take into account its political dimension, in addition to its erotic dimension, will be incomplete.

Phaedrus's concern expands into a fear that speechwriting as such is disgraceful or shameful. This cannot be a blanket indictment of speeches as such, because Phaedrus himself is a prodigious devotee and generator of speeches.[1] For him to indict speeches as such would be tantamount to his indicting himself as their cause (258c9-10). Phaedrus's indictment of speeches, then, is an indictment of *written* speeches, an indictment that he adopts from political persons (257c5) and that he has implicitly embodied from the beginning of the dialogue when he hid the scroll of Lysias's speech under his clothing.

Socrates is ὁ τῶν λόγων ἐραστής,[2] and even more, he is diseased with the capacity for hearing about speeches.[3] Hence, he rallies to the defense of speeches by pointing out that whatever political persons may say in their abuse of speechwriting, since they themselves write speeches (e.g., laws, resolutions), their indictment is not a blanket indictment of written speeches as such,[4] but only of shameful and bad written speeches:[5]

> *Socrates.* Then this is clear to all, that the writing [of] speeches itself, then, is not shameful.
> *Phaedrus.* What then?
> *Socrates.* But now I believe this to be shameful, [namely,] speaking and writing, not beautifully, but shamefully and badly.[6]

Socrates's defense is a defense of speaking as well as of writing, i. e., it is a defense of λόγος.[7] Every Socratic-Platonic defense is a defense against justifiable accusations, a defense that does justice to the accusations insofar as they are justifiable, but that simultaneously does justice to the accused insofar as it is justifiable.[8]

---

1 Cf. *Phaedrus* 242a7-b5; *Symposium* 177d2-5, esp. d5.

2 Cf. *Phaedrus* 228c1-2.

3 Cf. *Phaedrus* 228b6-7: τῷ νοσοῦντι περὶ λόγων ἀκοήν.

4 It should be noted here that what is presented externally as a confrontation between the anti-writing persons and the pro-writing persons must be considered internally with regard to any discussion of writing in the Platonic corpus. In particular, the explicit assertions of the anti-writing persons are belied by their very practice of writing, even if they write against writing. In accordance with the generalization of the discussion, Plato would be an example of an ostensible anti-writing person who explicitly in deed and implicitly in speech is pro-writing. Cf. Sallis, p. 162.

5 Of course, they may define a beautiful speech as one that glorifies themselves and their deeds and a shameful speech as one that denigrates them, but that does not affect the point that Socrates makes.

6 *Phaedrus* 258d1-5: ΣΩ. Τοῦτο μὲν ἄρα παντὶ δῆλον, ὅτι οὐκ αἰσχρὸν αὐτό γε τὸ γράφειν λόγους. ΦΑΙ. Τί γάρ? ΣΩ. Ἀλλ' ἐκεῖνο οἶμαι αἰσχρὸν ἤδη, τὸ μὴ καλῶς λέγειν τε καὶ γράφειν ἀλλ' αἰσχρῶς τε καὶ κακῶς.

7 The generality of the defense is also suggested at 258b1-5 when Socrates alludes briefly to the poet in the theater. Cf. Vries, note ad 258b2-3. Also cf. 272a8-b2: "[*Socrates.*] But if anyone speaking or teaching or writing leaves out any of them, and [still] asserts himself to speak by art, the person who is not persuaded [by his assertion that he speaks by art] is the master of the situation." (ἀλλ' ὅτι ἂν αὐτῶν τις ἐλλείπῃ λέγων ἢ διδάσκων ἢ γράφων, φῇ δὲ τέχνῃ λέγειν, ὁ μὴ πειθόμενος κρατεῖ.) Also cf. 277d6, λέγει ἢ γράφει, and context, and 278b7 ff. In addition, compare 259e1-2 to 258d7. Finally, especially consider 258a6-b1: "[*Socrates.*] Indeed after this next the writer speaks, showing off his own wisdom to his praisers, sometimes making an altogether long writing; or does the suchlike appear to you to be anything other than a [spoken] speech that has been writen down? *Phaedrus.* To me at any rate, it does not." ([ΣΩ.] Ὁ συγγραφεύς—ἔπειτα λέγει δὴ μετὰ τοῦτο, ἐπιδεικνύμενος τοῖς ἐπαινέταις τὴν ἑαυτοῦ σοφίαν, ἐνίοτε πάνυ μακρὸν ποιησάμενος σύγγραμμα· ἢ σοι ἄλλο τι φαίνεται τὸ τοιοῦτον ἢ λόγος συγγεγραμμένος; ΦΑΙ. Οὐκ ἔμοιγε.)

8 The same applies to Socratic-Platonic accusations, namely that they always (even if only as an undertone of the surface argument) contain a defense of the accused insofar as it can be defended. This is certainly the case with the ostensibly scathing attacks against democracy in *Republic* 8 and against poetry in *Republic* 10. The *Apology of Socrates* is no exception to this: cf. George Anastaplo, "Human Being and Citizen; a beginning to the study of Plato's *Apology of Socrates*," in *Ancients and Moderns*, p. 23 et passim.

Even before he denies that writing in itself is shameful, Socrates adumbrates the double-edged nature of the discussion that will follow:

> Whenever an orator or a king becomes sufficient [i.e., is up to his responsibility], so that having grasped the power of Lycurgus or Solon or Darius, he becomes an immortal speechwriter in a city, then does not he himself regard himself while still living to be the equal to a god, and do not the persons who come to be afterward [i.e., those in the future], when they behold his writings, customarily believe these same things about him?[1]

The use of Λόγος, then, has three consequences. First, it enables one to become immortal, i. e., it has a power even beyond the political or oratorical power alone of Lycurgus or Solon or Darius, and this power is implicitly more a power of written speeches over and above spoken speeches and political deeds. Although the specific examples here suggest self-glorifying writings, one must also consider writings that glorify and/or immortalize others. For example, how well would we know Socratic philosophizing without the writings of Aristophanes, Xenophon, and Plato? Moreover, in the case of Plato at least, the glorifying and immortalizing of Socrates[2] is an indirect glorifying and immortalizing of Plato himself.[3] In other words, although the explicit case here[4] is of one who makes writings that are self-praising and that praise one's praisers, one can conceive of a writing that is made as a praise of someone else, yet here too there would seem to have to be an element, however indirect, of self-praise.[5]

Second, it results in a deification of the speechwriter by the audience to such an extent that the speechwriter comes to regarding himself or herself as the equal of a god.[6] This is one of the dangers of speech, that the power that it gives one over others, whether to rule or to enchant, is reflected back from the others onto the writer, so as to evoke in the writer an excessive self-regard. The height of conceit or hybris is to regard oneself as equal to a god while living, something that is fitting for no human.[7]

Third, future readers of writings too will regard the speechwriter as an immortal equal to a god: it will be customary (νομίζουσι) for them to do so. Can there be a sober understanding of this apparently hyperbolic claim? There can, if one takes seriously the demand that is placed on writings in the *Phaedrus*,[8] namely that every writing must be composed as a ζῷον according to a logographic compulsion. As Socrates puts it elsewhere:

---

1 *Phaedrus* 258b10-c5: [ΣΩ.] ὅταν ἱκανὸς γένηται ῥήτωρ ἢ βασιλεύς, ὥστε λάβων τὴν Λυκούργου ἢ Σόλωνος ἢ Δαρείου δύναμιν ἀθάνατος γενέσθαι λογογράφος ἐν πόλει, ἆρ' οὐκ ἰσόθεον ἡγεῖται αὐτός τε αὐτὸν ἔτι ζῶν, καὶ οἱ ἔπειτα γιγνόμενοι ταὐτὰ ταῦτα περὶ αὐτοῦ νομίζουσι, θεώμενοι αὐτοῦ τὰ συγγράμματα;

2 Cf. *Epistles* 2. 314c4.

3 The Socratic philosophy could have remained an oral teaching—as the Pythagorean and Orphic traditions did—although there would have been an ultimate writing by someone, to the inexorability of which hints in the dialogues abound (as in the external settings of the *Theaetetus*, *Symposium*, and so forth). Better for it to be done, then, in the proper way.

4 Cf. *Phaedrus* 257e4-258a2.

5 This problem came up in connection with φιλοτιμία in the seventh epistle. One could also point to each speech delivered in the *Symposium* as an example of the compulsion, when praising another, to praise oneself (cf. *Philebus* 28b1-2). Another way in which this is suggested by Plato is that if all the so-called Platonic dialogues are actually the writings Σωκράτους καλοῦ καὶ νέου γεγονότος (cf. *Epistles* 2. 314c3 and context), then the bulk of the so-called Platonic corpus is a praise of a Socrates by a Socrates; hence, as writings, they are in principle no different in this respect from the writings of political persons. Perhaps it should be reemphasized here that when one considers any passage of the Platonic corpus that is concerned with writing, one must always hold before one the Platonic practice of writing.

6 That this is simply humorous or sarcastic, as Hackforth (p. 116) supposes, is debatable, to say the least.

7 *Phaedrus* 278d3-6. Of course, there is an equality to a god that is possible for humans, but it is not treated until after Socrates's palinode.

8 *Phaedrus* 264c2-5, cited above (ch. IV).

> For the speech now appears to me to be worked forth as some non-bodily cosmos for the purpose of beautifully ruling an ensouled body.[1]

If the making of a speech (whether spoken or written) is done properly only if one makes the speech as a ζῷον or κόσμος, and if making a ζῷον or κόσμος is a work for a god, or one who is similar to a god,[2] then the maker of a speech is, in a sense, ἰσόθεος[3] and must be regarded as such if, through time, the speechmaker is regarded as a writer who writes in a beautiful way.

Finally, the explicit question for the remaining discussion is asked:

> *Socrates.* Therefore, what is the manner of writing both beautifully and not [beautifully]?[4]

The discussion will apply to all writers, future as well as past, and it will make no difference whether their writings are political or private (ἰδιωτικόν), whether they are in meter, as a poet's are, or are without meter, as a prosewriter's (ἰδιώτης) are (258e8-11). In short, from Socrates's point of view at least, the discussion of writing in the *Phaedrus* is applicable to any writing whatsoever that deserves the name of writing.

Before the general question about writing is faced, Socrates deflects Phaedrus's attention, and that of the readers of the dialogue, toward the cicadas. Why? Socrates's remarks will provide an answer.

At first, Socrates says, there were humans, but no Muses. Then the Muses came to be, and by their coming to be (οὕτως), songs somehow appeared. What does this signify?

The Muses are the daughters of Zeus and Mnemosyne, i. e., of philosophy and memory.[5] That is, the Muses are philosophical reminders.[6] But what is the manner of this reminding? Socrates indicates it when he first mentions the cicadas (258e7-259a1): it is διαλέγεσθαι (conversing). Conversing, or conversation, is treated here as identical to singing.[7] Thus, when the cicadas are διαλεγόμενοι ἀλλήλοις, the sound of their conversation is what we regard as their singing (ᾄδοντες).

---

1 *Philebus* 64b6-8: ἐμοὶ μὲν γὰρ καθαπερεὶ κόσμος τις ἀσώματος ἄρξων καλῶς ἐμψύχου σώματος ὁ νῦν λόγος ἀπειργάσθαι φαίνεται.

2 Cf. *Republic* 10. 596a5-597e5; *Timaeus* 41a3-d3 et passim.

3 Cf. William Faulkner's remark: "I created a cosmos of my own. I can move these people around like God, not only in space but in time too." [*Writers at Work: the Paris Review interviews*, ed. Malcolm Cowley (NY, 1959), p. 141.] Also cf. *Phaedrus* 253a7-b1.

4 *Phaedrus* 258d7: ΣΩ. Τίς οὖν ὁ τρόπος τοῦ καλῶς τε καὶ μὴ γράφειν;

5 See Hesiod *Theogony* 915-917. Cf. *Phaedrus* 252e1-3.

6 Cf. H.J. Rose, *Handbook of Greek Mythology* (NY, 1959), p. 174.

7 Cf. *Republic* 7. 532d6-e3 (Glaucon speaking, italics mine): "Indeed let us go toward *the song itself* and narrate in this way as we narated the proemium. Therefore, speak what is the manner of *the power of conversing*, and indeed in accordance with what sorts of looks it has been separated [i.e.,analysed], and what in turn are its ways; for these now, as is likely, would be the ones leading toward it, [i. e., toward] where it would be for a person coming [to it] as a resting-up from the way and an end of the journey" (ἐπ' αὐτὸν δὴ τὸν νόμον ἴωμεν, καὶ διέλθωμεν οὕτως ὥσπερ τὸ προοίμιον διήλθομεν. λέγε οὖν τίς ὁ τρόπος τῆς τοῦ διαλέγεσθαι δυνάμεως, καὶ κατὰ ποῖα δὴ εἴδη διέστηκεν, καὶ τίνες αὖ ὁδοί· αὗται γὰρ ἂν ἤδη, ὡς ἔοικεν αἱ πρὸς αὐτὸ ἄγουσαι εἶεν, οἷ ἀφικομένῳ ὥσπερ ὁδοῦ ἀνάπαυλα ἂν εἴη καὶ τέλος τῆς πορείας.) This remark could almost be taken as a capsule summary of the setting and contents of the *Phaedrus*.

In the same way, one could suggest, the appearance of songs with the Muses is equivalent to the appearance among humans of διαλεκτική, both in the ordinary sense and in the service of philosophical inquiry.[1] Before the Muses came to be, then, speech must have been atomic or totally idiosyncratic or a chaotic manifold of noises. For speech to become a genuine means of interanthropic communication, memory had to arise, and the Muses as the progeny of memory (Mnemosyne) are the expressions of that.

One may restate the first stage in the account of the cicadas thus: at first, there were humans, but their speech was a chaotic manifold of noise, because they had neither memory nor διαλεκτική. This is reminiscent of the movement of the soul that Socrates describes in the *Republic*:

> Then only the skillfully conversational method proceeds in this way, taking out the hypotheses, to the beginning itself, so that it will become steadfast, and it gently drags the soul's seeing thing [i.e., the soul's 'eye'] which has been sunk down beingly in some barbaric bog and leads it up upward, using the arts which we narrated as [being its] co-laborers and co-leaders-around.[2]

The songs that arise, then, signify the dialectical method and the arts that it uses to reach an unhypothetical beginning of something.[3] This may explain why, in the account of the discussion between Theuth and Thamus (274e1-4), all the arts except writing are omitted, namely because, in the cicada interlude and the discussion that follows, their function at least has been adumbrated.

Once conversational skill (i. e., singing) comes to be among humans, some humans are smitten by the pleasure (ὑφ' ἡδονῆς) that they derive from it:

> They are gratified hearing humans being examined, and many times they themselves imitate me, and then they take it in hand to examine others . . .
> For it is not unpleasant.[4]

1 For the identification of τὸ διαλέγεσθαι and ἡ φιλοσοφία, cf. Parmenides 135b5-c7 (italics mine): "'But yet,' Parmenides spoke, 'indeed, oh Socrates, then if, having gazed off unto all the things [spoken] just now and other suchlike things, anyone in turn will not allow looks of the beings to be and does not delimit some look of each one thing, he will not even have [any place] whither he will turn his thinking, having disallowed the same look of each of the beings always to be, and thus *he all in all corrupts the power of conversing*. Thereefore, you, and very much so, seem to me to sense the suchlike.' 'You speak truly,' [Pythodorus asserted Socrates] to assert. 'Therefore, *what will you do about philosophy*? Where will you turn when these things are unrecognized?' 'I altogether do not seem to myself to see [where] in the present at any rate.'" ('Αλλὰ μέντοι, εἶπεν ὁ Παρμενίδης, εἴ γέ τις δή, ὦ Σώκρατες, αὖ μὴ ἐάσει εἴδη τῶν ὄντων εἶναι, εἰς πάντα τὰ νυνδὴ καὶ ἄλλα τοιαῦτα ἀποβλέψας, μηδέ τι ὁριεῖται εἶδος ἑνὸς ἑκάστου, οὐδὲ ὅποι τρέψει τὴν διάνοιαν ἕξει, μὴ ἐῶν ἰδέαν τῶν ὄντων ἑκάστου τὴν αὐτὴν ἀεὶ εἶναι, καὶ οὕτως τὴν τοῦ διαλέγεσθαι δύναμιν παντάπασι διαφθερεῖ. Τοῦ τοιούτου μὲν οὖν μοι δοκεῖς καὶ μᾶλλον ᾐσθῆσθαι. 'Αληθῆ λέγεις, φάναι. Τί οὖν ποιήσεις φιλοσοφίας πέρι; πῇ τρέψῃ ἀγνοουμένων τούτων; Οὐ πάνυ μοι δοκῶ καθορᾶν ἔν γε τῷ παρόντι.)

2 *Republic* 7. 533c7-d4: Οὐκοῦν, ἦν δ' ἐγώ, ἡ διαλεκτικὴ μέθοδος μόνη ταύτῃ πορεύεται, τὰς ὑποθέσεις ἀναιροῦσα, ἐπ' αὐτὴν τὴν ἀρχὴν ἵνα βεβαιώσηται, καὶ τῷ ὄντι ἐν βορβόρῳ βαρβαρικῷ τινι τὸ τῆς ὄμμα κατορωρυγμένον ἠρέμα ἕλκει καὶ ἀνάγει ἄνω, συνερίθοις καὶ συμπεριαγωγοῖς χρωμένη αἷς διήλθομεν τέχναις. Cf. *Phaedo* 69c5-7.

3 Cf. *Phaedrus* 264e7-266c8; *Republic* 6. 511b3-d5.

4 *Apology of Socrates* 23c4-5, 33c4: χαίρουσιν ἀκούοντες ἐξεταζομένων τῶν ἀνθρώπων, καὶ αὐτοὶ πολλάκις ἐμὲ μιμοῦνται, εἶτα ἐπιχειροῦσιν ἄλλους ἐξετάζειν . . . . ἔστι γὰρ οὐκ ἀηδές. Cf. 33b9-c3.

Those who are overcome by the pleasure of dialectic become unconcerned about food and drink. The most massive example of this in the Platonic corpus is the *Republic*, in which the interlocutors never partake of the dinner promised by Polemarchus.[1] The explicit connection between this attitude and philosophy is made by Socrates in the *Phaedo*:

> "Does it appear to you to be [proper] for a philosopher, who is a man, to have been serious in respect to suchlike so-called pleasures, such as about foods and drinks?"
> "Least so, oh Socrates," Simmias asserted.
> "And what of the [pleasures] of sexual activities?"
> "In no way."[2]

In the P*haedrus* interlude, although there is no explicit mention of τὰ ἀφροδίσια, they too are meant, as one can see if one considers that Aristophanes asserts in his λόγος at the banquet that before Zeus moved the genitals of humans to the front of their bodies, humans "used to generate and bring forth not into each other but into the earth, as cicadas do."[3] Whereas, to Aristophanes, distinctly human sexuality is the compulsory tragic way for approaching—without ever achieving—originary bodily unity, which as such is all that humans desire, to Socrates, human progress is toward a freedom from the tyranny of distinctly human sexuality (which is not an abstinence) toward a psychic sexuality, the full extent of which he sketches in his grand mythic palinode.

The singing humans, then, become unconcerned about sex,[4] food, and drink, and they sing (converse) until they come to their end without even noticing it, and then they metamorphose into cicadas. How could they experience death without noticing it? Their transformation into cicadas must have been instantaneous,[5] so that their singing (conversing) was uninterrupted; since they were aware of it, and of it alone, only if it were interrupted would they have noticed a change. Διαλεκτική, then, is a means to a sort of immortality, although certainly not to any individual immortality.

For the humans who were consumed by the pleasure of singing (conversing), their being themselves means their singing εὐθὺς . . . ἕως ἂν τελευτήσῃ (259c4-5), i. e., conversing from birth until death, and their knowing themselves means their becoming themselves only insofar as they are capable of continuously exhibiting their nature as singer-conversationalists. The continuous exhibiting of their nature means the abandonment of a human body for the body of a cicada, so that they are cicadas in body but still distinctly human in their νοῦς.

In other words, each is a monster, a monstrous nature, and although each may be "an animal both gentler and simpler [than Typhon], [an animal] partaking of a certain divine and non-fuming portion by nature,"[6] still each is one member of "a mob . . . of certain monstrous

---

1 Cf. *Republic* 1. 328a7-8; cf. 1. 352b3-6 et passim.

2 *Phaedo* 64d2-7: φαίνεταί σοι φιλοσόφου ἀνδρὸς εἶναι ἐσπουδακέναι περὶ τὰς ἡδονὰς καλουμένας τὰς τοιάσδε, οἷον σιτίων τε καὶ ποτῶν; Ἥκιστα, ὦ Σώκρατες, ἔφη ὁ Σιμμίας. Τί δὲ τὰς τῶν ἀφροδισίων; Οὐδαμῶς. Also cf. 116e1-6 and Socrates's reply.

3 *Symposium* 191b7-c2: ἐγέννων καὶ ἔτικτον οὐκ εἰς ἀλλήλους ἀλλ' εἰς γῆν, ὥσπερ οἱ τέττιγες.

4 If humans are indifferent to distinctly human sexual pleasure, then they are indifferent to whether or not they have a distinctly human body. If thinking or singing/conversing is one's be all and end all, then it can be carried on in any body, if psychic migration from one body to another—even of another sort—is assumed to be possible. Cf. *Odyssey* 10. 237-243, esp. 240.

5 Cf. Franz Kafka, "The Metamorphosis," in *The Penal Colony*, tr. Willa and Edwin Muir (NY, 1961), p. 67: "As Gregor Samsa awoke one morning from uneasy dreams he found himself transformed in his bed into a gigantic insect." Also consider the account of Gregor's death, p. 127.

6 *Phaedrus* 230a5-6: εἴτε ἡμερώτερόν τε καὶ ἁπλούστερον ζῷον, θείας τινὸς καὶ ἀτύφου μοίρας φύσει μετέχον.

natures."[1] The example of the cicadas suggests that to recognize (γνῶναι) oneself, κατὰ τὸ Δελφικὸν γράμμα (229e5-6), is to recognize in oneself the look, τὸ εἶδος (cf. 229d5-6), of a monster. The tasks of knowing oneself and σοφίζεσθαι τὰ μυθολογήματα (cf. 229c7) are not different, but rather to do one is to do the other.[2]

Furthermore, although the cicadas die, τὸ τεττίγων γένος (259c2) persists. The race, then, must perpetuate itself. How? As has been said, they generate into the earth: "the female lays her eggs in the sand, where the young are hatched out by the sun's heat."[3] It is now noon (ἐν μεσημβρίᾳ, 259a2), which means that the sun's heat is perfect for the propagation of the cicadas. But there is no laying of eggs.

What form, then, does their propagation take here? What do they bestow in order to perpetuate themselves? On humans who converse, i. e., on humans who act as the cicadas did when they were humans, the cicadas bestow the gift that they have from the gods, namely from the Muses.[4] That gift is the not needing of nurture (e.g., food and drink) in any way. Thus, ἄνθρωποι διαλεκτικοί are the recipients of a lack of concern for nurture. This unconcern will result in the metamorphosis of new humans into new cicadas.

Therefore, the perpetuation of the race of cicadas depends on the perpetuation of διαλεκτική among at least some humans,[5] a perpetuation that is difficult to achieve because most humans doze on account of the idleness[6] of their thinking. Indeed, most humans behave like slaves, i. e., like sheep or like "a horse [that is] more sluggish and needs to be wakened."[7]

However, some humans doze under the very influence of the cicadas' conversing. These humans are beguiled by the cicadas themselves,[8] which means—it seems—that if διαλεκτική is used as an empty method, it does not produce knowledge, but rather it produces a destructive skepticism and the conceit of believing oneself to know when one actually does not know.[9] Thus, whatever positive function it may serve, ἡ διαλεκτική can beguile humans into thoughtlessness, and it can lure them by its siren song to destruction.[10]

How is one to prevent this? By energizing, putting to work, one's διάνοια.[11] Thus, the discussion that follows the interlude is a discussion of the requirements for knowledge[12] in a speaker or writer. It culminates in a description of how "it is obligatory to think through about any nature whatever."[13]

Insofar as the speaking of Socrates and Phaedrus about this is a conversing that prevents the laughable dozing of their διάνοια, they are enacting the very method about which they are conversing (cf. 259d7-9). Only those who are capable of doing this should be called skilled conversationalists or dialecticians.[14]

---

1 *Phaedrus* 229d7: ὄχλος . . . τερατολόγων τινῶν φύσεων.

2 The image of were-cicadas is no more monstrous than the image of the were-gadfly that Socrates is (*Apology of Socrates* 30e1-6).

3 Plato, *The Symposium of Plato*, ed. with intro. and commentary by R.G. Bury, 2d ed. (Cambridge, Eng., 1973), note ad 191c. Bury also says, "This is not merely a piece of natural history; it contains also an allusion to the cicada [i. e., the cicada hair clasp] as the symbol of Athenian autochthony."

4 Compare *Phaedrus* 259b1 to c3-4; also see *Ion* 533e3-535a5.

5 Cf. *Symposium* 210d3-6: "but having turned toward the much open sea of the beautiful and beholding it, he brings forth many beautiful and magnificent speeches and thoughts in abundant philosophy" (ἀλλ' ἐπὶ τὸ πολὺ πέλαγος τετραμμένος του καλου καὶ θεωρῶν πολλοὺς καὶ καλοὺς λόγους καὶ μεγαλοπρεπεῖς τίκτῃ καὶ διανοήματα ἐν φιλοσοφίᾳ ἀφθόνῳ).

6 *Phaedrus* 259a3: ἀργίαν.

7 *Apology of Socrates* 30e4-5: ἵππῳ . . . νωθεστέρῳ καὶ δεομένῳ ἐγείρεσθαι.

8 *Phaedrus* 259a3: κηλουμένους ὑφ' αὐτῶν.

9 Cf. *Republic* 7. 538c4-539d2.

10 This is one of the lessons of Aristophanes's *Clouds*.

11 Cf. *Republic* 7. 523a10 ff.

12 *Phaedrus* 259e5: τὴν . . . διάνοιαν εἰδυῖαν.

13 *Phaedrus* 270c10-d1: δεῖ διανοεῖσθαι περὶ ὁτουοῦν φύσεως.

14 *Phaedrus* 266b7-c1: καὶ τοὺς δυναμένους αὐτὸ ὁρᾶν . . . καλῶ . . . διαλεκτικούς.

Before returning to this method, one first should consider the deities that preside over διάνοια κατὰ ἐνέργειαν, or τὸ διαλέγεσθαι, or ἡ φιλοσοφία. These deities are the Muses, or rather some of the Muses. When Socrates lists the Muses to whom the dead cicadas report, i. e., the Muses to whom disembodied conversing reports, he lists only four—Terpsichore, Erato, Kalliope, and Ourania—and apparently focuses on two—Kalliope and Ourania—as the Muses of philosophy.

Yet the context would suggest that all the Muses mentioned would have something to do with philosophy (ἡ φιλοσοφία, or ἡ διαλεκτική). Why else would Socrates mention them? After all, since he does not list all nine Muses, and since he is distinguishing humans who converse from humans who do not converse, humans who are dialectical from humans who are not dialectical, the suggestion is very strong that all the Muses whom he mentions explicitly are the Muses of philosophy.[1]

Why, then, does it seem that persons passing time in philosophy[2] are announced especially to the Kalliope-Ourania yoked pair of Muses? The answer lies in the precise way in which Socrates has phrased his remark. Socrates has said that the cicadas announce to the Muses "who of those here honor which of them."[3] He adds that the announcement is "in accordance with the look of each honor."[4] In other words, the determining factor is what one *honors*, not what one does. When Socrates speaks of those who are announced to Kalliope and Ourania, he speaks of them as honoring the music of Kalliope and Ourania.[5] Simply with respect to being announced to these two Muses, this latter criterion alone would seem to be sufficient.

But Socrates says that those are announced who *both* engage in philosophy *and* honor the music of these Muses.[6] Why? The double requirement indicates that the Muses for those who simply engage in philosophy are Terpsichore and Erato. Is there any other evidence to support this? There is.

First, Terpsichore, whose name means 'delight in choral activities,' and whose honorers are the honorers of choruses,[7] is intended as the Muse of ἡ διαλεκτική, i. e., τὸ διαλέγεσθαι. This function is suggested by the following considerations. When Socrates makes his Lysian speech, he begins with an invocation to shrill Muses.[8] The only other beings in the dialogue who are described by shrillness are the cicadas, whose song is said to produce a shrill echo.[9] Later (263d3-4), the cicadas are called those who talk for the Muses. Thus, there is an extremely close connection between the cicadas and the Muses, and in particular between the cicadas and Terpsichore, because the cicadas in their singing/conversing are called a chorus.[10] In other words, τὸ διαλέγεσθαι is a choral activity, and as such it falls within the province of Terpsichore, the dialectic Muse, who represents one aspect of engaging in philosophy. Insofar

---

1 One could go further and say that for Socrates's palinode at least, the four Muses whom Socrates mentions are all the Muses. For the connection between the Muses and philosophy, cf. *Cratylus* 406a3-5: "[*Socrates.*] And this name [i. e., "Muses"] nicknamed both the Muses and wholly music from searching, as is likely, and seeking and philosophy" (τὰς δὲ Μούσας τε καὶ ὅλως τὴν μουσικὴν ἀπὸ τοῦ μῶσθαι, ὡς ἔοικεν, καὶ τῆς ζητήσεως τε καὶ φιλοσοφίας τὸ ὄνομα τοῦτο ἐπωνόμασεν).

2 *Phaedrus* 259d4: τοὺς ἐν φιλοσοφίᾳ διάγοντας.

3 259c6: τίς τίνα αὐτῶν τιμᾷ τῶν ἐνθάδε.

4 259d2-3: κατὰ τὸ εἶδος ἑκάστης τιμῆς.

5 259d4-5: τιμῶντας τὴν ἐκείνων μουσικὴν.

6 *Phaedrus* 259d4-5: The structure of the clause is: τοὺς . . . διάγοντας τε καὶ τιμῶντας. The use of only one article to govern both participles and the emphatic τε καί connective between the participles demand that the clauses be rendered by an emphatic "both . . . and." Vries, note ad loc., takes the τε καί as self-evidently explanatory, although this is not the most typical use of the connective. Its most typical use is rather to connect clauses that are not identical but are either similar or contrary, and this use could be called amplificatory. Cf. J.D. Denniston, *The Greek Particles* (Oxford, 1970), pp. 512, 514, 515, 516.

7 259c7: τοὺς ἐν τοῖς χοροῖς τετιμηκότας αὐτὴν.

8 237a7: ὦ Μοῦσαι . . . λίγειαι.

9 230c1-3. So far as I know, the word λιγύς and its derivatives appear in no other Platonic writing than the *Phaedrus*.

10 230c2-3: τῷ τῶν τεττίγων χορῷ.

as Terpsichore presides over cicadian immortal dialectic, and insofar as the way of the cicadas is a dying and being dead, i. e., insofar as the proto-cicadian humans and the post-human cicadas represent the practice of dying and being dead in the service of the immortality of speech, the *Phaedo* is an elaboration of the Terpsichorean aspect of philosophy (cf. *Phaedo* 63e8 ff., 89b9-c1, 88e2).

Second, Erato, whose name means 'lovable' or 'lovely,' and whose honorers are the honorers of the erotic things,[1] is intended as the Muse of ἡ φιλοσοφία as the erotic striving to be with the beings themselves, to see the beings in their nature.[2] The identification of philosophy and erotics is a strong one in Plato, especially in the person of Socrates. Socrates goes so far as to claim that he knows nothing but the erotic things[3] and that he can recognize a lover or a beloved.[4] In addition, Socrates recognizes himself as a lover, a lover of speeches and of young men.[5] Not only is the philosopher an ἐραστής and ἐρωτικός, but philosophy too is an ἔρως and ἐρωτική. This is its Eratonic aspect.

In the *Symposium*, the speeches at the banquet are first called "erotic speeches,"[6] then "speeches about philosophy,"[7] thereby suggesting that philosophy is identical to the erotic.[8] In addition, Diotima explicitly demonstrates that Ἔρως is a philosopher:

> "For it holds thus. None of the gods philosophizes or desires to become wise—for [each] is [wise]—nor if any other is wise, does he philosophize or desire to become wise . . . ."
>
> "Therefore, who, oh Diotima," I asserted, "are the philosophizers, if they are neither the wise nor the unlearned?"
>
> "Indeed, this then is clear," she asserted, "already even to a child, that they are the persons between both, among whom also Eros would be. For indeed, wisdom is among the most beautiful things, and Eros is eros in respect to the beautiful, so that it is compulsory for Eros to be a philosopher, and [for Eros,] being a philosopher, to be between wise and unlearned."[9]

---

1 259d1-2: τοὺς ἐν τοῖς ἐρωτικοῖς.

2 Cf. *Symposium* 210e4-212a7, esp. 210e5, 211b1-2, c7-8, c8-d1, d3, d8, e1, e3.

3 *Symposium* 1777-8: "I . . . who assert myself to know nothing other than the erotic things" (ἐγὼ . . . ὃς οὐδέν φημι ἄλλο ἐπίστασθαι ἢ τὰ ἐρωτικά). Also consider *Theages* 128b3-6: "[*Socrates.*] I chance to know, so as to speak a word, nothing except a certain small learning, [namely the learning] of the erotic things. Yet with respect to this learning, I make the claim that I am formidable above and beyond anyone whomsoever of both the humans who have been born before [me] and those now." (ἐγὼ τυγχάνω ὡς ἔπος εἰπεῖν οὐδὲν ἐπιστάμενοις πλήν γε σμικροῦ τινος μαθήματος, τῶν ἐρωτικῶν. τοῦτο μεντοι τὸ μάθημα παρ' όντινοῦν ποιοῦμαι δεινὸς εἶναι καὶ τῶν προγεγονότων ἀνθρώπων καὶ τῶν νῦν.) Cf. *Symposium* 198d1-2, *Lysis* 205a1-2.

4 *Lysis* 204b8-c2: "[*Socrates.*] And I am mean and useless with respect to the other things, but this somehow has been given me from a god, [namely] being of such a sort as quickly to recognize both a lover and a beloved." (εἰμὶ δ' ἐγὼ τὰ ἄλλα φαῦλος καὶ ἄχρηστος, τοῦτο δέ μοί πως ἐκ θεοῦ δέδοται, ταχὺ οἵῳ τ' εἶναι γνῶναι ἐρῶντά τε καὶ ἐρώμενον.)

5 Cf. *Phaedrus* 228c1-2 (τοῦ τῶν λόγων ἐραστοῦ); *Charmides* 154b8 ff., esp. 155d3-4 ("and I saw the things inside his cloak and became inflamed and no longer was I inside myself": εἶδον τε τὰ ἐντὸς τοῦ ἱματίου καὶ ἐφλεγόμην καὶ οὐκέτ' ἐν ἐμαυτοῦ ἦν). Also cf. *Rival-lovers* 133a3-5; *Alcibiades I* 103a1-2, 104e4-6; *Symposium* 213c6 ff., 216d2-4. Further cf. Sallis, pp. 111-113.

6 *Symposium* 172b2: τῶν ἐρωτικῶν λόγων.

7 *Symposium* 173c3: περὶ φιλοσοφίας λόγους.

8 Diotima's speech, which initially is called a speech about Eros (τὸν . . . λόγον τὸν περὶ τοῦ Ἔρωτος, 201d1-2), turns out to be a λόγος περὶ τῆς φιλοσοφίας. Cf. 209e5.

9 *Symposium* 204a1-4, a8-b5: ἔχει γὰρ ὧδε. θεῶν οὐδεὶς φιλοσοφεῖ οὐδ' ἐπιθυμεῖ σοφὸς γενέσθαι—ἔστι γάρ—οὐδ' εἴ τις ἄλλος σοφός, οὐ φιλοσοφεῖ. οὐδ' αὖ οἱ ἀμαθεῖς φιλοσοφοῦσιν οὐδ' ἐπιθυμοῦσι σοφοὶ γενέσθαι . . . . Τίνες οὖν, ἔφην ἐγώ, ὦ Διοτίμα, οἱ φιλοσοφοῦντες, εἰ μήτε οἱ σοφοὶ μήτε οἱ ἀμαθεῖς; Δῆλον δή, ἔφη, τοῦτό γε ἤδη καὶ παιδί, ὅτι οἱ μεταξὺ τούτων ἀμφοτέρων, ὧν ἂν εἴη καὶ ὁ Ἔρως. ἔστιν γὰρ δὴ τῶν καλλίστων ἡ σοφία, Ἔρως δ' ἐστὶν ἔρως περὶ τὸ καλόν, ὥστε ἀναγκαῖον Ἔρωτα φιλόσοφον εἶναι, φιλόσοφον δὲ ὄντα μεταξὺ εἶναι σοφοῦ καὶ ἀμαθοῦς.

The *Symposium*, then, is an elaboration of the Eratonic aspect of philosophy.

If Terpsichore and Erato are the Muses of philosophy, of what are Kalliope and Ourania the Muses? They are not simply—as there is a tendency to assume[1]—concerned with the divine and the human heaven and the divine and human speeches.[2] All the Muses are concerned with these to some degree, although Kalliope and Ourania are concerned especially with them.[3] Nonetheless, their concern with divine and human heaven and speeches does not as such distinguish them by kind from the other Muses, but only by degree. Nor does their music,[4] namely, that they throw off the most beautiful sound,[5] distinguish them by kind from the other Muses, but only by degree.

Kalliope and Ourania, then, are the superlative Muses, superlative in their concern and in the beauty of their sound and in age (cf. 259d3-4). Since the other two Muses represent ἡ φιλοσοφία, what is the superlative, as it were, of philosophy?

The suggestion is that it is ἡ σοφία, and that Kalliope and Ourania are the Muses of wisdom. While philosophy may be the biggest music,[6] still "the most beautiful and biggest of the consonances would most justly be spoken to be the biggest wisdom."[7] If "the true Muse [is] the one [that is] together with both speeches and philosophy,"[8] then the truest Muse is the one that is together with wisdom.

What is wisdom? On the one hand, it is beholding or contemplating: this is presided over by Kalliope, as her name suggests. Although the usually assumed derivation is from 'beautiful voice (ὄψ),' one could equally well derive it from 'beautiful eye (ὄψ).'[9]

The derivation from 'beautiful eye' would be more consistent with the imagery of Socrates's mythic palinode, in which there is, it seems, a greater density of vision terms than in any other Socratic utterance. As Socrates says, "The beingness that beingly is, is a spectacle."[10] This spectacle is also a sight, an ὄψις,[11] i. e., an ὄψ, namely—to use the word in both its subjective and its objective meanings (cf. 250d3 to 250b6-7)—the seeing a sight.

It sees two things, both represented by Ourania, divine heaven and human heaven.[12] In other words, it sees the οὐρανὸς ὁρατός (τόπος ὁρατός[13] or οὐράνιος τόπος), and it sees the

---

1 See Vries, note ad 259d6-7; Hackforth, p. 118; Sallis, p. 165; Robin, "Notice," p. xxxvi.

2 I am baffled at the absolute unanimity among translators and commentators in assuming that the phrase τε οὐρανὸν καὶ λόγους . . . θείους τε καὶ ἀνθρωπίνους (259d6) is to be rendered as though the adjective 'divine' is to be construed with 'heaven' and the adjective 'human' with 'speeches.' The construction manifestly means for both adjectives to be taken with both nouns, as the emphatic τε καί connective and the plural θείους demand. See note 78 above.

3 *Phaedrus* 259d5: μάλιστα.

4 259d4-5: τὴν ἐκείνων μουσικὴν.

5 259d7: ἱᾶσιν καλλίστην φωνήν.

6 *Phaedo* 61a3-4: φιλοσοφίας . . . οὔσης μεγίστης μουσικῆς.

7 *Laws* 3. 689d6-7: ἡ καλλίστη καὶ μεγίστη τῶν συμφωνιῶν μεγίστη δικαιότατ᾽ ἂν λέγοιτο σοφία.

8 *Republic* 8. 548b8-c1: τῆς ἀληθινῆς Μούσης τῆς μετὰ λόγων τε καὶ φιλοσοφίας.

9 See JSJ; ὄψ, voice, is a poetic form unto itself, while ὄψ, eye or face, is a variant of the word ὄψις. Consider also *Phaedrus* 250c8 ff., esp. d3 ff.

10 247c7: οὐσία ὄντως οὖσα . . . θεατὴ. Cf. especially ὄψιν τε καὶ θέαν at 250b6-7. Also cf. ἰδοῦσα at 247d3, καθορᾷ at 247d5-6 (thrice), τῆς . . . θέας at 248b4, ἰδεῖν at 248b6, κατίδῃ at 248c3, ἴδί at 248c6, ἰδοῦσα at 249b6, εἶδεν at 249c2 (with which cf. εἴδει at 249b1 and εἶδος at b7), ὑπεριδοῦσα at 249c3, βλέπων at 249d7, τεθέαται at 249e5, εἶδον at 250a2 and 4, ἴδωσιν at 250a6, θεῶνται and ἰδεῖν at 250b5, εἶδον at 20b8, ἐποπτεύοντες at 250c4, and so forth.

11 See 250b6-7 and preceding two notes.

12 Cf. *Republic* 7. 532a2-3, b1-2

13 Cf. *Republic* 7. 516c1: τῷ ὁρωμένῳ τόπῳ.

οὐρανὸς νοητός (τόπος νοητός[1] or ὑπερουράνιος τόπος[2]).[3] Thus ἡ Οὐρανία represents τὰ οὐράνια, the heavenly things,[4] of which the beholding or contemplating constitutes wisdom,[5] and toward which the erotic striving and conversing constitute philosophy.

The final aspect of the Muses of wisdom is their special concern with divine and human speeches. To see what this means, one must look to the *Phaedo*, where the same two types of speeches are distinguished by Simmias, a superlative Phaedrus[6] (italics mine):

> For [it seems to me] to be obligatory to enact some one then of these things, either to learn [from someone else] in what way it holds or to find [it for oneself] or, if these things are impossible, [it seems to be obligatory] for a person who has grasped the best and hardest of *human speeches* to refute, being carried on this [speech] as on a float-raft to sail through his lifetime running a risk, unless someone should be capable of proceeding through more unfalteringly and in a less risky way on a more steadfast carriage, namely, a certain *divine speech*.[7]

The best way, the first sailing, as it were, is the way of divine speech, while the second best way, the second sailing (cf. διαπλεῦσαι at *Phaedo* 85d2 to τὸν δεύτερον πλοῦν at 99c9-d1), is the way of human speeches.

---

1 Cf. *Republic* 7. 517b5: τὸν νοητὸν τόπον.

2 Cf. *Phaedrus* 247c3.

3 Cf. *Republic* 6. 509d1-4: "'Then,' I said, 'intellect, as we speak, these two to be, and the one to be king of the intellectible class and place, and the one in turn of the seeable, so that, having spoken "of the heaven" [instead of "of the seeable"], I shall not seem to you to be a wise guy in respect to the name.'" (Νόησον τοίνυν, ἦν δ' ἐγώ, ὥσπερ λέγομεν, δύο αὐτὼ εἶναι, καὶ βασιλεύειν τὸ μὲν νοητοῦ γένους τε καὶ τόπου, τὸ δ' αὖ ὁρατοῦ, ἵνα μὴ οὐρανοῦ εἰπὼν δόξω σοι σοφίζεσθαι περὶ τὸ ὄνομα.)

4 The connection between Kalliope (ὄψις, sight) and Ourania (τὰ οὐράνια, the heavenly things) is suggested by the onomatology of Οὐρανός at *Cratylus* 396b7-c3: "[*Socrates.*] And he [i. e., Kronos] is the son of Ouranos, as the speech [speaks]; and in turn seeing toward that which is upward has to be called beautifully this name, 'ourania,' seeing those things which are upward, whence indeed also, oh Hermogenes, the speakers about things in midair assert pure intellect to become present, and [whence they assert] the name for the heaven to be laid down correctly" (ἔστι δὲ οὗτος Οὐρανοῦ ὑός, ὡς λόγος· ἡ δὲ αὖ ἐς τὸ ἄνω ὄψις καλῶς ἔχει τοῦτο τὸ ὄνομα καλεῖσθαι, "οὐρανία," ὁρῶσα τὰ ἄνω, ὅθεν δὴ και φασιν, ὦ Ἑρμόγενες, τὸν καθαρὸν νοῦν παραγίγνεσθαι οἱ μετεωρολόγοι, καὶ τῷ οὐρανῷ ὀρθῶς τὸ ὄνομα κεῖσθαι). One might add that, onomatogenetically at least, there is a close connection between τὰ οὐράνια and οἱ ἄνθρωποι, as suggested at *Cratylus* 399c1-6: "[*Socrates.*] This name 'human' signifies that none of the things that the other beasts see do they consider or reckon up or look up at, but the human simultaneously has seen—and this is the 'he had seen'—and looks up at and reckons this which he has seen. Indeed, thence, looking up at the things that he has seen, the human alone of the beasts was named 'human' correctly" (σημαίνει τοῦτο τὸ ὄνομα "ὁ ἄνθρωπος" ὅτι τὰ μὲν ἄλλα θηρία ὧν ὁρᾷ οὐδὲν ἐπισκοπεῖ οὐδὲ ἀναλογίζεται οὐδὲ ἀναθρεῖ, ὁ δὲ ἄνθρωπος ἅμα ἑώρακεν—τοῦτο δ' ἐστὶ τὸ "ὄπωπε"—καὶ ἀναθρεῖ καὶ λογίζεται τοῦτο ὃ ὄπωπεν. ἐντεῦθεν δὴ μόνον τῶν θηρίων ὀρθῶς ὁ ἄνθρωπος " ἄνθρωπος " ὠνομάσθη, ἀναθρῶν ἃ ὄπωπε).

5 Cf. *Republic* 7. 516a8-c3.

6 See *Phaedrus* 242a7-b4: "*Socrates.* Oh Phaedrus, at any rate you are divine in respect to speeches and absolutely wondrous. For of the speeches which have come to be in your lifetime, I believe no one to have made more come to be than you, either speaking yourself or compelling in addition others by some one manner then—I take out of the speech Simmias the Theban; but you altogether much overpower the others [i. e., all others but Simmias]" (ΣΩ. θεῖος γ' εἶ περὶ τοὺς λόγους, ὦ Φαῖδρε, καὶ ἀτεχνῶς θαυμάσιος. οἶμαι γὰρ ἐγὼ τῶν ἐπὶ τοῦ σοῦ βίου γεγονότων λόγων μηδένα πλείους ἢ σὲ πεποιηκέναι γεγενῆσθαι ἤτοι αὐτὸν λέγοντα ἢ ἄλλους ἑνί γέ τῳ τρόπῳ προσαναγκάζοντα—Σιμμίαν Θηβαῖον ἐξαιρῶ λόγου· τῶν δὲ ἄλλων πάμπολυ κρατεῖς).

7 *Phaedo* 85c7-d4: δεῖν γὰρ . . . ἕν γέ τι τούτων διαπράξασθαι, ἢ μαθεῖν ὅπῃ ἔχει ἢ εὑρεῖν ἤ, εἰ ταῦτα ἀδύνατον, τὸν γοῦν βέλτιστον τῶν ἀνθρωπίνων λόγων λαβόντα καὶ δυσεξελεγκτότατον, ἐπὶ τούτου ὀχούμενον ὥσπερ ἐπὶ σχεδίας κινδυνεύοντα διαπλεῦσαι τὸν βίον, εἰ μή τις δύναιτο ἀσφαλέστερον καὶ ἀκινδυνότερον ἐπὶ βεβαιοτέρου ὀχήματος, λόγου θείου τινός, διαπορευθῆναι. (I accept, with Burnet, note ad *Phaedo* 85d3, Heindorf's seclension of ἤ.)

What is the difference between divine speech and human speech, between a divine λόγος and a human λόγος? The answer to this is suggested in Socrates's philosophical autobiography, in the contrast that he draws between his first and second sailings, which could be regarded as his searches first for divine and then for human λογοί. If this is so, then divine speeches would be speeches that concern the final causes of phenomena, the causes of their being better in the way that they are.[1] Ultimately, this means that *the* λόγος θεῖος is the μῦθος λέγων τὸ αγαθὸν αὐτό, the myth that bespeaks the good itself.[2] Perhaps such a μῦθος is utopian:

> "But, oh blessed ones, let us let go for the now being [i.e., for the time being] of whatever is the good itself—for it appears to me more than in accordance with our present impulse to hit what seems so to me for the things now—but I am willing to speak what appears to me to be a progeny of the good, and most similar to it, if it is also friendly to you, but if not, to let it go."
>
> "But speak," [Glaucon] said, "for you will pay off the narrating of the father at another time."
>
> "I would wish," I spoke, "for me to be capable of giving it [i.e., the narrating] forth and for you [to be capable] of receiving it itself, but not, as now, only the interest. And therefore, indeed receive this interest and progeny of the good itself."[3]

The promise of a future narrating of the good itself seems to be an unfulfilled promise for the Platonic corpus, and that makes the suggestion that such a μῦθος is utopian very strong indeed.[4]

In the *Phaedrus*, it is suggested that the μῦθος of the soul is as utopian as the μῦθος of the good itself seems to be, and that the divine μῦθος of soul must be abandoned in favor of a human μῦθος:

> What sort it is, is for a narrating which is everywhere in every way divine and long, but for what it is like [the narrating is] both human and lesser; therefore, in this way [i. e., in the human and lesser way], let us speak.[5]

However, the μῦθος of the superheavenly place *is* suggested to be a divine μῦθος:

---

1 Cf. βέλτιστα at 97c6, βέλτιστον at 97c8; τὸ ἄριστον καὶ τὸ βέλτιστον at 97d3; τὸ χεῖρον at 97d4; τὸ ἄμεινον at 97e2 (bis), e4, 98a5; βέλτιστον at 98a8, b2; τὸ βέλτιστον at 98b5-6; τὸ χεῖρον at 98b6; βέλτιον at 98e2, 3; τοῦ βελτίστου at 99a2, b1; βέλτιστα at 99c1. Also cf. δικαιότερον at 98e4, 99a2.

2 Cf. τὸ κοινὸν . . . ἀγαθόν at 98b2-3; τὸ ἀγαθὸν at 99c5. Also cf. Republic 7. 516b5-6.

3 *Republic* 6. 506d8-507a4: ἀλλ', ὦ μακάριοι, αὐτὸ μὲν τί ποτ' ἐστὶ τἀγαθὸν ἐάσωμεν τὸ νῦν εἶναι—πλέον γάρ μοι φαίνεται ἢ κατὰ τὴν παροῦσαν ὁρμὴν ἐφικέσθαι τοῦ γε δοκοῦντος ἐμοὶ τὰ νῦν—ὃς δὲ ἔκγονός τε τοῦ ἀγαθοῦ φαίνεται καὶ ὁμοιότατος ἐκείνῳ, λέγειν ἐθέλω, εἰ καὶ ὑμῖν φίλον, εἰ δὲ μή, ἐαν. 'Αλλ', ἔφη, λέγε· εἰς αὖθις γὰρ τοῦ πατρὸς ἀποτείσεις τὴν διήγησιν. Βουλοίμην ἄν, εἶπον, ἐμέ τε δύνασθαι αὐτὴν ἀποδοῦναι καὶ ὑμᾶς κομίσασθαι, ἀλλὰ μὴ ὥσπερ νῦν τοὺς τόκους μόνον. τοῦτον δὲ δὴ οὖν τὸν τόκον τε καὶ ἔκγονον αὐτοῦ τοῦ ἀ ἀγαθοῦ κομίσασθε.

4 Cf. Adam, note ad *Republic* 6. 506e: "The emphasis on τὸ νῦν εἶναι and τὰ νῦν seems to hint that a description of the ἀγαθόν, as it is in itself, may be expected on some future occasion. But there is no dialogue in which the Idea of the Good is so clearly described as in the *Republic*, and it is not without reason that every historian of Philosophy regards this passage as the *locus classicus* on the subject." Also cf. Plato, *Plato's Phaedo*, tr. with intro. and comm. by R. Hackforth (Cambridge, Eng., 1972), p. 132.

5 *Phaedrus* 246a4-6: οἷον μέν ἐστι, πάντῃ πάντως θείας εἶναι καὶ μακρᾶς διηγήσεως, ὧ δὲ ἔοικεν, ἀνθρωπίνης τε καὶ ἐλάττονος· ταύτῃ οὖν λέγομεν. Cf. 245c2-3.

> But not any poet, of those here [and now], hymned yet, or ever will hymn, the superheavenly place in accordance with its worth. But it holds thus—for one must dare to speak the true thing then, both otherwise and [especially] for a person speaking about the truth.[1]

Socrates's mythic palinode, then, is a combination of a human and a divine Λόγος ᾗ μῦθος, and hence it especially does honor to Kalliope and Ourania.

In addition, insofar as it is Stesichorean (cf. 244a2), i. e., insofar as it is for the purpose of setting up choruses or choral activities,[2] it does honor to Terpsichore;[3] and insofar as it is concerned with erotic things, it does honor to Erato. Therefore, it is not surprising that when it is completed, the conversing of the cicadas is heard, presumably announcing to these Muses that they have been honored.

The speech by which they have been honored is the mythic palinode. The palinode may be subdivided in the following way:

I. 243e9-245c4: introduction
  A. 243e9-244a3: genealogy
  B. 244a3-245c4: kinds of craziness
II. 245c5-256e2: the myth (cf. 253c7), ἀπόδειξις of the soul
  A. 245c5-246e4: soul
    1. 245c5-246a3: soul's deathlessness
    2. 246a3-e4: soul's ἰδέα
  B. 246e4-247e6: heaven
    1. 246e4-247c2: the subheavenly loop
    2. 247c3-e6: the superheavenly place
  C. 248a1-249d3: human soul types
    1. 248a1-249b6: seeing human souls
    2. 249b6-d3: the superseeing human soul, the philosopher
  D. 249d4-252b1: longing
    1. 249d4-250c8: memory
    2. 250c8-252b1: seeing
  E. 252b1-256e2: soul
    1. 252b1-253c6: soul's gods
    2. 253c7-256e2: soul's εἴδη
III. 256e3-257b6: conclusion
  A. 256e3-257a2: to the boy
  B. 257a3-b6: to friend Eros

The occasion for the palinode is Socrates's realization that his Lysian myth-speech was shameful and wrong, and that he, the progenitor of the speech, needs to purify himself so as to forestall the punishment of blindness that is meted out to those who tell lies in published speech, whether the lies be about something divine (e.g., Eros or nature) or about something human (e.g., Helen). Later in the myth, it will turn out that blindness as a punishment for telling lies is severe in the extreme.

---

1 *Phaedrus* 247c3-6: Τὸν δὲ ὑπερουράνιον τόπον οὔτε τις ὕμνησέ πω τῶν τῇδε ποιητὴς οὔτε ποτὲ ὑμνήσει κατ' ἀξίαν, ἔχει δὲ ὧδε—τολμητέον γὰρ οὖν τό γε ἀληθὲς εἰπεῖν, ἄλλως τε καὶ περὶ ἀληθείας λέγοντα.

2 The meaning of the names is discussed in what follows.

3 The dialogic character of the speech is another aspect of this.

The two liars to whom Socrates refers in this connection are Homer and Stesichorus: Homer failed to recant his lie, and hence he remained blind; Stesichorus, "having made all the so-called Palinode on the spot, gazed again."[1]

Since—for readers today, as undoubtedly for the Hellenes too—the Homeric lie prevailed over the Stesichorean recantation, and since Socrates surely would have known this, one must wonder whether the Socratic Lysian myth-error—all recantation notwithstanding—will prevail over the Socratic Stesichorean myth-correction of that error. In other words, one must wonder whether the view of eros and nature as animated by a low predatoriness and desire for success will prevail over the view of eros and nature as animated and nourished by a lofty eidetic vision and banquet.[2]

The introduction to the palinode is in two parts, a genealogy and a classification.[3]

The genealogy re-stresses the contrast between the Lysian perspective and the Socratic perspective. The progeneration of Socrates's Lysian speech—and, by extension, insofar as Socrates's Lysian speech reveals the genesis of the perspective of Lysias's own epideictic speech, the progeneration of Lysias's enscrolled speech—is attributed to the desire of a man (ανδρός) for the radiantly beautiful (Φαίδρου) body of another man, and its inspiration is Apollonian (τοῦ Πυθοκλέους), i. e., its inspiration issues from the traditional muses,[4] the muses of Homer,[5]

1 *Phaedrus* 243b2-3: ποιήσας . . . πᾶσαν τὴν καλουμένην Παλινῳδίαν παραχρῆμα ἀνέβλεξεν.

2 The development of modern philosophy, at least of modern political philosophy, from its inception in Machiavelli, Bacon, and Hobbes, seems to suggest that the former prevailed. In like manner, in the terminology of the *Symposium*, in modern philosophy, the penultimate level of Diotima's narration, namely the desire for immortality through fame and glory (208b7-209e4), prevailed over the ultimate level, namely the desire for immortality through the love and beholding of the beautiful itself (209e5-212c3). In the terms of the *Phaedo*, in modern philosophy, the fear of death is in principle eradicated in a physico-political way rather than in the psychico-transpolitical way suggested by Socrates's incantations. For a lucid account of the modern development in relation to the ancient position, cf. Leo Strauss, *NRH*, pp. 161-162, and the chapter "Modern Natural Right," pp. 165-251, esp. pp. 165-202 and 249-251. In some sense, this theme in all its variations is the theme of Leo Strauss's corpus as a whole.

3 This is roughly also the structure of Diotima's major speech in the penultimate section of the *Symposium*, except that there one finds a genealogy of Eros followed by a classification of eros. The genealogy there is as little meant literally as is the genealogy here. This is not only a recurring intradialogic structure, but also it is a recurring interdialogic structural feature. For example, within the sequence of eight dialogues surrounding Socrates's trial and death (*Theaetetus*, *Euthyphro*, *Cratylus*, *Sophist*, *Statesman*, *Apology of Socrates*, *Crito*, and *Phaedo*, in that chronological order: compare *Theaetetus* 210d1-4 to *Euthyphro* 2a1-6; also consider *Cratylus* 396d4-8; κατὰ τὴν χθὲς ὁμολογίαν at *Sophist* 216a1; and *Cratylus* 396e3-397a1)—within that sequence, the *Cratylus* as a genealogy (of names) is followed by the classification of the projected *Sophist-Statesman-Philosopher* trilogy (the last of which is either not extant or was never written, either because its purpose was achieved in the two that were written or because it could not be written or because of some other circumstance, to speculate upon which alternatives goes beyond the scope of this work). Or, in analogous manner, in the dramatic sequence of the *Republic*, the *Timaeus*, the incomplete *Critias*, and the projected (but non-existent) *Hermocrates*, the *Republic* and *Timaeus* are genetic accounts of the city and the cosmos respectively, while the *Critias* is a descriptive account of the city, and the *Hermocrates*, if the parallel were to hold, would have been a descriptive account of the cosmos (although its absence in the sequence after it has been projected explicitly may have been Plato's way of obliquely suggesting that such an account is impossible). I shall return to this in Chapter VI, "THE *REPUBLIC* TETRALOGY."

4 Cf. *Iliad* 1. 603-604. For the close connection between Apollo and the traditional Muses, see Pindar, *Pythian* 1. 1-2, Hesiod, *Theogony* 94-95. Also cf. *Cratylus* 404d8 ff.; *Hymn to Apollo* 189-193, 516-519. Furthermore, compare *Iliad* 1. 603-604 to *Hymn to Apollo* 130 ff. Finally, cf. *Pythian* 5. 65.

5 For the close connection between Homer and Apollo, see *The Contest of Homer and Hesiod* [in the LCL volume, *Hesiod, the Homeric Hymns and Homerica* (Cambridge, MA, 1936)], 324, Homer's inscription to Apollo: "Lord Phoebus—I, Homer, gave you then a beautiful gift for the thoughts [which you gave me]; and would that you might make fame follow me always" (Φοῖβε ἄναξ, δῶρόν τοι Ὅμηρος καλὸν ἔδωκα / σῇσιν ἐπιφροσύναις· σὺ δέ μοι κλέος αἰὲν ὀπάζοις). The *Contest* is contemporary with Plato. That Plato knew it is suggested by the occurrence later in the *Phaedrus* (246d3-6) of a series of verses that precede the Homeric inscription in the same work. Also cf. Vries, note ad 264d3 ff.

who—it is suggested—are amusical by contrast to the truly musical Stesichorean muses.[1] The Apollonian muses, who are identical to the Homeric muses, are concerned with the power of song and low erotic success (both heterosexual and homosexual),[2] and they are concerned with fame.[3] In addition, Apollo became identified with sobriety (μηδὲν ἄγαν) after leading a life of excess.[4]

Apollo is an appropriate god for a lover whose desire is a compulsion[5] in a world characterized by compulsion, a lover who uses sobriety in the service of excess,[6] namely a coldly calculating lover of the type that Lysias and Socrates pretend to be in their combined speeches. On the other hand, the progeneration of Socrates's Socratic speech is grounded in the establishment of of choral activities (Στησιχόρου), which means grounded in dialectic,[7] and it contains no blasphemy (τοῦ Εὐφήμου).[8] Furthermore, it is Himeraian (Ἱμεραίου), i. e., it expresses the gentle (ἥμερος) longing (ἵμερος)[9] for day (ἡμέρα) to come out of darkness,[10] i. e., for knowledge to dissipate ignorance.

The Lysian perspective of savage sobriety will be replaced by the Socratic perspective of gentle craziness, but with the implicit suggestion that these two perspectives, the low and the high, are not simply unrelated, but rather that the high is a purified[11] version of the low.

Socrates turns to his classification of the kinds of craziness,[12] and he begins by denying that it is obligatory for the non-lover to be gratified, because the non-lover is sober or moderate (σωφρονεῖ), while the lover is crazy (μαίνεται). To assert such a thing is to assert what is both not beautiful and not true: the not beautiful is the assertion that craziness is simply bad;[13] and the not true is the assertion that one should gratify a non-lover. The truth of the simple goodness or badness of craziness is not decided explicitly, but it is certain that even if craziness is not simply bad, it does not follow that it is simply good. Indeed, the craziness that generates the biggest

1 This is why Socrates preceded his palinode with this remark (243a2-7): "Therefore, there is a compulsion for me, oh friend, to purify myself; and there is for those who err in respect to myth-speaking an originary purification, which Homer did not sense, but [which] Stesichorus [sensed]. For, having been deprived of his eyes because of his badmouthing of Helen, he [i. e., Stesichorus] did not unrecognize [the cause], as Homer [failed to do], but since he [i.e., Stesichorus] was musical, he recognized the cause" (ἐμοὶ μὲν οὖν, ὦ φίλε, καθήρασθαι ἀνάγκη· ἔστιν δὲ τοῖς ἁμαρτάνουσι περὶ μυθολογίαν καθαρμὸς ἀρχαῖος, ὃν Ὅμηρος μὲν οὐκ ᾔσθετο, Στησίχορος δέ. τῶν γὰρ ὀμμάτων στερηθεὶς διὰ τὴν Ἑλένης κακηγορίαν οὐκ ἠγνόησεν ὥσπερ Ὅμηρος, ἀλλ' ἅτε μουσικὸς ὢν ἔγνω τὴν αἰτίαν). In other words, Homer and his muses are amusical, whereas Stesichorus and the Socratic muses (cf. *Phaedrus* 259b60-d7) are truly musical. This adumbrates the private Socratic victory over the poets in the *Symposium*, a victory that depends not only on the truth and comprehensiveness of the Socratic perspective but also on the more 'poetic' and more musical Socratic presentation of his perspective. The suggestion there, as here in the *Phaedrus* and elsewhere, is that the Socratic victory can only be a private one and never the public victory that inevitably goes to the so-called—but not truly musical, because not truly philosophical—poetry of Homer and his tribe.

2 Cf. Robert Graves, *The Greek Myths* (Baltimore, 1955), vol. 1. 21. i-m, p. 78. Also cf. *Hymn to Apollo* 208.

3 κλέος: cf. τοῦ Πυθοκλέους (*Phaedrus* 244a1) and last note on preceding page.

4 Cf. Graves, 21. o, p. 79.

5 That Phaedrus is Μυρρινουσίου suggests this. As Thompson (note ad loc.) rightly suggests, this is a reference to *Republic* 2. 372b5-6, but not (as he wrongly concludes) to the love of festivity that is alien to the description there of the city of sows (ὑῶν πόλιν: 2. 372d4). Rather the reference is to the city itself, the most compulsory city (ἥ γε ἀναγκαιοτάτη πόλις: 2. 369d11), the city that is founded precisely and only to meet needs.

6 Cf. *Republic* 6. 509c1-2.

7 Cf. Sallis, pp. 133-134.

8 Cf. *Phaedrus* 265c1.

9 Cf. *Phaedrus* 251c8.

10 Cf. *Cratylus* 418c5-d7.

11 Cf. *Phaedrus* 243a2 (καθήρασθαι), 3 (καθαρμὸς).

12 How little Phaedrus will learn from this and the rest of the palinode is indicated in his reply at 268c2-4, especially his use of μαίνεται at c2.

13 Cf. *Phaedrus* 244a5-6: "For if being crazy were simply bad, it [i.e., the assertion] would have been spoken beautifully" (εἰ μὲν γὰρ ἦν ἁπλοῦν τὸ μανίαν κακὸν εἶναι, καλῶς ἂν ἐλέγετο). This is put conditionally to indicate that being crazy is not simply bad, and that therefore the speech was not spoken beautifully

goods is the craziness that is bestowed by a divine gift.This in turn suggests that there is a human craziness[1] that at least generates lesser goods and at most generates bads.[2]

The διαίρεσις of craziness into human and divine yields to a further διαίρεσις of divine craziness alone[3] into three: (1) 244a8-d5, divination (μαντική); (2) 244d5-245a1, solvent (λύσις); (3) 245a1-8, poetizing (ποίησις). Then (245b1-c4), in what appears to be a conclusion from the other three, Socrates adds what appears to be a fourth, love (ἔρως).[4]

Several things should be observed about this classification.

First, an implicit bisection runs through it, so as to suggest the following two sets of categories:

craziness	
(1) divine (or by divine portion/gift)	human[5]
(2) τὸ κεκινῆσθαι	moderation[6]
(3) beautiful	ugly[7]
(4) complete	incomplete[8]
(5) inspiration and τέχνη together	τέχνη alone[9]
(6) correct	in error[10]
(7) ancient	new[11]

Presumably such a division could be made of each of the four types of craziness.[12]

Second, the four kinds look very much like Apollo's four powers,[13] with the exception that ἔρως replaces τοξική.[14] Is there some connection between erotic activity and archery? Perhaps there is, if one considers the analogy between them that could be based on the arrow's trajectory, an ascent followed by a descent, much like the course of the soul that is described in the palinode or like the journey of the released prisoner in the image of the cave. The difference would be that for eros, the target would be at the peak of the curve rather than at the end of its

1 Cf. Sallis, pp. 132-133.

2 There is always the possibility that divine craziness generates the biggest goods and the biggest bads, while human craziness generates littler goods and littler bads. Cf. *Republic* 2. 379b1-380c10, esp. 379c2-7.

3 However, the other leg of the διαίρεσις is not forgotten: cf. θείᾳ . . . δόσει (244a7-8) and ὅταν θείᾳ μοίρᾳ γίγνηται (244c3). Also cf. ἐκ θεοῦ . . . παρ' ἀνθρώπων (244d4-5), τῷ ὀρθῶς μανέντι (244e4), ἐκ τέχνης (i. e., from art alone, a sober human method: 245a6; cf. 244b3-4, c1-2), and ψυχῆς φύσεως πέρι θείας τε καὶ ἀνθρωπίνης (245c2-3).

4 Cf. *Timaeus* 17a1-3; also *Statesman* 257a1-b4.

5 Cf. *Phaedrus* 244a7-8, c3, d4-5, 245b1-2, c2-3.

6 Cf. 245b3-4; also cf. 244a5, b2, c5, 245a8, b4-5.

7 Cf. 244a5-6, b1-2, 7, c1, 2-3, 4, d3-4, 245b1-2; also cf. 245a4.

8 Compare 244d2-3 to 245a7.

9 Compare 244b3-4 and c1-2 to 245a6-7.

10 Cf. 244e4; also cf. 244b4-5. Included here would be self-deception: cf. 245a6-7.

11 Cf. 244b7-c4, d1; also cf. 245a4.

12 On the basis of this division, one might also suggest that Lysias's enscrolled speech is the product of human sobriety, Socrates's Lysian speech the product of human craziness, and Socrates's Stesichorean speech the product of divine craziness. Only the category of divine sobriety, if there be any such thing, would be missing, although it is possible that the discussion of writing and speaking with which the *Phaedrus* concludes is meant to be the symmetrically required product of divine sobriety or moderation. On the other hand, as Emily Dickinson suggests, divine craziness and divine sobriety may be identical ("Much Madness is divinest Sense— /To a discerning Eye— /Much Sense—the starkest Madness—").

13 Cf. *Cratylus* 404d8-406a3: μουσική (= ποίησις here), μαντική, ιατρική (= λύσις here), τοξική. Cf. Pindar *Pythians* 5. 60 ff., *Hymn to Apollo* 130 ff.. Also see note 123 above.

14 The regular association of Eros (or Cupid) with the bow does not arise until very late in antiquity, although there is the first vague suggestion of it in Euripides, *Trojan Women* 255, but there it is in opposition to Apollonian divination.

descent—where the arrow becomes fixed and untransmovable—and the target and the arrow together would keep moving. The difference in the placing of the targets roughly corresponds to the difference between the Apollonian-Lysian perspective (target low) and the Stesichorean-Socratic perspective (target high).

The difference between the way of ἔρως and the way of ἡ τοῦ Ἀπόλλωνος τοξική is the difference between the way of knowledge and the way of opinion,[1] as Socrates suggests (italics mine):

> *Socrates. "Opinion" indeed has been so nicknamed* either because of chasing with respect to which the soul proceeds to chase envisioning [i.e., understanding] in whatever way things hold, or *because of throwing from the bow.* And it is more like this latter.[2]

The way of the bow, of Apollo, of the arrow fixed in the target, is the way of δόξα.

Finally, although the kinds are presented as four, the equivocal way in which ἔρως appears suggests that it is the fundamental kind, that erotic craziness is the root of the other three.

Divine craziness is that through which the biggest goods and beautifuls come to humans (244a6-8), and through which bads are loosed from humans (244d5-245a1). It is that through which the soul is awakened and intoxicated (245a3-4). It is that through which the biggest good luck comes to humans (245b7-c1). In addition, it is that which corrects humans (244b4-5),[3] educates humans (245a4-5), and benefits humans (245b4-6).

Furthermore—although this is not stated explicitly here—divine craziness is a craziness of the soul. Hence, in order to understand it, it is necessaary to see the soul's πάθη and ἔργα (245c3-4) and to intuit intellectually the truth about the nature of divine and human soul.[4] This intellective seeing and intuition will be a showing forth (ἀπόδειξις).[5] The beginning of this ἀπόδειξις is the conclusion that "all soul is deathless,"[6]

What follows is a dense and elliptical triad of arguments (argument 1 at 245c5-8; argument 2 at 245c8-e2; and argument 3 at 245e2-6) capped off by a concluding statement (245e6-246a3).

Argument 1 is the most elliptical of the three:

Conclusion: All soul is deathless.

(1) The always movable is deathless.
(2) (a) The other-moving and other–moved is not always moving.
(2) (b) The not moving is the not living.
(3) The self-moving is always itself.

What is missing here is a series of steps that involve the double character, κατὰ φύσιν, of soul as cause of life and soul as cause of motion, i. e., a series of steps based on Socrates's analysis of the name "soul:"

1 Cf. Parmenides Fr. 8. 50-52: "Here I cease my trustable speech and intellectual intuition to you / about truth; and from here the opinions of mortals / learn, hearing the deceptive order of my sayings" (ἐν τῶι σοι παύω πιστὸν λόγον ἠδὲ νόημα/ ἀμφὶς ἀληθείης· δόξας δ' ἀπὸ τοῦδε βροτείας/ μάνθανε κόσμον ἐμῶν ἐπέων ἀπατηλὸν ἀκούων). The text is from Parmenides, *Parmenides: a text with tr., comm., and crit. essays*, by Leonardo Tarán (Princeton, 1965); the translation is mine.

2 *Cratylus* 420b7-9: ΣΩ. "Δόξα" δὴ ἤτοι τῇ διώξει ἐπωνόμασται, ἣν ἡ ψυχὴ διώκουσα τὸ εἰδέναι ὅπῃ ἔχει τὰ πράγματα πορεύεται. ἢ τῇ απο τοῦ τόξου βολῇ. ἔοικε δὲ τούτῳ μᾶλλον.

3 In other words, it does precisely what Socrates disclaimed: cf. ὤρθωσαν at 244b5 to ἐπανορθοῦσθαι at 229d6.

4 This too contains an implicit διαίρεσις: first, there is Ψυχή, and then there is ψυχή θεία and ψυχή ἀνθρωπίνη.

5 Cf. ἀποδεικτέον at 245b7, ἀπόδειξις at 245c1, and ἀποδείξεως at 245c4. Also cf. Sallis, pp. 135-136.

6 Ψυχὴ πᾶσα ἀθάνατος: 245c5. Cf. Vries, note ad loc., on πᾶσα as simultaneously collective (all) and distributive (every).

[*Socrates.*] I believe the persons who named the soul intellected something suchlike, how then this, when it is present to the body, is the cause of living for it, furnishing it the power of breathing-in and re-cooling [i. e., reviving] it, and simultaneously when the re-cooling is left out of it, the body both is destroyed and comes to an end; whence indeed they seem to me to have called it "soul" . . . . What seems to you both to hold and to carry the nature of all the body, so as for it both to live and to go-around, other than soul?

Hermogenes. None other.

Socrates. And what [of this]? Do you not also trust Anaxagoras [who asserted] intellect and soul to be that which thoroughly orders and holds the nature of all other things?

Hermogenes. I at any rate do.

Socrates. Then this name would hold beautifully [for] nicknaming this power which carries and holds nature, [namely,] "nature-holder." And it is permissible also for a person who is refined to speak [this to be] "soul."

Hermogenes. Therefore, altogether so, and this seems, to me at any rate, to be more artful than that [i. e., than onomatogenesis 1].

Socrates. For also it is; yet how it, being named so truly, was posited appears laughable.[1]

Soul as a nature has a double character (life and motion), but both the *Phaedrus* and the *Cratylus* agree that motion is more fundamental than life. On this basis, the first *Phaedrus* argument would have to be completed thus (additions in brackets):

(1) The always movable is deathless.
(2) (a) The other-moving and other–moved is not always moving.
(2) (b) The not moving is the not living.
[(c) The other-moving and other–moved is not (always) living.]
[(d) The other-moving and other–moved (sometimes) dies.]
[(e) The other-moving and other–moved is not deathless.]
(3) (a) The self-moving is always itself.
[(b) The always movable is always moving.]
[(c) The moving is the living.]
[(d) The always movable is always living.]
[(e) The self-moving always itself is the self-movable always itself.]
[(f) The self-movable always itself is always movable.][2]
[(g) The self-movable always itself is always living.]
[(h) The self-movable always itself never dies.]
[(i) The self-movable always itself is deathless.]
[(j) The soul is the self-movable always itself.]
[(k) The soul is deathless.]

---

1 *Cratylus* 399d10–e3, 400a5–b7: [ΣΩ.] οἶμαί τι τοιοῦτον νοεῖν τοὺς τὴν ψυχὴν ὀνομάσαντας, ὡς τοῦτο ἄρα, ὅταν παρῇ τῷ σώματι, αἴτιόν ἐστι τοῦ ζῆν αὐτῷ, τὴν τοῦ ἀναπνεῖν δύναμιν παρέχον καὶ ἀναψῦχον, ἅμα δὲ ἐκλείποντος τοῦ ἀναψύχοντος τὸ σῶμα ἀπόλλυταί τε καὶ τελευτᾷ· ὅθεν δή μοι δοκοῦσιν αὐτὸ 'ψυχὴν' καλέσαι . . . . Τὴν φύσιν παντὸς τοῦ σώματος, ὥστε καὶ ζῆν καὶ περιιέναι, τί σοι δοκεῖ ἔχειν τε καὶ ὀχεῖν ἄλλο ἢ ψυχή; ΕΡΜ. Οὐδεν ἄλλο. ΣΩ. Τί δέ; καὶ τὴν τῶν ἄλλων ἁπάντων φύσιν οὐ πιστεύεις Ἀναξαγόρᾳ νοῦν καὶ ψυχὴν εἶναι τὴν διακοσμοῦσαν καὶ ἔχουσαν; ΕΡΜ. Ἔγωγε. ΣΩ. Καλῶς ἄρα ἂν τὸ ὄνομα τοῦτο ἔχοι τῇ δυνάμει ταύτῃ ἣ φύσιν ὀχεῖ καὶ ἔχει "φυσέχην" ἐπονομάζειν. ἔξεστι δὲ καὶ "ψυχὴν" κομψευόμενον λέγειν. ΕΡΜ. Πάνυ μὲν οὖν, καὶ δοκεῖ γέ μοι τοῦτο ἐκείνου τεχνικώτερον εἶναι. ΣΩ. Καὶ γὰρ ἔστιν· γελοῖον μέντοι φαίνεται ὡς ἀληθῶς ὀνομαζόμενον ὡς ἐτέθη. Cf. Sallis, pp. 136–138.

2 I. e., the self that the self-moving always is, is movability.

The problem with the argument is that it does not prove that soul is deathless, because such a conclusion depends upon the undemonstrated step (3) (j) that the soul is the self-movable always itself. One expects the second argument to provide a demonstration of this, but that expectation is unfulfilled, although the third argument returns to it with the tentative—and still apparently undemonstrated—assertion (245e2-3) that the thing that is moved by itself has appeared to be deathless and that the soul's beingness/speech is self-moving, an assertion that is made in such a way as to suggest that it *has* been demonstrated.

Consider the second argument with this in mind. The second argument is composed of an introductory statement (245c8-9) followed by three parts, one part (245d1-6) that positively elaborates the double character of the ἀρχή of moving (ungeneratable, d1-3; incorruptible, d3-6), a second part (245d6-8) that positively returns to the self-moving always itself, and a third part (245d8-e2) that apparently negatively establishes what has already been positively established. The second argument is full by comparison to the bareness of the first argument. Its fullness may derive from its tautological generality. The structure of the second argument is the following (additions in brackets):

Introductory statement: The moving self-movable always itself is the ἀρχή and fountain[1] of the moving of the other-movable.

(1) (a) The ἀρχή of moving is ungeneratable.

(a.1) Everything that becomes, becomes from an ἀρχή.

(a.2) The ἀρχή itself becomes from nothing.

(a.3) If an ἀρχή became from anything, it could not have become fron an ἀρχή.[2]

(b) The ἀρχή of moving is incorruptible.

(b.1) The ungeneratable is incorruptible.

(b.2) If (1) (a.1), then if the ἀρχή is destroyed, i. e., if it is totally corrupted, the ἀρχή itself will not become again, and none of the things that would have become from it will become from it.

(2) The self-moving always itself is the ἀρχή of moving.

(a) The ἀρχή of moving is indestructible and unbecomable.

[(b) The self-moving always itself is indestructible and unbecomable.]

[(c) The indestructible/unbecomable is deathless.]

[(d) The self-moving always itself is deathless (cf. arg. 1, (3)(g)-(i).]

---

1 *Phaedrus* 245c9: πηγή. Cf. *Phaedrus* 255c1, 2-7: "Then already the fountain of that flow [i. e., the flow of beauty] . . .which [fountain] is borne much toward the lover, on the one hand sank into him, and on the other hand flows off outside [when] he is filled; and such as breath or a certain echo springing from things both smooth and solid is borne again whence it set out, thus the flow of beauty [is borne] again unto the beautiful person, going through the things through which one sees" (τότ' ἤδη ἡ τοῦ ῥεύματος ἐκείνου πηγή . . .πολλὴ φερομένη πρὸς τὸν ἐραστήν, ἡ μὲν εἰς αὐτὸν ἔδυ, ἡ δ' ἀπομεστουμένου ἔξω ἀπορρεῖ· καὶ οἷον πνεῦμα ἤ τις ἠχὼ ἀπὸ λείων τε καὶ στερεῶν ἁλλομένη πάλιν ὅθεν ὡρμήθη φέρεται, οὕτω τὸ τοῦ κάλλους ῥεῦμα πάλιν εἰς τὸν καλὸν διὰ τῶν ὀμμάτων ἰόν). In other words, as a fountain flows back to its source, so too the ἀρχή of moving moves back upon itself, and the whole is no less characterized by its erotically self-reflexive flow than is the soul.

2 *Phaedrus* 245d2-3: εἰ γὰρ ἔκ του ἀρχὴ γίγνοιτο, οὐκ ἂν ἐξ ἀρχῆς γίγνοιτο. With Vries (cf. note ad loc.), but against Burnet (cf. OCT, emended text and apparatus criticus ad loc.) and Hackforth (cf. p. 63, n. 1), I accept the manuscript reading as intelligible. What it suggests is that there is a source that is not the fountain itself, i. e., there is a source that is beyond an ἀρχή, as the good is beyond beingness. Cf. *Republic* 6. 509b6-10: "Then also assert not only having been recognized to be present to the things which are recognized by [means of] the good, but also both being and beingness in addition to be present to them by [means of] it, although the good is not beingness but holds itself over beyond beingness by its venerability and power." (Καὶ τοῖς γιγνωσκομένοις τοίνυν μὴ μόνον τὸ γιγνώσκεσθαι φάναι ὑπὸ τοῦ ἀγαθοῦ παρεῖναι, ἀλλὰ καὶ τὸ εἶναι τε καὶ τὴν οὐσίαν ὑπ' ἐκείνου αὐτοῖς προσεῖναι, οὐκ οὐσίας ὄντος τοῦ ἀγαθοῦ, ἀλλ' ἔτι ἐπέκεινα τῆς οὐσίας πρεσβείᾳ καὶ δυνάμει ὑπερέχοντος.) (For the infinitive φάναι as the imperative, cf. Adam note ad *Rep*. 473a.)

[(e) The soul is the self-moving always itself (cf. arg. 1, (3)(e)&(j).]
[(f) The soul is deathless.]

(3) [*Reductio ad absurdum.*]

(a) The self-moving always itself (= the ἀρχή of moving) would be destroyed or would become.

[(b) The moving would be destroyed.]

(c) All heaven and all genesis would fall together and stand still.[1]

(d) The still-standing all will have nothing from which ever to come to be moving again.

[(e) The self-moving always itself is always moving (cf. arg. 1, (3)(a),(b),&(e)).]
[(f) The ἀρχή of moving can neither be destroyed nor become.]
[(g) The indestructible/unbecomable is deathless.]
[(h) The ἀρχή of moving is deathless.]
[(i) The soul is the ἀρχή of moving.]
[(j) The soul is deathless.]

The second argument generalizes the showing of the soul's deathlessness in such a way as to suggest (α) that the deathlessness of every (distributive 'all') soul is derived from the deathlessness of all (collective 'all') soul, (β) that all soul is the cosmic soul, and (γ) that the cosmos is a living thing.[2]

The third, and final, argument consists not of syllogistic reasoning but rather of two sets of assertions (the self-moving at 245e2-4, the other-moving at 245e4-6):

(1) The self-moving:
- (a) The self-moving has appeared to be deathless.
- (b) The self-moving is the beingness and speech of soul.

(2) The other-moving:
- (a) All body that is moved only from outside is unsouled.[3]
- (b) All body that is moved from inside is ensouled.
- (c) Moving from inside is the nature of soul.

This argument adds a new dimension to the discussion of soul by asserting what has been implicit all along, namely that in addition to its double natural character, soul has a non-natural character.

---

1 245d8-e1: πάντα τε οὐρανὸν πᾶσαν τε γένεσιν σμπεσοῦσαν στῆναι. With Vries (cf. note ad loc.) and Hackforth (cf. p. 63, n. 2), but against Burnet (cf. OCT, emended text and apparatus criticus ad loc.), I retain the manuscript reading, because it is intelligible in itself and accords with Timaeus's usage in the *Timaeus*, in which τὸ πᾶν and ὁ κόσμος and ὁ οὐρανός are used interchangeably (cf. Tim. 92c4, 6, 8; 28b2-4 and ff.) and are coupled with ἡ γένεσις (cf. γένεσιν καὶ τὸ πᾶν at 29d7, and γενέσεως καὶ κόσμου at 29e4). In addition, I should note that, as above at *Phaedrus* 245c5, the πάντα and πᾶσαν are used as simultaneously collective and distributive: cf. Vries, note ad loc.; Hackforth, p. 66, n. 3; note 157 above.

2 This too is consonant with Timaeus's teaching in the *Timaeus*. Cf. 30b6-c1: "Therefore, indeed, in this way, in accordance with the likely speech, it is obligatory to speak this cosmos to have become a living thing, having within it, in truth, soul and intellectual intuition because of the god's prescience" (οὕτως οὖν δὴ κατὰ λόγον τὸν εἰκότα δεῖ λέγειν τόνδε τὸν κόσμον ζῷον ἔμψυχον ἔννουν τε τῇ ἀληθείᾳ διὰ τὴν τοῦ θεοῦ γενέσθαι πρόνοιαν). Also consider *Philebus* 30a3-b7.

3 Again, here and in (b), the πᾶν is used as simultaneously collective and distributive.

In other words, soul may be regarded as a nature, on the one hand, and as an οὐσία and λόγος,[1] on the other. These two aspects of soul roughly correspond to soul insofar as it is partititve and embodied (nature), on the one hand, and soul insofar as it is simple unembodied intellectual intuition (οὐσία and λόγος), on the other.[2] This is the problem of the soul in its being in the world and the soul as the knower of its own being in the world, the problem of the soul as other-moving and the soul as self-moving.

Broadly speaking, the *Timaeus* treats the soul in its genesis as a nature (and hence it is a physiological myth),[3] whereas the rest of Socrates's palinode here treats the soul in its genesis as a beingness and speech (and hence it is an ousiological myth). Whether these two aspects of soul can ever be put together satisfactorily is a problem that, in the present context, must be left open,[4] as Socrates does implicitly by concluding (245e6-246a2: italics mine):

> And *if* this holds thus, [namely] *if the same thing moving itself is* nothing other than *soul,* soul—from compulsion—would be both ungenerated and deathless.[5]

He means that if soul were *only* self-moving, then it would be deathless, but since it is not, its deathlessness, in any literal sense at least, is problematic at best. This may explain why[6]—when the gods and their followers ascend to the subheavenly loop (τὴν ὑπερουράνιον ἁψῖδα, 247a8-b1) on their way to the divine meal and feast[7] in the superheavenly place (Τὸν . . . ὑπερουράνιον τόπον, 247c3), where intellectual intuition may feed on the beingly being[8] and the true (cf. τἀληθῆ, 247d4)[9]—"Hestia remains alone in the house of the gods."[10]

---

1 For a brief discussion of the parallels between this and the treatment of the soul in *Laws* 10, see Sallis, pp. 139-140, esp. n. 20.

2 In other words, these two aspects of soul correspond to the discussions of soul found respectively in *Republic* 4 (nature) and *Republic 10* (beingness and speech).

3 Cf. *Timaeus* 29b2-3: "Indeed, biggest of all is for a beginning to begin in accordance with nature" (μέγιστον δὴ παντὸς ἄρξασθαι κατὰ φύσιν ἀρχήν).

4 The elaboration of this problem is central both to the Platonic corpus and to the Aristotelian corpus. In a way, this is the central theme of Aristotle's *De Anima*, which begins by treating soul as an οὐσία (Book 1) and ends by treating soul as a nature (Books 2 and 3). These two treatments roughly correspond to the soul as the object of study of the dialectician and the soul as the object of study of the physicist. Cf. *De Anima* 3. 5. 430a10-14; 1. 1. Et passim.

5 εἰ δ' ἔστιν τοῦτο οὕτως ἔχον, μὴ ἄλλο τι εἶναι τὸ αὐτὸ ἑαυτὸ κινοῦν ἢ ψυχήν, ἐξ ἀνάγκης ἀγένητόν τε καὶ ἀθάνατον ψυχὴ ἂν εἴη.

6 For a discussion of the intervening section, see Sallis, pp. 140-144.

7 *Phaedrus* 247a8: δαῖτα καὶ . . . θοίνην. Cf. Kenneth Dorter, "Imagery and Philosophy in Plato's *Phaedrus*," *Journal of the History of Philosophy*, vol. 9, July 1971, p. 280, n. 3: "The *Phaedrus* abounds in culinary terminology which recurs throughout with the regularity of a leitmotif: 227b6, [230d6-8,] 235d1, 238a6, b2, 241c8, 243d4, 246e2, 247a8, d2-4, e3, 6, 248b5, 7, c2, 251c8, 255d1, 259c1-4, 260d1, 265e3, 270b6, 276d6."

8 Cf. οὐσία ὄντως οὖσα at 247c7, τὸ ὄν at 247d3, ὅ ἐστιν ὂν ὄντως at 247e2, τἆλλα . . . τὰ ὄντα ὄντως at 247e2-3.

9 Cf. *Republic* 6. 508d4-6: "Thus then also the one [aspect] of the soul intellects thus; whenever it supports itself on this on which truth and being shine down, it both intellected and recognized it and it appears to have intellect" (Οὕτω τοίνυν καὶ τὸ τῆς ψυχῆς ὧδε νόει· ὅταν μὲν οὗ καταλάμπει ἀλήθειά τε καὶ τὸ ὄν, εἰς τοῦτο ἀπερείσηται, ἐνόησέν τε καὶ ἔγνω αὐτὸ καὶ νοῦν ἔχειν φαίνεται).

10 *Phaedrus* 247a1-2: μένει γὰρ Ἑστία ἐν θεῶν οἴκῳ μόνη.

To flesh out this explanation, one must again turn to the *Cratylus*:[1]

> *Socrates.* Therefore, are we not to begin from Hestia, in accordance with law?
>
> *Hermogenes.* Therefore, it is just [to do so] at any rate.
>
> *Socrates.* Therefore, what would someone assert the person who has named Hestia to have thought through to name [her]?
>
> *Hermogenes.* By Zeus, I believe not even this to be easy.
>
> *Socrates.* Therefore, then, oh good Hermogenes, the first name-positers run the risk of being, not mean, but speakers about highfalutin things and idle chatterers.
>
> *Hermogenes.* Indeed what?
>
> *Socrates.* The positing of names appears to me [to be the work] of certain such humans, and if anyone reconsiders foreign names, nonetheless he will find again what each [name] wishes [to be, i.e., what each name means]. Such as also in this which we call "beingness," there are those who call [it] "be-ness," and [there are those] who in turn [call it] "pushiness." Therefore, first, in accordance with the other [i.e., second] name of these, the beingness of things has a speech [i.e., a good explanation] for being called "Hestia," and in that then in turn we assert [with respect to] the thing partaking of beingness "it is," also in accordance with this, Hestia would be called so correctly; for we too are likely to call beingness the ancient "be-ness." And in addition also, in accordance with sacrifices, anyone who has intellected would regard the positers to intellect these things thus; for sacrificing to Hestia first before all gods would be likely for those persons who nicknamed the beingness of all things "be-ness." And in turn, as many persons as [nicknamed it] "pushiness," these persons in turn almost somehow, in accordance [i.e., agreement] with Herakleitos, would regard all the beings to go [i.e., to move] and none to remain [still]; therefore, [they would regard] the cause and leading-ruling-beginning of them to be the thing pushing, whence indeed [they would regard] its having been named "pushiness" to hold beautifully. And indeed, let these things be spoken in this way, as though by [i.e., since we are] persons having envisioned [i.e., understood] next to nothing.[2]

Hestia represents the two apparently irreconcilable, but equally compelling, aspects of soul: (1) the ousiological as represented by the "is" (the ἔστιν); and (2) the physiological as represented by

---

1 Perhaps the closeness of the *Phaedrus* and the *Cratylus* has something to do with Socrates's assertions in both dialogues that his speech is the product of inspiration or inspired wisdom: cf. *Cratylus* 396d2-e2; also consider 399a1, 409d1-2, 428c6-8. In addition, see *Phaedrus* 241e1-5, 249c4-d3, 252e5-253a5, 263d1-3.

2 *Cratylus* 401b1-e1: ΣΩ. Ἄλλο τι οὖν ἀφ' Ἑστίας ἀρχώμεθα κατὰ τὸν νόμον; ΕΡΜ. Δίκαιον γοῦν. ΣΩ. Τί οὖν ἄν τις φαίη διανοούμενον τὸν ὀνομάσαντα Ἑστίαν ὀνομάσαι; ΕΡΜ. Οὐ μὰ τὸν Δία οὐδὲ τοῦτο οἶμαι ῥᾴδιον εἶναι. ΣΩ. Κινδυνεύουσι γοῦν, ὠγαθὲ Ἑρμόγενες, οἱ πρῶτοι τὰ ὀνόματα τιθέμενοι οὐ φαῦλοι εἶναι ἀλλὰ μετεωρολόγοι καὶ ἀδολέσχαι τινές. ΕΡΜ. Τί δή? ΣΩ. Καταφαίνεταί μοι ἡ θέσις τῶν ὀνομάτων τοιούτων τινῶν ἀνθρώπων, καὶ ἐάν τις τὰ ξενικὰ ὀνόματα ἀνασκοπῇ, οὐχ ἧττον ἀνευρίσκεται ὃ ἕκαστον βούλεται. οἷον καὶ ἐν τούτῳ ὃ ἡμεῖς "οὐσίαν" καλοῦμεν, εἰσὶν οἳ "ἐσσίαν" καλοῦσιν, οἳ δ' αὖ "ὠσίαν." πρῶτον μὲν οὖν κατὰ τὸ ἕτερον ὄνομα τούτων ἡ τῶν πραγμάτων οὐσία "Ἑστία" καλεῖσθαι ἔχει λόγον, καὶ ὅτι γε αὖ ἡμεῖς τὸ τῆς οὐσίας μετέχον "ἔστιν" φαμέν, καὶ κατὰ τοῦτο ὀρθῶς ἂν καλοῖτο "Ἑστία"· ἐοίκαμεν γὰρ καὶ ἡμεῖς τὸ παλαιὸν "ἐσσίαν" καλεῖν τὴν οὐσίαν. ἔτι δὲ καὶ κατὰ τὰς θυσίας ἄν τις ἐννοήσας ἡγήσαιτο οὕτω νοεῖν ταῦτα τοὺς τιθεμένους· τὸ γὰρ πρὸ πάντων θεῶν τῇ Ἑστίᾳ πρώτῃ προθύειν εἰκὸς ἐκείνους οἵτινες τὴν πάντων οὐσίαν "ἐσσίαν" ἐπωνόμασαν. ὅσοι δ' αὖ "ὠσίαν," σχεδόν τι αὖ οὗτοι καθ' Ἡράκλειτον ἂν ἡγοῖτο τὰ ὄντα ἰέναι τε πάντα καὶ μένειν οὐδέν· τὸ οὖν αἴτιον καὶ τὸ ἀρχηγὸν αὐτῶν εἶναι τὸ ὠθοῦν, ὅθεν δὴ καλῶς ἔχειν αὐτὸ "ὠσίαν" ὠνομάσθαι. καὶ ταῦτα μὲν δὴ ταύτῃ ὡς παρὰ μηδὲν εἰδότων εἰρήσθω.

the "pushiness" (the ὠσία). To these two aspects of soul, there correspond two apparently irreconcilable, but equally compelling, accounts of the whole:[1] (1) the Parmenidean; and (2) the Herakleitean. The conjunction of these two aspects in Hestia finds its living embdiment in Socrates:

> [*Euthyphro*.] For he [i. e., Meletus], by taking it in hand to do injustice to you [i. e., Socrates], absolutely seems to me to begin to work something bad for the city [beginning] from its Hestia [i. e., from Socrates].[2]

So, Socrates mediates—and by mediating, he somehow unifies—the Parmenidean and Herakleitean perspectives.

One example of this mediation is Socrates's conversation with Cratylus and Hermogenes:[3] Cratylus begins with an onomatic crypto-Parmenideanism and ends with an onomatic Herakleiteanism; and Hermogenes undergoes the reverse movement. It is Socrates who effects the change. Only Socrates can be, as it were, in both places at the same time, whereas Cratylus and Hermogenes can be in only one or the other. Being in two places at the same time seems to be the essential characteristic of eros, which is simultaneously a lack and a fullness,[4] a poverty and a resource,[5] the first born (the oldest) and the youngest,[6] a capability and a willingness,[7] a reins-holder and two good and beautiful horses (cf. 246a6-8).

In the likeness of the soul that Socrates constructs, if the reins-holderr is νοῦς, then the good horse would be purified ἔρως (thymoeidetic epithymia).[8] The divine soul—the soul to which the philosopher is near (cf. 249c5-6, d1)—is a soul that consists of νοῦς and purified ἔρως moving together toward a vision[9] of the beingly being beingness,[10] a vision that eventuates in the energizing (inspiring) of the philosopher's διάνοια by memory or re-remembering[11] of the divinely serious things, by comparison to which the humanly serious things are moving askew, so that the non-philosophical many—who do not notice the truth of the situation and who are

1 For the relationship between the soul and the whole, cf. *Phaedrus* 270c1-2: "*Socrates*. Therefore, do you believe it to be possible in a way worthy of speech to intellect the nature of soul without the nature of the whole?" (ΣΩ. Ψυχῆς οὖν φύσιν ἀξίως λόγου κατανοῆσαι οἴει δυνατὸν εἶναι ἄνευ τῆς τοῦ ὅλου φύσεως;)

2 *Euthyphro* 3a7-8: ἀτεχνῶς γάρ μοι δοκεῖ ἀφ' Ἑστίας ἄρχεσθαι κακουργεῖν τὴν πόλιν, ἐπιχειρῶν ἀδικεῖν σέ. Cf. Burnet, note ad loc.

3 Cf. Sallis, pp. 183 ff.

4 Cf. *Philebus* 34c10-35d7.

5 Cf. *Symposium* 199c3-201c9, 201e3-202e2, 203a9-204b7.

6 Cf. *Hymn to Aphrodite* 22-23, according to which Hestia was both the first and the last of Kronos's children, both the oldest and the youngest (see LCL, note ad loc.). In the *Symposium*, this range is embodied in the figures of Phaedrus (cf. 178a9-c3), for whom Eros is the oldest god, and Agathon (cf. 195a8-c7), for whom Eros is the youngest god. There too, the extremes are united only in Socrates.

7 Cf. *Phaedrus* 247a6-7: "and the person who is always both willing and capable follows" (ἕπεται δὲ ὁ ἀεὶ ἐθέλων τε καὶ δυνάμενος).

8 Cf. *Republic* 4. 435e1-441c8, esp. 439e2-440d7. This represents a revision of the politically appropriate, but otherwise inaccurate, tripartite account of soul in the *Republic*. What is said here indicates that it is rather that (as Glaucon suggests) spiritedness and desire work together against intellect than that (as Socrates suggests) intellect and spiritedness work together against desire. The revision retains the tripartition of soul, but it does so by fusing spiritedness and desire (as—in the sense of the *Republic*—the δῆμος of low desires) and interposing a purified erotic part of the soul.

9 There is an extraordinary density of vision terms at 247c3-252b1: 247c7, d3, 4, 5, 6, e3, 248a4, 6, b4, 6, c3, 6, d2, 249b6, c2, 3, 5, 250a2, 4, 6, b5, 6-7, 8, d3, 4, 6, e3, 3-4, 251a3, 5, 7, b2, c6, e2, 3. This emphasizes the seriousness of blindness as a punishment.

10 247c7: οὐσία ὄντως οὖσα.

11 Cf. ἀνάμνησις at 249c2, μνήμη at 249c5, and ὑπομνήμασιν at 249c7.

chained[1] to the humanly serious—see the philosopher as moving askew and try to set him straight.[2]

Since no soul is humanly embodied without a prior vision of the beings, every presently living human is—by nature, and simply in accordance with being human—the possessor of that vision. The difference in strict anamnetic ability among humans derives from the relative length or brevity of the vision, according to which one is more or less blinded by immersion in injustice, i. e., in unpurified ἔρως.

With regard to why humans must have the prior vision, Socrates offers the following explanation:

> For the [soul] then which has never seen the truth will not come unto this shaped-surface [i.e, the human one]. For it is obligatory for a human to be cognizant in accordance with that which is spoken[to be] the look, going from many sensings unto one thing which is taken together by reckoning; and this is re-remembering those things which our soul once saw when it proceeded with and looked down on the things which we now assert to be, and when it lifted its head unto the beingly being.[3]

The process that is described here has the following steps:

(1) the soul sees (supersees) the truth (= the beingly being);

(2) the soul is humanly embodied;

(3) the human senses many sensings;

(4) the human reckons (speaks out) the many to be one (= the human re-remembers the truth/the beingly being);

(5) the human is cognizant that the one that is spoken (reckoned) is in accordance with a look.

Therefore, speech presupposes an already existing eidetic organization that is formulated by the speech. To speak at all bespeaks an eidetic unity that is stretched through all things about which speaking is. A speech is a taking together into one of an aisthetic many that is visible as the kind of many that it is. Such a speech is the product of ἡ διαλεκτική, the energized speaking-through, that corresponds to ἡ διάνοια, the energized thinking-through. In both ἡ διαλεκτική and ἡ διάνοια, the εἶδος (look) radiantly shines through its εἴδωλον (look-alike).

Hence, insofar as every human by nature speaks, every human is more or less cognizant of the eidetic unity in things. The difference between the philosopher and the many is that while the many is only operatively cognizant of it, the philosopher is thematically cognizant of it.[4] The person who engages in this thematizing activity is the skilled conversationalist, the dialectical person, the lover of dividings and leadings-together.

---

1 Cf. *Republic* 7. 514a1 ff. The chained prisoners in the cave are like oysters, the most mindless and most ignorant of living things: cf. *Timaeus* 92a7-c1; *Phaedrus* 250c6; *Cratylus* 400b8-c9.

2 Cf. *Phaedrus* 249c6-d3: "And indeed using the suchlike reminders correctly, a man who always is perfected by (is initiated into) the perfect (initiating) perfections (initiations)—[such a man] alone becomes beingly perfect (initiated); and having stood himself outside the human serious things and coming to be near the divine, he is excoriated by the many as though he were moving askew, and he has escaped the notice of the many [as actually] being inspired." (τοῖς δὲ δὴ τοιούτοις ἀνὴρ ὑπομνήμασιν ὀρθῶς χρώμενος, τελέους ἀεὶ τελετὰς τελούμενος, τέλεος ὄντως μόνος γίγνεται· ἐξιστάμενος δὲ τῶν ἀνθρωπίνων σπουδασμάτων καὶ πρὸς τῷ θείῳ γιγνόμενος, νουθετεῖται μὲν ὑπὸ τῶν πολλῶν ὡς παρακινῶν, ἐνθουσιάζων δὲ λέληθεν τοὺς πολλούς.) Cf. Vries, note ad 249c7-8.

3 *Phaedrus* 249b5-c4: οὐ γὰρ ἥ γε μήποτε ἰδοῦσα τὴν ἀλήθειαν εἰς τόδε ἥξει τὸ σχῆμα. δεῖ γὰρ ἄνθρωπον συνιέναι κατ' εἶδος λεγόμενον, ἐκ πολλῶν ἰὸν αἰσθήσεων εἰς ἓν λογισμῷ συναιρούμενον· τοῦτο δ' ἐστιν ἀνάμνησις ἐκείνων ἅ ποτ' εἶδεν ἡμῶν ἡ ψυχὴ συμπορευθεῖσα θεῷ καὶ ὑπεριδοῦσα ἃ νῦν εἶναί φαμεν, καὶ ἀνακύψασα εἰς τὸ ὂν ὄντως.

4 I have adapted the distinction between operative and thematic from Eugen Fink, as cited in Richard Zaner, *The Way of Phenomenology* (NY, 1970), pp. 115, 160-163.

It is time now to turn outside the mythic palinode to the discussion of dialectic that follows it,[1] a discussion in which Socrates descends from the divine childishly playful craziness of eros to the human soberly serious method of art.[2]

Socrates begins by recapitulating his fourfold classification of divine craziness, although—as with every Socratic recapitulation—there are refinements:

> *Socrates.* And then of craziness, [there are] two looks, the one [coming to be] by human diseases, and the one coming to be by a divine release from the accustomed lawful things.
> *Phaedrus.* Altogether so then.
> *Socrates.* And of the divine, we—having divided four parts of four gods, having posited divinative inspiration of Apollo, and initiatory [inspiration] of Dionysus, and in turn poetic [inspiration] of the Muses, and a fourth [inspiration] of Aphrodite and Eros—[having done this,] we asserted erotic craziness to be best.[3]

The refinement that is introduced here is that the value of craziness lies in its ability to release humans from the fetters of their habits, customs, and laws. This is no less characteristic of poetry, for example, than it is of philosophy.[4]

---

1 The delimited scope of the present inquiry makes it impossible to consider exhaustively the remainder of the palinode (250c8-257b6). As a whole, it is about the experience of love. Here, a few of its themes must be noted, at least briefly.

First, at 250c8-e1, the hierarchy of the lovable is treated as equivalent to the hierarchy of being, and the criterion for rank in the hierarchy is vivacity (cf. τῆς ἐναργεστάτης at 250d2, ἐναργέστατα at 250d3, ἐναργὲς at 250d5).

Second, in the discussion of the corrupt lover (250e1-251a1), homosexuality is condemned explicitly as unnatural, while heterosexuality in the service of procreation is regarded implicitly as natural: the corrupt lover sows children only because he regards it as a conventional compulsion (250e4-251a1): "But, after he has given himself over to pleasure, [the corrupt lover] takes it in hand to mount [a woman] and to sow children with respect to the law of the quadruped, and since he has had commerce in addition with insolence, he neither has feared nor is ashamed of chasing—outside nature—pleasure which is outside nature [i.e, both heterosexual acts that are not in the service of procreation and all homosexual acts]" (ἀλλ' ἡδονῇ παραδοὺς τετράποδος νόμον βαίνειν ἐπιχειρεῖ καὶ παιδοσπορεῖν, καὶ ὕβρει προσομιλῶν οὐ δέδοικεν ουδ' αἰσχύνεται παρὰ φύσιν ἡδονὴν διώκων). (Cf. Vries, note ad 251a1, for the double construing of παρὰ φύσιν and for references to related passages in the *Laws.*)

Third, the description of the corrupt lover's wing (251a1-c5)—its shiver (251a2-7), fever (251a7-b5), swelling (251b5-7), and boiling (251c1-5)—is simultaneously a description of a phallus in all stages of sexual arousal through orgasm. It is a complete somatization of the psychic. Hence, it suggeests the ease with which a lover may become corrupted. In the erotic things, the step from imaged somatization to behavioral somatization is an easy one to take: the itching (κνῆσις, 251c3) of eros beckons virtually irresistibly to be scratched. This explains, to some extent, the enormous power of the hybristic horse, the virtually irresistible itch that thymoeidetic epithymia is.

As to the rest of the palinode, cf. Sallis, p. 157: "all that remains is for Socrates to describe the course which the development of love follows and then, finally, to bring the entire speech explicitly to bear on the question inherited from the speech of Lysias." Also see Sallis, pp. 157-159.

2 Cf. *Phaedrus* 265c8-d1: "*Socrates.* The other things appear to me to have been childish play by that which *is* childish play; and of these certain things which have been uttered from luck, [there are] two looks which would not be ungratifying, if anyone were capable of grasping their power by art." (ΣΩ. Ἐμοὶ μὲν φαίνεται τὰ μὲν ἄλλα τῷ ὄντι παιδιᾷ πεπαῖσθαι· τούτων δέ τινων ἐκ τύχης ῥηθέντων δυοῖν εἰδοῖν εἰ αὐτοῖν τὴν δύναμιν τέχνῃ λαβεῖν δύναιτό τις, οὐκ ἄχαρι.)

3 *Phaedrus* 265a9-b5: ΣΩ. Μανίας δέ γε εἴδη δύο, τὴν μὲν ὑπὸ νοσημάτων ἀνθρωπίνων, τὴν δὲ ὑπὸ θείας ἐξαλλαγῆς τῶν εἰωθότων νομίμων γιγνομένην. ΦΑΙ. Πάνυ γε. ΣΩ. Τῆς δὲ θείας τετάρων θεῶν τέτταρα μέρη διελόμενοι, μαντικὴν μὲν ἐπίπνοιαν Ἀπόλλωνος θέντες, Διονύσου δὲ τελεστικήν, Μουσῶν δ' αὖ ποιητικήν, τεττάρτην δὲ Ἀφροδίτης καὶ Ἔρωτος, ἐρωτικὴν μανίαν ἐφήσαμέν τε ἀρίστην εἶναι. (In the initial classification, only the Muses were mentioned explicitly.)

4 *Republic* 10. 604a1-607a9.

The instrument of release—as Socrates is about to explain before identifying it explicitly—is ἡ διαλεκτική,[1] whose two looks are ἡ συναγωγή and ἡ διαίρεσις,[2] which he discusses in that order, and all too briefly.[3]

First, and more briefly,[4] he outlines ἡ συναγωγή, leading-together (collecting):

> And [the one look is] for the person who sees-together to lead the [things-] having-been-dispersed in many ways into one look so that the person defining it makes clear each [thing] about which [the person] always is willing to teach. As in the [things spoken] just now about eros—which is the [thing] having-been-defined—whether it was spoken well or badly, because of these [things], therefore then, the speech had [this] to speak, [namely] that which is distinct and the same [thing] agreeing with itself [i.e., clarity and consistency].[5]

Socrates partially repeats and partially amplifies his earlier statement regarding leading-together (collecting). The person who practices this method must be synoptic.[6] Furthermore, the

---

1 The identification is not made until 266c1.

2 Cf. *Timaeus* 71d5-72b5: "For remembering [their] father's missive—when he commissioned [them] to make the mortal class the best possible unto their power—correcting thus indeed even the mean [part] of us—so that in some way it should in addition touch the truth—the ones composing us set up the divinative in this [i.e., in the mean part of humans]. And a sufficient sign [of] how the god has given divination to human thoughtlessness [is this]; for no one in [his right] intellect touches upon inspired and true divination, but [only] either having been shackled [in] the power of his prudence either by sleep or because of disease, or having altered because of some inspiration. But it is for the person to conceive in [his right] intentions the re-remembered things which have been uttered either adream or awake by divination and inspired nature, and by reckoning to divide all, as many apparitions as were seen, in whatever way and to whom they signify when bad or good is about to be or already has come or is present; and when the crazy person still also remains in this [visionary condition], it is not his work to judge by himself the things which appeared and were voiced, but acting and recognizing his own things and himself, are spoken well and anciently to be fitting to the moderate person alone [to do]. Whence indeed also law has set up over inspired divinations the class of prophets as judges; which very persons some name "diviners," [the namers] being altogether unrecognizing that these persons are actors-out of riddling assertion and apparition, and they are not in any way diviners, and they most justly would be named prophets of the things which are divined." (μεμνημένοι γὰρ τῆς τοῦ πατρὸς ἐπιστολῆς οἱ συστήσαντες ἡμᾶς, ὅτε τὸ θνητὸν ἐπέστελλεν γένος ὡς ἄριστον εἰς δύναμιν ποιεῖν, οὕτω δὴ κατορθοῦντες καὶ τὸ φαῦλον ἡμῶν, ἵνα ἀληθείας πῃ προσάπτοιτο, κατέστησαν ἐν τούτῳ τὸ μαντεῖον. ἱκανὸν δὲ σημεῖον ὡς μαντικὴν ἀφροσύνῃ θεὸς ἀνθρωπίνῃ δέδωκεν· οὐδεὶς γὰρ ἔννους ἐφάπτεται μαντικῆς ἐνθέου καὶ ἀληθοῦς, ἀλλ' ἢ καθ' ὕπνον τὴν τῆς φρονήσεως πεδηθεὶς δύναμιν ἢ διὰ νόσον, ἢ διὰ τινα ἐνθουσιασμὸν παραλλάξας. ἀλλὰ συννοῆσαι μὲν ἔμφρονος τά τε ῥηθέντα ἀναμνησθέντα ὄναρ ἢ ὕπαρ ὑπὸ τῆς μαντικῆς τε καὶ ἐνθουσιαστικῆς φύσεως, καὶ ὅσα ἂν φαντάσματα ὀφθῇ, πάντα λογισμῷ διελέσθαι ὅπῃ τι σημαίνει καὶ ὅτῳ μέλλοντος ἢ παρελθόντος ἢ παρόντος κακοῦ ἢ ἀγαθοῦ· τοῦ δὲ μανέντος ἔτι τε ἐν τούτῳ μένοντος οὐκ ἔργον τὰ φανέντα καὶ φωνηθέντα ὑφ' ἑαυτοῦ κρίνειν, ἀλλ' εὖ καὶ πάλαι λέγεται τὸ πράττειν καὶ γνῶναι τά τε αὑτοῦ καὶ ἑαυτὸν σώφρονι μόνῳ προσήκειν. ὅθεν δὴ καὶ τὸ τῶν προφητῶν γένος ἐπὶ ταῖς ἐνθέοις μαντείας κριτὰς ἐπικαθιστάναι νόμος· οὓς μάντεις αὐτοὺς ὀνομάζουσίν τινες, τὸ πᾶν ἠγνοηκότες ὅτι τῆς δι' αἰνιγμῶν οὗτοι φήμης καὶ φαντάσεως ὑποκριταί, καὶ οὔτι μάντεις, προφῆται δὲ μαντευομένων δικαιότατα ὀνομάζοιντ' ἄν.)

3 Here the following apology is apt: "The very brief discussion of collection and division in the *Phaedrus* hardly provides a sufficient basis for a thorough consideration, which, instead, must take its bearings primarily from the *Sophist* and the *Statesman*." (Sallis, p. 171, n. 37) Sallis might have added the *Republic*.

4 This is the briefer of the two because it already has been discussed explicitly: cf. *Phaedrus* 249b5-c4 and the discussion of it above.

5 *Phaedrus* 265d3-7: ΣΩ. Εἰς μίαν τε ἰδέαν συνορῶντα ἄγειν τὰ πολλαχῇ διεσπαρμένα, ἵνα ἕκαστον ὁριζόμενος δῆλον ποιῇ περὶ οὗ ἂν ἀεὶ διδάσκειν ἐθέλῃ. ὥσπερ τὰ νυνδὴ περὶ Ἔρωτος—ὃ ἔστιν ὁρισθέν—εἴτ' εὖ εἴτε κακῶς ἐλέχθη, τὸ γοῦν σαφὲς καὶ τὸ αὐτὸ αὑτῷ ὁμολογούμενον διὰ ταῦτα ἔσχεν εἰπεῖν ὁ λόγος. (I have altered Burnet's punctuation slightly.)

6 Cf. συνορῶντα at 265d3 to σύνοψιν at *Republic* 7. 537c2. Also consider Republic 7. 537c7: "For the synoptic person is dialectical, but the non[-synoptic] is not." (ὁ μὲν γὰρ συνοπτικὸς διαλεκτικός, ὁ δὲ μὴ οὔ.)

unifying of a manifold is a delimiting, i. e., a horizoning, and the εἶδος of a manifold, its whither, is its horizonal schema.[1]

The context of bringing together a manifold into a unity is pedagogical. In addition, the method is productive of distinctness and internal consistency, although the price that it pays for achieving that twofold gain is that it may lose the particular phenomena that are being gathered together, i. e., it may not see the mountains for the range.

However, ἡ συναγωγή alone is not sufficient. Another method is required to supplement it.

Socrates now turns to that other method, ἡ διαίρεσις:

> The reverse is being capable, in accordance with looks, of cutting through at joints, where they are by nature, and not taking it in hand to break down any part, using the manner of a bad butcher; but as the [two] speeches just now grasped the meaninglessness of thinking-through to be some one look in common, and as, of a body, from one thing there are, by nature, two homonymous things—the ones having been called left, and the ones right—so also the [two] speeches, having regarded the look of dementedness as though it were by nature in us, the one who cut a part on the left, [then] cutting this again, did not leave off until it—having found in them that which is named a certain left eros—reviled it very much with justice, and the one—having led us unto the things of craziness on the right and it in turn having a certain divine eros [which was] homonymous to that one and having stretched it forth—praised it as the cause of the biggest goods for us.[2]

The striking thing about Socrates's description is the assertion of what the two methods have in common: they are both in accordance with looks.[3] The looks are the natural articulations of beings. For a good butcher of being, the cutting of being is only at these points.

In addition, it clearly makes a difference if the method is used badly—in contradistinction to synoptic delimiting or collecting—although precisely what the difference is, is not so clear. That the butcher is called κακός cannot mean (as Hackforth renders it) "clumsy."[4] Rather, it must mean either not knowing or disregarding the εἴδη in accordance with which one must cut. In the bad butcher, capability is not in question, but doing is, as the language itself strongly suggests.[5] The same butcher of being could cut a leg of being or make ground being, but in the former, the butcher would be cutting κατ' ἄρθρα ᾗ πέφυκεν, while in the latter, the butcher would not. However, in neither procedure would the butcher be clumsy.

Socrates gives two examples. However different they may seem, Socrates presents them as identical in import: both are introduced by a ὥσπερ (265e3, 4), and the double ὥσπερ is

---

1 Cf. Martin Heidegger, *Being and Time*, tr. John Macquarrie and Edward Robinson (NY, 1962), pp. 416 (H365) and 19 (H1). Also see his *Discourse on Thinking*, tr. John M. Anderson and E. Hans Freund (NY, 1968), pp. 64 ff.

2 *Phaedrus* 265e1-266b1: ΣΩ. Τὸ πάλιν κατ' εἴδη δύνασθαι διατέμνειν κατ' ἄρθρα ᾗ πέφυκεν, καὶ μὴ ἐπιχειρεῖν καταγνύναι μέρος μηδέν, κακοῦ μαγείρου τρόπῳ χρώμενον· ἀλλ' ὥσπερ ἄρτι τὼ λόγω τὸ μὲν ἄφρον τῆς διανοίας ἕν τι κοινῇ εἶδος ἐλαβέτην, ὥσπερ δὲ σώματος ἐξ ἑνὸς διπλᾶ καὶ ὁμώνυμα πέφυκε, σκαιά, τὰ δὲ δεξιὰ κληθέντα, οὕτω καὶ τὸ τῆς παρανοίας ὡς ἐν ἡμιν πεφυκὸς εἶδος ἡγησαμένω τὼ λόγω, ὁ μὲν τὸ ἐπ' ἀριστερὰ τεμνόμενος μέρος, πάλιν τοῦτο τέμνων οὐκ ἐπανῆκεν πρὶν ἐν αὐτοῖς ἐφευρὼν ὀνομαζόμενον σκαιόν τινα ἔρωτα ἐλοιδόρησεν μάλ' ἐν δίκῃ, ὁ δ' εἰς τὰ ἐν δεξιᾷ τῆς μανίας ἀγαγὼν ἡμᾶς, ὁμώνυμον μὲν ἐκείνῳ, θεῖον δ' αὖ τινα ἔρωτα ἐφευρὼν καὶ προτεινάμενος ἐπῄνεσεν ὡς μεγίστων αἴτιον ἡμῖν ἀγαθῶν. (I have removed from the text Heindorf's addition of ἕν at 266a2: cf. Burnet, OCT, apparatus criticus ad loc.)

3 Cf. κατ' εἶδος at 249b7 and Εἰς μίαν . . . ἰδέαν at 265d3 to κατ' εἴδη at 265e1, εν τι . . . εἶδος at 265e4, and τὸ . . . εἶδος at 266a2–3.

4 Cf. Sallis, p. 170, who adopts this rendering.

5 Cf. δύνασθαι at e1 to ἐπιχειρεῖν at e2.

answered by the οὕτω (266a2) that signifies the consequence of the two together. So, Socrates gives a two that—he suggests—is a one, and from them as a one, he draws a conclusion.

The example of the two speeches—and this seems rather curious—adumbrates their embodiment of the method of συναγωγή, in which the manifold "meaninglessness of thinking-through" is collected into one common look, a method that Socrates himself exemplifies in his explanation by using three names for the single phenomenon of craziness,[1] and by suggesting that the two examples be fused together as one.

The example of the body adumbrates the method of διαίρεσις, in which, in the case of the body, a natural one presents itself as a natural two. The example of the body is striking. The body is symmetrical, at least from the front and back,[2] having symmetrically corresponding similarly named pairs of parts: (right) leg and (left) leg, (right) ear and (left) ear, and so forth. However, this must not simply be taken for granted, especially if "the navel [is] the memorial of the ancient [human] affection,"[3] or if we reflect upon the placement of male and female genitals that Aristophanes suggests in his λόγος,[4] because the human sphere would not be symmetrical—if indeed one can speak strictly of any sphere as symmetrical—in the way in which the human trunk is symmetrical. This indicates an insufficiency in the method of διαίρεσις, a sterility, as it were, in that διαίρεσις can reveal εἶδος only as γένος, but not as γένεσις.

Indeed, the Aristophanean account of the result of bodily τμῆσις can be taken as a caricature of the consequences of the employment of διαίρεσις alone:

> Therefore, when the nature was cut in two, each—yearning for the [other] half of itself—used to go with [it], and throwing their arms around and being interwoven with each other, desiring to co-nature, they died by humger and other idleness because of their being unwilling to do anything separate from each other.[5]

The splitting fails to provide a natural fulfillment, a natural τροφή and ἔργον, for the yearning which that same splitting activates. This, by the way, is the failure of Aristophanes's own account as well.[6] One of the purposes of both Diotima's account in the *Symposium* and Socrates's mythic palinode in the *Phaedrus* is to adumbrate the natural τροφή and ἐνέργεια of humans.

---

1 τὸ . . . ἄφρον at 265e4, τῆς παρανοίας at 266a2, and τῆς μανίας at 266a6. Cf. Sallis, p. 170, n. 36.

2 Cf. William Blake, *Songs of Experience*, "The Tyger," lines 1-4: "Tyger! Tyger! Burning bright / In the forests of the night, / What immortal hand or eye / Could frame thy fearful symmetry?" [*The Complete Writings of William Blake with all variant readings*, ed. Geoffrey Keynes (NY, 1957), p. 214.] Although Blake's speaker does not say so explicitly, the tiger is taken as symmetrical because it is seen from the front.

3 Cf. *Symposium* 191a3-5: "and he [i. e., Apollo] left behind a few [wrinkles], the ones around the belly itself and the navel, to be a memorial of the ancient affection" (ὀλίγας δὲ κατέλιπε, τὰς περὶ αὐτὴν τὴν γαστέρα καὶ τὸν ὀμφαλόν, μνημεῖον εἶναι τοῦ παλαιοῦ πάθους). In addition, consider the suggestion at *Philebus* 35b1-d7 that desire is memory.

4 Cf. *Symposium* 191b5 ff. Also consider Iago's loathsomely rich remark: 'your Daughter and the Moore, are making the Beast with two backs." [Shakespeare, *Othello, a new variorum edition*, ed. Horace Howard Furness (NY, 1963), I. 1. 128-129.] In connection with Aristophanes's speech, one could raise the question whether Apollo was a good butcher or a bad butcher.

5 Symposium 191a5-b1: ἐπειδὴ οὖν ἡ φύσις δίχα ἐτμήθη, ποθοῦν ἕκαστον τὸ ἥμισυ τὸ αὑτοῦ συνῄει, καὶ περιβάλλοντες τὰς χεῖρας καὶ συμπλεκόμενοι ἀλλήλοις. ἐπιθυμοῦντες συμφῦναι, ἀπέθνῃσκον ὑπὸ λιμοῦ καὶ τῆς ἄλλης ἀργίας διὰ τὸ μηδὲν ἐθέλειν χωρὶς ἀλλήλων ποιεῖν.

6 Therefore, as Aristophanes presents Eros (cf. *Symposium* 189d1-3), far from being a "healer of these things which, when they have been healed, would be the biggest happiness for the human race" (ἰατρὸς ὧν ἰαθέντων μεγίστη εὐδαιμονία ἂν τῷ ἀνθρωπείῳ γένει εἴη), it is that which infects the human race with an ineradicable disease and is thereby productive of the greatest unhappiness. The darkness of Aristophanean comedy is exceeded only by the darkness of the Platonic comedy that presents so darkly comic a figure.

Διαίρεσις, then is purely or abstractly descriptive, i. e., it is a λόγος in the narrow sense,[1] but it is not, and cannot be, a μῦθος, a genetic accoount. This is why, in the *Statesman*, the Elean Stranger must supplement his διαίρεσις (258a7-267c4) with a μῦθος (267c5-277a2), a μῦθος that he introduces (268e8 ff.) as a συναγωγή of a previously cut many (including the strife between Atreus and Thyestes, with the concomitant change in the rising and setting of the heavenly bodies, Kronos's kingdom, and the earth-born):

> *Stranger.* Then these [accounts] all together are from the same affection, and in addition to these, ten thousand others even still more wondrous than these [are from the same affection], but through a multitude of time, the ones of them have extinguished [i.e., been forgotten], and the ones having been thoroughly dispersed have been spoken, [but] each severally separate from each other. But the affection which is the cause of all these things no one has spoken, but now indeed it must be spoken.[2]

The *Statesman* myth, then, that perfects the preceding διαίρεσις,[3] is an implicit συναγωγή.

In like manner, Socrates's Aesopic myth about the pleasant and the painful is a small paradigm designed to illustrate that a μῦθος is a genetic συναγωγή:

> And sitting up on the bed, Socrates both bent his leg and rubbed [it] with his hand, and simultaneously as [he was] rubbing, he asserted, "How eccentric, oh men, is likely to be this something which humans call pleasant; how wonderfully it is naturally related to the thing seeming to be its contrary, [namely] the painful, so as for them not to be willing to come to be present to a human simultaneously, and [yet] if anyone chases and catches one of the two, [he seems] in some way almost to be compelled always to catch also the other of the two, as though the two are fastened to one head. And it seems to me," he [further] asserted, "if Aesop had intellected these things, he would have composed a myth [about] how, wishing to release them from warring, since he was not capable [of doing so], the god fastened their heads together for them into the same thing, and because of these things, if the one of the two comes to be present to anyone, also the other of the two follows later."[4]

---

1 Cf. *Philebus* 57a9 ff., where λόγος is personified as διαίρεσις.

2 *Statesman* 269b5-c1: ΞΕ. Ταῦτα τοίνυν ἔστι μὲν σύμπαντα ἐκ ταὐτοῦ πάθους, καὶ πρὸς τούτοις ἕτερα μυρία καὶ τούτων ἔτι θαυμαστότερα, διὰ δὲ χρόνου πλῆθος τὰ μὲν αὐτῶν ἀπέσβηκε, τὰ δὲ διεσπαρμένα εἴρηται χωρὶς ἕκαστα ἀπ' ἀλλήλων. ὁ δ' ἐστὶν πᾶσι τούτοις αἴτιον τὸ πάθος οὐδεὶς εἴρηκεν. νῦν δὲ δὴ λέκτεον.

3 Cf. Seth Benardete, "Eidos and Diairesis in Plato's *Statesman*," *Philologus*, vol. 107, 1963, p. 203: "The myth gives the conditions under which the diairesis would be true." He also refers to the "myth as the perfection of the diairesis" (p. 204).

4 *Phaedo* 60b1-c7: ὁ δὲ Σωκράτης ἀνακαθιζόμενος εἰς τὴν κλίνην συνέκαμψέ τε τὸ σκέλος καὶ ἐξέτριψε τῇ χειρί, καὶ τρίβων ἅμα, Ὡς ἄτοπον, ἔφη ὦ ἄνδρες, ἔοικέ τι εἶναι τοῦτο ὃ καλοῦσιν οἱ ἄνθρωποι ἡδύ· ὡς θαυμασίως πέφυκε πρὸς τὸ δοκοῦν ἐναντίον εἶναι, τὸ λυπηρόν, τὸ ἅμα μὲν αὐτὼ μὴ 'θέλειν παραγίγνεσθαι τῷ ἀνθρώπῳ, ἐὰν δέ τις διώκῃ τὸ ἕτερον καὶ λαμβάνῃ, σχεδόν τι ἀναγκάζεσθαι ἀεὶ λαμβάνειν καὶ τὸ ἕτερον, ὥσπερ ἐκ μιᾶς κορυφῆς ἡμμένω δύ' ὄντε. καί μοι δοκεῖ, ἔφη εἰ ἐνενόησεν αὐτὰ Αἴσωπος, μῦθον ἂν συνθεῖναι ὡς ὁ θεὸς βουλόμενος αὐτὰ διαλλάξαι πολεμοῦντα, ἐπειδὴ οὐκ ἐδύνατο, συνῆψεν εἰς ταὐτὸν αὐτοῖς τὰς κορυφάς, καὶ διὰ ταῦτα ᾧ ἂν τὸ ἕτερον παραγένηται ἐπακολουθεῖ ὕστερον καὶ τὸ ἕτερον.

The Socratic Aesopic myth[1] here is an attempt to account for the genesis of the concomitance, without coincidence, of the pleasant and the painful. Its method is synagogic, i. e., it adumbrates their unitary source that depends on an underlying natural relatedness that their manifest contrariety belies. Who is the god? As will be seen from the *Phaedrus*—although perhaps it can be suggested now—the synagogic god is ὁ διαλεκτικός, who is also the diairetic god (cf. *Sophist* 216a1-c4).

Neither διαίρεσις nor συναγωγή alone is sufficient. What is required is a combination of the two,[2] of λόγος in the narrow sense of classificatory description and μῦθος in its sense of genetic accoount. In some of the dialogues, the one or the other method predominates, e.g., in the *Republic* συναγωγή[3] or in the *Sophist* διαίρεσις.[4] In other dialogues, e.g., the *Statesman*, the two methods are used side by side as supplementary to each other. In the rare case, they interpenetrate, as they seem to do in the *Phaedrus*, as Socrates suggests when he says:

> Indeed, I at any rate am a lover, oh Phaedrus, of these dividings and leadings-together, so that I may be able both to speak and to think; and if we regard anyone else [to be] capable of seeing that which is by nature into one and over many, I shall chase this person from behind, after his track, as though he were a god. And yet also therefore, up to now, I call persons who are capable of doing it, whether I proclaim them correctly or not god knows, "dialectical persons."[5]

In his usual allusive and elliptical way, Socrates indicates the importance of διαιρέσεις and συναγωγαί. Without them, no speech or thinking would be possible.

Hence, διαίρεσις/συναγωγή and λέγειν/φρονεῖν are coeval:

> Somehow we assert the one and the many which come to be the same by speeches to run around in every way in accordance with each of the things which are spoken, [and we assert them to do so] always, both anciently and now. And this neither ever ceases nor now began, but the suchlike is, as it appears to me, a certain deathless and old-ageless affection in us of speeches themselves.[6]

Therefore, διαίρεσις and συναγωγή are an affection of Λόγος itself.

---

1 Cebes seems to understand that Socrates's usage of myth as genetic account makes Aesop's tales no longer myths, but rather λόγοι. Hence, he refers to them in his interruption as Aesop's speeches (τοὺς τοῦ Αἰσώπου λόγους, 60d1), even though when Socrates next refers to them, he refers to them as myths (μύθους . . . τοὺς Αἰσώπου, 61b6) in the context of their general accessibility, as though to emphasize that these things that are generally regarded as myths differ from Socrates's own myths.

2 Cf. *Philebus* 16b5-17a5 and ff.

3 One could say that *the* result of *the* synoptic συναγωγή is the good.

4 One could say that the constant shifting of the sophist from γένος to γένος, which makes it impossible to capture him, is grounded in his artful ability to render himself immune to any considerations rooted in natural articulations.

5 *Phaedrus* 266b3-c1: Τούτων δὴ ἔγωγε αὐτός τε ἐραστής, ὦ Φαῖδρε, τῶν διαιρέσεων καὶ συναγωγῶν, ἵνα οἷός τε ὦ λέγειν τε καὶ φρονεῖν· ἐάν τε τιν' ἄλλον ἡγήσωμαι δυνατὸν εἰς ἓν καὶ ἐπὶ πολλὰ πεφυκόθ' ὁρᾶν, τοῦτον διώκω "κατόπισθε μετ' ἴχνιον ὥστε θεοῖο. " καὶ μέντοι καὶ τοὺς δυναμένους αὐτὸ ὁρᾶν εἰ μὲν ὀρθῶς ἢ μὴ προσαγορεύω, θεὸς οἶδε, καλῶ δὲ οὖν μέχρι τοῦδε διαλεκτικούς.

6 *Philebus* 15d4-8: Φαμέν που ταὐτὸν ἓν καὶ πολλὰ ὑπὸ λόγων γιγνόμενα περιτρέχειν πάντῃ καθ' ἕκαστον τῶν λεγομένων ἀεί, καὶ πάλαι καὶ νῦν. καὶ τοῦτο οὔτε μὴ παύσηταί ποτε οὔτε ἤρξατο νῦν, ἀλλ' ἔστι τὸ τοιοῦτον, ὡς ἐμοὶ φαίνεται τῶν λόγων αὐτῶν ἀθάνατόν τι καὶ ἀγήρων πάθος ἐν ἡμῖν. (This would suggest that what immortality humans have is the immortality of this πάθος in them that manifests itself in speeches, i. e., the immortality of an affection of Λόγος. Such a possibility must be kept in the back of one's mind when one reads the demonstrations of the immortality of human soul in the *Phaedo*.)`

In addition, Socrates's divine erotic craziness, his ἔρως, is no less of dividings and leadings-together than it is of speaking and thinking. This ἔρως eventuates in seeing the natural ones that are over natural manies. Such seeing is a seeing of monsters, as Socrates indicates in the *Philebus*:

> Having divided by speech simultaneously both the limbs and parts of each thing, having agreed all these things to be that one thing, someone may refute [himself], laughing because he has been compelled to assert monsters, [such monsters as that] there is a way in which the one is many and unlimited, and a way in which the many is only one.[1]

Socrates, then, constantly employs the very monster methodology, synagogic diairesis, that he disclaims early in the *Phaedrus*. His ἔργον in this respect simply reflects the essential character of Λόγος itself.

Any person whose ἐνέργεια this is, any person for whom this is the πρᾶγμα, is the equal of a god. Therefore, the god (or demigod, if one prefers) who knows whether Socrates's proclaiming is correct or not is none other than ὁ διαλεκτικός, namely Socrates himself.[2] In chasing the tracks of such a god, Socrates is chasing himself: the synagogic diairesis of which dialectic consists is nothing other than the trail of self-knowledge. Self-knowledge is the knowledge of the good[3] and of the beingness of the nature of the soul.[4] This is the knowledge that the serious and perfect rhetorical artist[5] must possess[6] in order to convey it to another soul[7] or to persuade[8] or to teach[9] another soul in speeches or in writings.[10]

---

1 *Philebus* 14d8-e4: τις ἑκάστου τὰ μέλη τε καὶ ἅμα μέρη διελὼν τῷ λόγῳ, πάντα ταῦτα τὸ ἓν ἐκεῖνο εἶναι διομολογησάμενος, ἐλέγχῃ καταγελῶν ὅτι τέρατα διηνάγκασται φάναι, τό τε ἓν ὡς πολλά ἐστι καὶ ἄπειρα, καὶ τὰ πολλὰ ὡς ἓν μόνον.

2 One would ultimately have to consider whether any of the other references to gods in the Platonic corpus are also to be taken, not as simple adoptions of Hellenic theological figures, but rather as idealized human types or idealized individual humans. Cf. Milton, "Lycidas," line 15 to lines 19-20. In addition, even when a contrast is drawn between ἄνθρωποι and θεοί, one would have to consider whether the ultimate distinction is between merely human (ἄνθρωποι) and truly human (θεοί): cf. *Timaeus* 68d4-7: "the god is sufficiently knowing and simultaneously capable to mix together the many into one and again to dissolve from one into many, and no one of humans either is now or ever will be at any time hereafter sufficient for either of these things." (θεὸς μὲν τὰ πολλὰ εἰς ἓν συγκεραννύναι καὶ πάλιν ἐξ ἑνὸς εὸς πολλὰ διαλύειν ἱκανῶς ἐπιστάμενος ἅμα καὶ δυνατός, ἀνθρώπων δὲ οὐδεὶς οὐδέτερα τούτων ἱκανὸς οὔτε ἔστι νῦν οὔτε εἰς αὖθίς ποτε ἔσται.) Also cf. *Timaeus* 3d6-7: "and in addition, a god—and whoever of men be friendly to that [god]—has envisioned [i.e., understood] the ruling-beginnings which are above these." (τὰς δ' ἔτι τούτων ἀρχὰς ἄνωθεν θεὸς οἶδεν καὶ ἀνδρῶν ὃς ἂν ἐκείνῳ φίλος ᾖ.)

3 Cf. *Charmides* 174d3-7, 167a1 ff., 169e2-7 et passim.

4 Cf. *Phaedrus* 270e2-5: "[*Socrates*.] But it is clear how, if anyone gives speeches to anyone by art, he will show precisely the beingness of the nature of this in regard to which he will bear forth the speeches; and this will be somehow soul." (ἀλλὰ δῆλον ὡς, ἄν τῳ τις τέχνῃ λόγους διδῷ, τὴν οὐσίαν δείξει ἀκριβῶς τῆς φύσεως τούτου πρὸς ὃ τοὺς λόγους προσοίσει· ἔσται δέ που ψυχὴ τοῦτο.)

5 Cf. "the art of the beingly rhetorical and persuasive person" (τὴν τοῦ τῷ ὄντι ῥητορικοῦ τε καὶ πιθανοῦ τέχνην, 269c9-d1), "a perfect competitor" (ἀγωνιστὴν τέλεον, 269d2; cf. ἀτελὴς, 269d6), "the most perfect of all in regard to rhetoric" (πάντων τελεώτατος εἰς τὴν ῥητορικὴν, 269e1-2), "work-perfecting" (τελεσιουργὸν, 270a2), "and whoever else seriously gives the rhetorical art" (καὶ ὃς ἂν ἄλλος σπουδῇ τέχνην ῥητορικὴν διδῷ, 271a4-5), "perfectly" (τελέως, 272a7).

6 If there is such a most perfect art, its method must be informed by, and lead toward, the most perfect. The most perfect is the good: cf. *Philebus* 20c8-d11, 60b7-c5.

7 Cf. "he will make [others] see soul" (ποιήσει ψυχὴν ἰδεῖν, 271a6).

8 Cf. πιθανοῦ at 269c9; πειθὼ at 270b8, 271a2; πείθεται . . . ἀπειθεῖ at 271b4-5; εὐπειθεῖς at 271d6; δυσπειθεῖς at 271d7; πείθεται at 271e3; πειθὼ at 272 a3; πειθόμενος at 272b2.

9 Cf. διδάσκουσιν at 269c8, διδάσκων at 271b3, ψυχαγωγία at 271c10, διδάσκων at 272b2.

10 Cf. γράφουσιν at 269c8, γράψει at 271a5, γραφήσεται at 271b8, οἱ νῦν γράφοντες at 271c1, γράφωσι and γράφειν at 271c4, γράφειν at 271c7, γράφων at 272b1, ὁ συγγραφεύς at 272b2-3.

The *Phaedrus* concludes with an elaboration of what perfect writing is, what appropriate or beautiful[1] writing is, an elaboration that is consonant with the view of writing sggested by Plato himself in his own myth in the seventh epistle (see Chapter IV), except that what there was presented in terms of its genesis in the form of a μῦθος here is presented in terms of classificatory description or λόγος in the narrow sense.

What is perfect writing? In the first place, it is a τέχνη[2] that is by nature[3] and about nature.[4] However—and in this it differs from most writing—it shows nature[5] through likeness for which the ground is truth and beingness:

> everywhere the person who has envisioned [i.e., understood] the truth knows how to find [the similarities]. So that . . . if anyone does not enumerate the natures of the persons who hear, and if he be not capable of both dividing the beings in accordance with looks and embracing with one look in accordance with each one [severally], he will never be skilled in art about speeches in accordance with as much as is possible for a human.[6]

So, in addition to διαίρεσις and συναγωγή, perfect writing prerequires a vision of the truth such as Socrates described in his palinode, a vision that leads to knowledge of the similes for truth,[7] and a classification of human soul types and speeches that leads to knowledge of how to adapt one's utterances to those types.

In brief, it prerequires a complete knowledge of soul:

> *Socrates.* Then it is clear that . . . whoever . . . seriously gives [others, i.e., teaches] the rhetorical art, first both will write [soul] with all precision and will make [others] see soul, whether it is by nature one and similar or multi-looked in accordance with [i. e., as is] the shape of the body; for we assert this to be to show nature.
>
> *Phaedrus.* Therefore, [it is] all in all so [as you speak].
>
> *Socrates.* And second then, what it is its nature to do to what and to be affected by what.
>
> *Phaedrus.* What then?

1 Cf. *Phaedrus* 274b6-7: "[*Socrates.*] And the thing about appropriateness and inappropriateness of writing, [namely] coming to be in what way it would be beautiful and in what way inappropriate, is left." (ΣΩ. Τὸ δ' εὐπρεπείας δὴ γραφῆς πέρι καὶ ἀπρεπείας, πῇ γιγνόμενον καλῶς ἂν ἔχοι καὶ ὅπῃ ἀπρεπῶς, λοιπόν.)

2 Cf. τῆς τέχνης at 269c7, τέχνην at 269d1, τέχνη at 269d6, τῶν τεχνῶν at 269e4, τέχνης at 270b1, τέχνῃ at 270b6, τεχνικοὶ at 270d2, τέχνῃ at 270e1, τέχνην at 271a5, τέχνῃ at 271b8, τέχνας at 271c2, τέχνῃ at 271c4, τεχνικῶς at 271c7, τέχνῃ at 272b1, τέχνης at 272b4, τέχνῃ at 272e2, τεχνικοὶ at 273a3, τεχνικὸν at 273b3, τέχνῃ at 273c5, τέχνην at 273c7, τέχνης at 273d7, τεχνικὸς at 273e3, τέχνης τε καὶ ἀτεχνίας at 274b3.

3 Cf. φύσει at 269d4, εὐφυὴς at 270a3, τὰς φύσεις at 273e1.

4 Cf. φύσεως πέρι at 270a1, φύσιν . . . ὧν δὴ πέρι at 270a5-6, φύσιν at 270b4 and c1, φύσεως at 270c2, περὶ φύσεως at 270c9, περὶ ότουοῦν φύσεως at 270d1, σκοπεῖν τὴν δύναμιν αὐτοῦ, τίνα πρὸς τί πέφυκεν . . . ἔχον ("to consider its power, what it had by nature") at 270d3-4, πέφυκεν at 270d7, τῆς φύσεως at 270e3-4, φύσιν at 271a7, αὕτη ἡ φύσις περὶ ἧς at 272a1, φύσει at 272d6.

5 Cf. τὴν ουσίαν δείξει . . . τῆς φύσεως at 270e3-4 and φύσιν . . . δεικνύμαι at 271a7-8.

6 *Phaedrus* 273d5-6, 8-e4: πανταχοῦ ὁ τὴν ἀλήθειαν εἰδὼς κάλλιστα ἐπίσταται εὑρίσκειν [τὰς ὁμοιότητας], ὥστ . . . ἐὰν μή τις τῶν τε ἀκουσομένων τὰς φύσεις διαριθμήσηται, καὶ κατ' εἴδη τε διαιρεῖσθαι τὰ ὄντα καὶ μιᾷ ἰδέᾳ δυνατὸς ᾖ καθ' ἓν ἕκαστον περιλαμβάνειν, οὔ ποτ' ἔσται τεχνικὸς λόγων πέρι καθ' ὅσον δυνατὸν ἀνθρώπῳ.

7 Cf. *Phaedrus* 273d4: ὁμοιότητα τοῦ ἀληθοῦς.

> *Socrates.* And indeed third, [the writer], who has thoroughly ordered for himself the classes of both speeches and soul and the affections of these, will go through all the causes, in addition harmonizing each to each and teaching which sort of being [soul] [and] by which sorts of speeches [and] because of which cause, is persuaded and which unpersuaded.[1]

So, knowledge of soul is needed because writing or speaking is soul-leading (ψυχαγωγία)[2] through speeches,[3] whether in public or in private.[4]

It is significant that the only two occurrences of the word ψυχαγωγία in Plato are in the *Phaedrus*,[5] although the process is described in the *Republic*.[6] In other words, *the* way of leading the soul is by speech, in particular by writing. Not all souls can be led (i. e., persuaded), and not all souls that can be led can be led in the same way. Therefore, a perfect writing must be constructed in such a way as to lead different souls simultaneously in different ways, i. e., in such a way as to speak different things simultaneously to different persons, and at the same time to leave unled or unpersuaded those souls that cannot be led or persuaded. "And yet," as Phaedrus remarks with marvellous understatement, "it does not appear to be, then, a small work."[7] The ultimate audience for whose gratification such a writing is composed is an audience of gods, of "masters who are both good themselves and from good [progenitors]."[8] Whether by "gods" Socrates means the gods of the traditional Hellenic pantheon or perfectly dialectical humans is at least an open question.[9]

The account[10] of Theuth and Ammon that Socrates presents next could almost be taken as a dialogue between the Socratic ἔργον (Ammon) and the Platonic ἔργον (Theuth) on the basis of an implicit identity between the Socratic Λόγος and the Platonic Λόγος. In addition, the account is rather, as its prologue in the *Philebus* (18b6-d2) indicates, a λόγος in the narrow sense than a μῦθος.

In the *Philebus*, Theuth is credited with having invented written equivalents of spoken sounds by intellecting that although an unlimited aisthetic (i. e., acoustic) multiplicity could not be reduced to a noetic oneness, it could be rendered intelligible by reducing it to a limited noetic manyness. Faced with the choice between a Herakleitean aisthetic heterogeneity and a Parmenidean eidetic homogeneity, Theuth decided that a mediation was possible by means of a finite eidetic heterogeneity. Then Theuth saw what his discovery meant:

---

1 *Phaedrus* 271a4-b5: ΣΩ. Δῆλον ἄρα ὅτι . . . ὃς ἂν . . . σπουδῇ τέχνην ῥητορικὴν διδῷ, πρῶτον πάσῃ ἀκριβείᾳ γράψει τε καὶ ποιήσει ψυχὴν ἰδεῖν, πότερον ἓν καὶ ὅμοιον πέφυκεν ἢ κατὰ σώματος μορφὴν πολυειδές· τοῦτο γάρ φαμεν φύσιν εἶναι δεικνύναι. ΦΑΙ. Παντάπασι μὲν οὖν. ΣΩ. Δεύτερον δέ γε, ὅτῳ τί ποιεῖν ἢ παθεῖν ὑπὸ τοῦ πέφυκεν. ΦΑΙ. Τί μήν; ΣΩ. Τρίτον δὲ δὴ διαταξάμενος τὰ λόγων τε καὶ ψυχῆς γένη καὶ τὰ τούτων παθήματα δίεισι πάσας αἰτίας, προσαρμόττων ἕκαστον ἑκάστῳ καὶ διδάσκων οἵα οὖσα ὑφ' οἵων λόγων δι' ἣν αἰτίαν ἐξ ἀνάγκης ἡ μὲν πείθεται, ἡ δὲ ἀπειθεῖ. Cf. 272c10 ff.

2 *Phaedrus* 271c10. Cf. *Republic* 7. 518b6 ff.

3 Cf. *Phaedrus* 261a8: ψυχαγωγία τις διὰ λόγων.

4 Cf. 261a8-9: "not only in courts of justice and as many other colloquia as are public, but also in private [places]" (οὐ μόνον ἐν δικαστηρίοις καὶ ὅσοι ἄλλοι δημόσιοι σύλλογοι, ἀλλὰ καὶ ἐν ἰδίοις).

5 *Phaedrus* 261a8, 271c10.

6 *Republic* 7. 518b6 ff.

7 *Phaedrus* 272b5-6: καίτοι οὐ σμικρόν γε φαίνεται ἔργον.

8 *Phaedrus* 274a1-2: δεσπόταις ἀγαθοῖς τε καὶ ἐξ ἀγαθῶν (cf. 273e7). This is the same phrase that Socrates uses to describe the souls of gods in his mythic palinode (246a8). Also cf. 274b9.

9 See above on the *Statesman* myth and the monster methodology. Also consider *Philebus* 18b6-7.

10 'Ακοήν, 274c1. The word ἀκοή is the closest Platonic equivalent to our 'tale,' but whether a given tale in the Platonic corpus is a λόγος or a μῦθος depends on how else the tale is characterized. However, one could formulate the general rule of thumb that when an ἀκοή is not otherwise characterized as a μῦθος—and it is not so characterized here—it is to be regarded as a λόγος.

> And seeing how none of us would learn [any] one itself in accordance with itself without all of them, having reckoned in turn this bond as being one and somehow making all these things one, having spoken in addition, [Theuth] uttered the one art over them as being grammar.[1]

This contains a strong caveat for everyone who reads Plato in that it indicates that no one of the εἴδη can be learned without all the others. In other words, no partial whole can be discerned without discerning the whole whole of which it is a part, just as no single Platonic dialogue can be discerned without discerning all the others.

Presumably it was after making his decision about the letters as symbols of the eidetic structure of the unlimited continuum of articulate sound that Theuth presented himself before Ammon. Between them they confront one of the key questions about written things, the question of harm and benefit.[2] On this basis, Ammon rejects written things as harmful to memory and productive of an incorrect or harsh contempt.[3] This is the presentation of the problem without any solution within the tale itself. However, in the sequel, the following solution is drawn out. Written things may have been superfluous, even dangerous, when humans were filled with naiveté,[4] i. e., when humans listened to an oak and a rock.[5] However, because Socrates as a representative current human is not "from an oak or from a rock,"[6] and because regimes now do not come to be from an oak or a rock,[7] writing may be desirable, even salutary.

What is the character of such writing? In what follows, Socrates answers that question partially by repetition of what he has said already, partially by amplification. Most writing (analogously to painting) has speeches that one would think could speak and teach, but they cannot.[8] If you try to engage them in conversation, they say only the same one thing, and they say it in the same way indiscriminately, both to those who can and should understand it and to those for whom it is not fitting to hear such a thing (cf. 275d4-e2). In short, most writing "does not know to whom then it is obligatory to speak and not [to speak]."[9] However, there is a kind of speech that does know to whom it should speak and to whom it should not speak, namely "the one which is written with knowledge in the soul of the learner."[10]

As to whether writing should be a playful and festive planting in the soul, such as farmers do in window boxes for a festival, or whether it should be serious, Socrates asserts that it is a childishly playful reminder both for himself and for everyone who follows him (cf. 276b1-c4). Therefore, when the truly dialectical person writes with ink on paper, such a person will write playfully an imitation of what the same person writes seriously in the soul of someone with

---

1 Philebus 18c7-d2: καθορῶν δὲ ὡς οὐδεὶς ἡμῶν οὐδ' ἂν ἓν αὐτὸ καθ' αὐτὸ ἄνευ πάντων αὐτῶν μάθοι, τοῦτον τὸν δεσμὸν αὖ λογισάμενος ὡς ὄντα ἕνα καὶ πάντα ταῦτα ἕν πως ποιοῦντα μίαν ἐπ' αὐτοῖς ὡς οὖσαν γραμματικὴν τέχνην ἐπεφθέγξατο προσειπών.

2 *Phaedrus* 274e9: βλάβης τε καὶ ὠφελίας. Cf. Chapter IV above.

3 Cf. *Epistles* 7. 341e1-342a1, and Chapter IV above.

4 Cf. εὐηθείας at *Phaedrus* 275b8, c7.

5 *Phaedrus* 275b8: δρυὸς καὶ πέτρας.

6 *Apol. Socr.* 34d4-5: οὐδ' . . . ἀπὸ δρυὸς οὐδ' ἀπὸ πέτρης.

7 Cf. *Republic* 8. 544d7-8.

8 Cf. *Protagoras* 329a3-4: "as books, they themselves have nothing to answer or to ask" (ὥσπερ βιβλία οὐδὲν ἔχουσιν οὔτε ἀποκρίνασθαι οὔτε αὐτοὶ ἐρέσθαι).

9 *Phaedrus* 275e3: οὐκ ἐπίσταται λέγειν οἷς δεῖ γε καὶ μή.

10 *Phaedrus* 276a5-6: ΣΩ. Ὃς μετ' ἐπιστήμης γράφεται ἐν τῇ τοῦ μανθάνοντος ψυχῇ. Cf. Vries, note ad loc.

whom the dialectical person converses directly (cf. 276c3-277a5). Perfect writing, then, is a playful μίμησις of the serious activity of the skilled conversationalist, the dialectician.[1]

The relationship between serious spoken conversations and playful written conversations—if the playful written conversations are written perfectly—is the relationship between a father and his legitimate progeny (cf. 277a6-279b4). In other words, the relationship between Socrates in Athens and the Platonic dialogues is analogous to the relationship between the good and the sun.

It is appropriate that Socrates should conclude his only thorough discussion of writing with a prayer to Pan,[2] who "is either speech or the sibling of speech,"[3] and whose double nature[4] is reflected in the doubleness of Socratic speech and Platonic writing.

Therefore, there is nothing wondrous in the tradition that has arisen that regards the *Phaedrus* as the first Platonic dialogue.[5]

Before turning to other myths in the Platonic corpus, it would be appropriate briefly to summarize the classification, however incomplete, of the kinds of accounts that have been found in the Platonic dialogues.

The most expansive category is Λόγος in the broad sense, which is used to designate any articulated verbal utterance, whether audible or not, i. e., whether spoken to another or to oneself in the soul.

Within the genus Λόγος, there have emerged three species: (1) λόγος in the narrow sense, which is used to designate a classificatory descriptive account, a διαίρεσις; (2) μῦθος, which is used to designate a synoptic genetic account, a συναγωγή; (3) ἀκοή, which straddles the distinction between λόγος and μῦθος, and which is used to designate a tale or story, although it may be further distinguished with regard to whether it is a λόγος or a μῦθος.[6]

---

1 Cf. *Protagoras* 347e1-348a6: "And thus also the suchlike beings-together, if they take [in] men of the very sort which the many of us assert ourselves to be, in no way are in need of another sort of sound or even of poets, whom it is not even possible to ask about the things which they speak; and the many leading them in [i. e., citing the poets] in their speeches, some assert the poet to intellect these things, and some [assert the poet to intellect] other things, they conversing about a business which they are incapable of refuting; but they [i. e., our sort] bid goodbye to the suchlike beings-together, and they themselves are together with themselves through themselves, taking and giving in their own speeches a test of each other. It seems to me to be useful for both me and you rather to imitate the suchlike persons, [we] putting aside the poets themselves to make the speeches through ourselves to each other, taking a test of the truth and ourselves" (οὕτω δὲ καὶ αἱ τοιαίδε συνουσίαι, ἐὰν μὲν λάβωνται ἀνδρῶν οἷοίπερ ἡμῶν οἱ πολλοί φασιν εἶναι, οὐδὲν δέονται ἀλλοτρίας φωνῆς οὐδὲ ποιητῶν, οὓς οὔτε ἀνερέσθαι οἷον τ' ἐστὶν περὶ ὧν λέγουσιν, ἐπαγόμενοί τε αὐτοὺς οἱ πολλοὶ ἐν τοῖς λόγοις οἱ μὲν ταῦτά φασιν τὸν ποιητὴν νοεῖν, οἱ δ' ἕτερα, περὶ πράγματος διαλεγόμενοι ὃ ἀδυνατοῦσι ἐξελέγξαι· ἀλλὰ τὰς μὲν τοιαύτας συνουσίας ἐῶσιν χαίρειν, αὐτοὶ δ' ἑαυτοῖς σύνεισιν δι' ἑαυτῶν, ἐν τοῖς ἑαυτῶν λόγοις πεῖραν ἀλλήλων λαμβάνοντες καὶ διδόντες. τοὺς τοιούτους μοι δοκεῖ χρῆναι μᾶλλον μιμεῖσθαι ἐμέ τε καὶ σέ, καταθεμένους τοὺς ποιητὰς αὐτοὺς δι' ἡμῶν αὐτῶν πρὸς ἀλλήλους τοὺς λόγους ποιεῖσθαι, τῆς ἀληθείας καὶ ἡμῶν αὐτῶν πεῖραν λαμβάνοντας).

2 In a way this final ὦ φίλε vocative culminates the movement of the dialogue, which can be schematized around Socrates's three such vocatives: Ὦ φίλε Φαῖδρε (227a1, 230c5, 238c5; cf. 276e4), ὦ φίλε Ἔρως (257a3), Ὦ φίλε Πάν (279b8). The dialogue deals with the soul's movement from aisthetic *radiance* by means of divine *erotic* craziness to a vision of *the all*, speech about the all, and speech about the speech about the all (cf. *Cratylus* 408c5-d4).

3 *Cratylus* 408d2-3: ἔστιν ἤτοι λόγος ἢ λόγου ἀδελφὸς.

4 Cf., in the *Cratylus*, διφυῆ at 408b8 and διφυὴς at 408d1 and context.

5 Cf. Diogenes Laertius III. 38; Robin, "Notice," pp. vi-vii.

6 Of course, this classification is not—no classification can be—composed of mutually exclusive categories, but of distinct yet occasionally overlapping categories. For example, a given διαίρεσις may require a pre-estabished συναγωγή which one can then divide, and a given συναγωγή may require a pre-delineated manifold which is then brought together. However, as with all categories, their interpenetration does not invalidate them as categories, any more than the difficuslty, say, of determining whether a given person is sane or crazy invalidates the categories of sanity and craziness, or of determining whether a given person is healthy or sick invalidaes the categories of health and sickness.

In none of these categories does the designation depend upon the truth or falsity of the account: if one were to formulate a false λόγος or a hypothetical λόγος, one could formulate a corresponding false μῦθος or hypothetical μῦθος, and the accounts—whatever their 'truth value'—would still be the kinds of accounts that they are.

Now that, however tentatively, a classification has developed, it is time to rub it on the touchstone of other Platonic dialogic accounts to see if the Platonic dialogic usage is as consistent as it seems.

VI. THE *REPUBLIC* TETRALOGY: *Republic, Timaeus, Critias, [Hermocrates]*[1]

The dramatic sequence of dialogues initiated by the *Republic* contains the longest myths in the Platonic corpus. Not only is the bulk of the *Timaeus*, for whatever various reasons, universally and correctly acknowledged to be a myth,[2] but also the suggestions are very strong that the bulk of the *Republic* is also to be regarded as a myth.

First, one must establish at least the dramatic connection between the *Republic* and what Cornford calls "the *Timaeus* trilogy,"[3] and one must do so precisely because so influential a commentator as Cornford himself denies such a connection.[4] On the other hand, Henri Martin presupposes the connection: "In Plato's dialogue titled Πολιτεία, i. e., Republic, or rather State, Socrates finding himself in Athens with Critias, Timaeus, Hermocrates, and a fourth person, who is not named, had related to them a philosophical conversation which had taken place the day before in the Piraeus between Glaucon, Polemarchus, Thrasymachus, Adeimantus, Cephalus, and Socrates himself."[5]

---

1 The *Republic* tetralogy designates the dramatic sequence of dialogues that consists of the *Republic*, the *Timaeus*, the incomplete *Critias*, and the projected *Hermocrates*. The last of these is included because the internal references to it are suficient to make it a necessary consideration, at least as an abandoned project. Such a consideration may lead to some understanding of the reasons for its abandonment. The dramatic connection between these dialogues, about which there has been some controversy, will be examined in the body of the text.

2 Cf., for example, R. G. Bury, "Introduction to the *Timaeus*," in the LCL, p. 3: "the literary genius displayed in the style and diction of its central Myth has compelled . . . admiration." Frutiger, pp. 209-211, treats the *Timaeus* as one of what he calls Plato's "mythes parascientifiques." J. A. Stewart, *The Myths of Plato* (Carbondale, IL, 1960), p. 273 remarks that "the whole Discourse delivered by Timaeus is a Myth." Léon Robin, *Platon* (Paris, 1968), p. 143, refers to "le mythe cosmologique du *Timée*." Also consider the following: Pierre-Maxime Schuhl, *La Fabulation Platonicienne* (Paris, 1968), p. 108: "La biologie de Platon s'insère dans sa cosmologie qui, tout entière, présente un aspect mythique." Paul Friedländer, *Plato; an introduction*, tr. Hans Meyerhoff (NY, 1958), p. 248: "the *Timaeus* was to have the form . . . of a myth." Plato, *Plato's Cosmology: the* Timaeus *of Plato*, tr. with comm. by F. M. Cornford (Indianapolis, n. d.), p. 37: "the *Timaeus* is a 'myth' or 'story' (μῦθος)." One could multiply such citations.

3 Cornford, *Cosmology*, p. 5.

4 Cornford, *Cosmology*, pp. 4-5. Cornford goes so far as to say (p. 5): "The design of the present trilogy is thus completely independent of the *Republic*."

5 Henri Martin, *Études sur le Timée de Platon* (Paris, 1841), tome 1, p. 1: "Dans le dialogue de Platon intitulé Πολιτεία, c'est-à-dire la République, ou plutôt l'Etat, Socrate se trouvant à Athènes avec Critias, Timée, Hermocrate et un quatrième personnage, qui n'est pas nommé, leur avait raconté une conversation philosophique qui avait eu lieu la veille au Pirée entre Glaucon, Polémarque, Thrasymaque, Adimante, Céphale et Socrate lui-même." Also consider A. E. Taylor, *A Commentary on Plato's* Timaeus (Oxford, 1928), who discusses "the connexion between the *Timaeus* and the *Republic*" (p. 27). And cf. Plato, *ΠΛΑΤΩΝΟΣ ΤΙΜΑΙΟΣ: the* Timaeus *of Plato*, ed. with intro. and notes by R. D. Archer-Hind (London, 1888), initial note: "Sokrates meets by appointment three of the friends to whom he has on the previous day narrated the conversation recorded in the *Republic*. After the absence of the fourth member of the party has been explained, he proceeds to summarize the social and political theories propounded in that dialogue. It will be observed that the unusually long introductory passage . . . has its application not to the *Timaeus* only, but to the whole trilogy, *Republic, Timaeus, Critias*. The recapitulation of the *Republic* indicates the precise position of that work in the series . . . . The supposed date of the present discussion is two days after the meeting in the house of Kephalos . . . . On the following day Sokrates reports to the four friends what passed at the house of Kephalos; and on the next the present dialogue takes place." And cf. Stewart, p. 252: "The assumed chronological order of the pieces is *Republic, Timaeus, Critias* . . . . But, of course, the logical order is *Timaeus, Republic, Critias*."

One must now, in agreement with Martin,[1] but against Cornford,[2] indicate the evidence that compels one to treat the *Republic* and the *Timaeus* as connected both dramatically and substantively. First, there is the massive datum that the speeches of the day before[3] that Socrates summarizes—and he emphasizes that it is a summary[4]—are the same as, or at the very least equivalent to, the discussion in Books 2-5 of the *Republic*.[5]

In addition, as its form indicates, the *Republic* is a dialogue narrated by Socrates to an indeterminate audience, an audience that Socrates, in the *Timaeus*, goes out of his way to make numerically determinate (17a1-2): "One, two, three; and indeed where, oh friend Timaeus, is our fourth?" The words "meal-guest" (ὁ δαιτυμών) and "hearth-feast-host" (ὁ ἑστιάτωρ), that occur in Socrates's first speech, occur in the Platonic corpus only there and in the *Republic* (respectively at 1. 345c5 and 4. 421b3).

Finally, there is the description of Timaeus himself:

> For also this Timaeus, being of the most-goodly-lawed city of Locris in Italy, and being last to none of those there by property [= beingness] or by class, has taken in hand the biggest ruling-offices and honors of those in the city, and in turn, in accordance with my opinion, has come upon the height of all philosophy.[6]

---

1 Also consider the notes of Bury (LCL) ad 17c ff.

2 Even Cornford grudgingly cites the *Republic* in his note ad 18c (p. 10, n. 1), and he asserts (p. 3, italics mine): "Socrates, we are told, had been describing the institutions of a city *on the lines of* the *Republic*." It is striking in Cornford that he very uncharacteristically derives substantive disconnection from dramatic disconnection rather than simply relying on his apparently preternatural ability to see into Plato's motives: "we may regard his doctrine simply as Plato's own" (p. 3), "Plato's design" (p. 4, cf. p. 5), "No doubt Plato was thinking of" (p. 4), and so forth. Cornford (pp. 4-4) also adduces the festival of the Thracian goddess Bendis (cf. *Rep.* 1. 327a1-5). However, what festival would have taken place two days later? It would have to be a festival in honor of "the goddess who is both a lover of war and a lover of wisdom" (φιλοπόλεμός τε καὶ φιλόσοφος ἡ θεὸς οὖσα, *Timaeus* 24c7-d1), namely Athene, who is in a way the goddess who implicitly presides over the central books of the *Republic*, which indeed deal with both war and wisdom. It has been widely assumed that the festival must be the Lesser Panathenaea: cf. Martin, p. 1; Archer-Hind, p. 66, note ad ἐν τῇ πανηγύρει; and Cornford, *Cosmology*, loc. cit. Although Martin and Archer-Hind see this as no obstacle to a closeness of dramatic date between the dialogues, Cornford points out—and he cites (p. 4, n. 1) Proclus in support—that the Lesser Panathenaea was at least two months after the Bendidea (cf. Taylor, note ad 17a1), and he concludes from this that the *Timaeus* cannot be the dramatic sequel to the *Republic*. Even though Cornford seems correct about the relative dates of the Bendidea and the Lesser Panathenaea, it still does not follow that the *Timaeus* could not have taken place two days after the *Republic*. Cornford is incorrect when he says (p. 5, n. 1) that the word πανήγυρις (literally "a gathering of all," from πᾶς + ἄγυρις: cf. LSJ; *Timaeus* 21a2) "implies an important festival," because it is used in a much lesser sense by Socrates at *Rep.* 4. 421b2, 10. 604e4, 614e3. Therefore, it seems best to agree with Taylor (note ad 17a1): "It has been suggested that Plato has made an oversight, but this is not likely. A modern writer would hardly be capable of making Epiphany and Good Friday, or Trinity Sunday and Michaelmas, fall in the same week. It is more natural to suppose that the reference . . . is not to the lesser Panathenaea but to some other festival connected with Athena." Therefore, one needs to go no further than this in identifying the festival, which, it is plausible to assume, is as historically non-existent as the dialogue's major interlocutor.

3 At the beginning of the *Timaeus*, the extraordinary density of occurrences of χθές (yesterday), which seem to echo cavernously the χθές that is the second word of the *Republic*, suggests a connection between the two dialogues. Cf. *Tim.* 17a2, b2, c1, 19a7, 20b1, c6, 25e2, 26a4, 7, b4, c8, e7. The only other Platonic dialogue that has an initial χθές equal in prominence to that of the *Republic* is the *Sophist* 216a1, from which the reference back is clearly to the *Theaetetus*, and to which there is no subsequent χθές referring back, as there is in the *Timaeus* to the *Republic*. Finally, there is a χθές at the very beginning of the *Euthydemus* (271a1), but there the prominent word is the interrogative Τίς that Crito uses out of his curiosity to discover the identity of Socrates's conversational interlocutor of the previous day.

4 Cf. τὸ κεφάλαιον at 17c2 and ἐν κεφαλαίοις at 19a8.

5 The reference back to the *Republic* is continued in the *Critias* too: cf. *Critias* 110c3-d4, esp. χθές at d3.

6 *Timaeus* 20a1-5: Τίμαιός τε γὰρ ὅδε, εὐνομωτάτης ὢν πόλεως τῆς ἐν Ἰταλίᾳ Λοκρίδας, οὐσίᾳ καὶ γένει οὐδενὸς ὕστερος ὢν τῶν ἐκεῖ, τὰς μεγίστας μὲν ἀρχάς τε καὶ τιμὰς τῶν ἐν τῇ πόλει μετακεχείρισται, φιλοσοφίας δ' αὖ κατ' ἐμὴν δόξαν ἐπ' ἄκρον ἁπάσης ἐλήλυθεν.

In short, Timaeus is a philosopher-ruler, i. e., he is "among the men who are both philosophers and politically skilled."[1] As such, he is the embodiment of the third wave[2] with which Socrates completes the founding of the best city in the *Republic*, namely the coincidence of political power and philosophy, but which he omits from his summary here in the *Timaeus*.

Since Timaeus is described as a philosopher-ruler, and "since he is the person of the [group] who is most skilled in astronomy and who has especially made it his work to have envisioned [i.e., understood] about the nature of the all,"[3] he seems the ideal person to provide the necessary cosmological foundation for the best city, a foundation that is as utopian in its way as the best city is in its. The utopian character of the whole enterprise is emphasized by Plato's selection of a utopian, i. e., a non-historically-existent, spokesperson.[4]

Furthermore, the *Republic* and the *Timaeus* have more substantive themes in common. In particular, they both, one in the service of poitical stability (the best city) and the one in the service of cosmic stability (the best cosmos), employ τέχνη as the model, and they both systematically suppress the one force that is most destructive of stability, namely ἔρως. In other words, both the best city and the best cosmos that is its ground depend upon an elevation of τέχνη and a denigration of ἔρως,[5] or an elevation of mathematized body and a denigration of the lived human body.

In the *Republic*, this is present throughout: in Book 1, in Cephalus's freedom from τὰ ἀφροδίσια (1. 329a1 ff.), and in the pervasiveness of examples from the arts (1. 332c5 ff.); in Book 2, in the basis of the founding of the city in speech on needs from which procreation is conspicuously absent (2. 369c9-e1), and in the founded city as a city of artisans (2. 369e2); in Book 3, in the well-born (gennaic) falsehood (3. 414b8 ff.) that substitutes autochthony for sexual generation and in which knowledge of soul is reduced to assaying of metals; in Book 4, in the assertion of the superiority of spiritedness to desire (4. 440b3-4 and context), and in the positing of the principle 'one person, one work' (4. 423d2 ff.); in Book 5, in the elimination of privacy from the way of life that is characterized by communism and equality of the sexes;[6] in Book 7, in the presentation of the philosopher's leaving the cave as an external compulsion[7] rather than as an internal and natural desire or ἔρως for the truth; in Book 8, in the nuptial

---

1 *Timaeus* 19e5-6: ἅμα φιλοσόφων ἀνδρῶν ᾖ καὶ πολιτικῶν. Cf. *Republic* 5. 473c11-e2, 474b3-c3.

2 Cf. *Republic* 5. 472a1-7, 473c6-8.

3 *Timaeus* 27a3-5: ἅτε ὄντα ἀστρονομικώτατον ἡμῶν καὶ περὶ φύσεως τοῦ παντὸς εἰδέναι μάλιστα ἔργον πεποιημένον.

4 Cf. Cornford, *Cosmology*, pp. 2-3: "There is no evidence for the historic existence of Timaeus of Locri . . . . The very fact that a man of such distinction has left not the faintest trace in political or philosophic history is against his claim to be a real person. The probability is that Plato invented him." Cf. Martin, p. 50. The utopianism of the best city, the best cosmos, and Timaeus himself is further matched by the utopianism of Atlantis: cf. Frutiger, pp. 244 ff. In addition, one could add that the two major non-historically existent speakers with names in the Platonic dialogues, Diotima and Timaeus, both have names containing the stem τιμ-.

5 Cf. Leo Strauss, *The City and Man* (Chicago, 1964), pp. 110-113, 116-118, 128, 133, 138; Allan Bloom, "Interpretive Essay," in Plato, *The Republic of Plato*, tr. with notes and an interpretive essay by Allan Bloom (NY, 1968), p. 378 et passim.

6 The case for the equality of the sexes is made on the basis of an undeniable psychic equality and a suppression of any somatic difference: cf. 454c1-5, where the somatic difference between the sexes is reduced to the difference between the hairy and the bald (but also cf. 455e1 ff.). In the discussion of procreation, the guardians are bred as beasts are bred, and there is no mention of pregnancy. It is as though the political implementation of the psychic equality of the sexes requires an extremely sophisticated eugenic technology, in which the foetus is removed from the womb after conception, to be returned to the mother for nursing when it reaches full term—and even that only in a very limited way (cf. 460c8-d7). What is required, then, is a suppression of erotic compulsions by geometric compulsions (cf. 458d5), a redefinition of the sacred as the politically beneficial or useful (cf. 458e4). Cf. Bloom, pp. 468 ff., n. 5.

7 Cf. ἀναγκάζοιτο at 515c6, ἀναγκάζοι at 515e1, ἕλκοι at 515e6, μὴ ἀνείη πρὶν ἐξελκύσειεν at 515e7-8, ἑλκόμενον at 516a1.

number (8. 546a1 ff.) that represents simultaneously the complete mathematization of ἔρως and the impossibility of the complete mathematization of ἔρως; in Book 9, in the presentation of the tyrant as the complete erotic πανοῦργος (cf. 9. 571c7-8 and context) and of ἔρως as the complete tyrant (cf. 9. 573b6-7, d4); and in Book 10, in the description of the εἴδη as made.

The *Timaeus* reproduces these motifs on the cosmic level: in its virtual elimination of the so-called sacred;[1] in its assertion that the κόσμος (οὐρανός or τὸ πᾶν) is made (cf. 28c3 et passim);[2] in its assertion of the superiority of spiritedness to desire (70a2-c1); in its explanation that the human body was made only to keep the head from rolling around on the ground (44d3-45a3); in its assertion that the genitals were created almost as an afterthought (91a1-d6); in its presentation of the receptacle (cf. 49a6, 51a5) as a χώρα (52a8, b4, d3; cf. *Rep.* 3. 414e3) that is the mother (cf. *Tim.* 50d3, 51a4-5) of the cosmos in a way analogous to the way in which the earth as the land is the mother of the city in the well-born (gennaic) falsehood (cf. *Rep.* 3. 414e2, 3).[3]

In short, the parallel between the city and the human (cf. *Rep.* 2. 368c7 to 4. end) is matched by the parallel between the cosmos and the ζῷον; and just as the founding of the city arises out of the needs of the body (*Rep.* 2. 369c9 ff.), i. e., out of a city/human body parallel, only to culminate in a psychology, i. e., in a city/human soul parallel, so too Timaeus's account moves from a somatology (31b4-34a7) to a psychology (34a8 ff.).

Since the substantive links between the *Republic* and the *Timaeus* so strongly support the dramatic link between them, the two dialogues—or rather the total sequence of dialogues that they establish—must be read together.

Turning now to this sequence insofar as it bears on the problem of myth in Plato means beginning briefly with the *Timaeus.*

Timaeus's account of the genesis of the all[4] is, as a whole, a likely myth,[5] but what that means needs to be explained. The tendency among commentators is to assert it to mean that

---

1 Consider Timaeus's perfunctory and compulsory invocation at 27c4-d1; also cf. 40d6-41a3 (italics mine): "And about the other daimons [i. e., other than the planets and stars], to speak and to recognize their genesis is bigger than in accordance with us, and one must be persuaded by the persons who have spoken before [i.e.,in the past], since they are, as they asserted, progenies of gods, and since somehow they distinctly have envisioned [i.e., understood] their own progenitors at any rate; *therefore, it is impossible to distrust the children of gods, although they speak without likely and compulsory showings-forth* [i.e., probable and necessary demonstrations], but following the law, we must trust them [i.e., those in the past] as we would persons declaring themselves to announce household things. Therefore, let the genesis of these gods hold and be spoken for us in accordance with them in this way. Ocean and Tethys, the children of Earth and Heaven, were generated, and of these Phorkys and Kronos and Rhea, and as many as are with these, [were generated], and from Kronos and Rhea [were generated] Zeus and Hera and all whom we know to be spoken as their siblings, and still other progenies of these" (Περὶ δὲ τῶν ἄλλων δαιμόνων εἰπεῖν καὶ γνῶναι τὴν γένεσιν μεῖζον ἢ καθ' ἡμᾶς, πειστέον δὲ τοῖς εἰρηκόσιν ἔμπροσθεν, ἐκγόνοις μὲν θεῶν οὖσιν, ὡς ἔφασαν, σαφῶς δέ που τούς γε αὐτῶν προγόνους εἰδόσιν· ἀδύνατον οὖν θεῶν παισὶν ἀπιστεῖν, καίπερ ἄνευ τε εἰκότων καὶ ἀναγκαίων ἀποδείξεων λέγουσιν, ἀλλ' ὡς οἰκεῖα φασκόντων ἀπαγγέλλειν ἑπομένους τῷ νόμῳ πιστευτέον. οὕτως οὖν κατ' ἐκείνους ἡμῖν ἡ γένεσις περὶ τούτων τῶν θεῶν ἐχέτω καὶ λεγέσθω. Γῆς τε καὶ Οὐρανοῦ παῖδες Ὠκεανός τε καὶ Τηθὺς ἐγενέσθην, τούτων δὲ Φόρκυς Κρόνος τε καὶ Ῥέα καὶ ὅσοι μετὰ τούτων, ἐκ δὲ Κρόνου καὶ Ῥέας Ζεὺς Ἥρα τε καὶ πάντες ὅσους ἴσμεν ἀδελφοὺς λεγομένους αὐτῶν, ἔτι τε τούτων ἄλλους ἐκγόνους). That this is the only place in Timaeus's narration where the traditional Greek pantheon is even alluded to makes the 'godlessness' of the dialogue stand out all the more. In other words, the perspective of Timaeus—and presumably his interlocutors too—is one of complete 'religious' enlightenment.

2 The possibility that the all is ἀγενές (27c5) is mentioned only to be forgotten immediately. The cosmos is presented as the work of a δημιουργός (cf. 28a6 et passim) of whose beautiful cosmos (cf. 29a2) the καλλίπολις (beautiful city) of the *Republic* (7. 527c2) is an analogue, and of whom each citizen of the best city is an analogue (cf. *Rep.* 3. 395c1).

3 In a sense, Timaeus's entire account is a lengthy cosmic elaboration of the founding lie of Socrates's best city.

4 29c4-5: πέρι . . . τῆς τοῦ παντὸς γενέσεως. He says here that it is also about the gods (πέρι θεῶν, 29c4) but, as becomes clear later, by the gods he means first and foremost the planets and stars, not the traditional Greek pantheon.

5 Cf. τὸν εἰκότα μῦθον at 29d2. Also cf. των εἰκότων μύθων at 59c6 and τὸν εἰκότα μῦθον at 68d2.

physics is likely because it is a myth or a myth because it is likely, or else it is assumed to be simpy a thinly disguised scientific treatise.[1]

Since those who adopt the latter perspective ignore the dialogue form and the dramatic context, and since Timaeus—even though he speaks uninterruptedly from 27d7 to the end of the dialogue—alludes repeatedly to his interlocutors and their common task,[2] even if the scientific analysis by these commentators of the scientific content of the dialogue is sound, they still do not clarify the dramatic status of that content. Insofar as dramatic status is an essential component of—a necessary prerequisite for understanding—substantive status, they also do not clarify that content's substantive role in the Platonic corpus.

Those who adopt the former perspective, on the other hand, implicitly accuse Plato—or, to be more precise, Timaeus—of a most unilluminating redundancy.

What, then, is meant by the appellation "likely myth"? Its likeliness does not derive from its being a myth. In the seventh epistle, Plato called his myth "a certain true speech." Throughout the *Timaeus* itself, there are repeated references to a likely λόγος,[3] and it is no accident that all but one of these occurs in the part of Timaeus's account (53b7-58a2) that is a classificatory description of bodies.

When Timaeus comes (58a2 ff.) to the genesis of compound bodies, to the change and motion from which elemental bodily compounds arise, he refers to the standard of "likely myths":

> And in addition, it is in no way intricate to reckon through [i.e., to explain] the other suchlike things, chasing after the look of likely myths; with respect to which [look], whenever, for the sake of resting up—having put aside the speeches about the things which always are, beholding the likely [myths] about genesis—anyone possesses an unregrettable pleasure, [such a person] would make in a lifetime a measured and prudent childlike-playing. Indeed, having hurled forth also the [preceding] things now in this way, we shall go through, with respect to the thing after this, the successive likelihoods about them in this way.[4]

Either a μῦθος or a λόγος may be likely. Likeliness is not an automatic characteristic of myths. Rather, it is one of the characteristics—along with ὀρθός, ἀληθής, ἄτοπος, τέλειος[5]—of

1 Cornford's position (*Cosmology*, pp. 30-31) is that it is likely because it is poetic, and it is a myth because there is no certainty in physics, and because it is a myth or story: "The cosmology of the *Timaeus* is poetry" (p. 30); "The *Timaeus* is a poem" (p. 31); "There are two senses in which the *Timaeus* is a 'myth' or 'story' (μῦθος). One . . . no account of the material world can ever amount to an exact and self-consistent statement of unchangeable truth. In the second place, the cosmology is cast in the form of a cosmogony, a 'story' of events spread out in time" (p. 31). Cf. Frutiger, pp. 173-175, 210-211. Also consider Taylor, general note ad 27d5-29d3, pp. 59-61. And cf. Friedländer, p. 248: "We cannot speak with exactness about the world of change," "About changing nature we can, at the utmost, give 'plausible accounts'." Also cf. G. Vlastos, *Plato's Universe* (Seattle, 1975), p. 49: "The creation story of the *Timaeus*, despite its allegorical tincture, attests Plato's assimilation of the results obtained by this science [i. e., empirically oriented science, esp. astronomy] in which theory and practice were now successfully interacting." It is striking that, on the whole, in these commentaries, one could form the impression that the major interlocutor of the *Timaeus* is Plato himself, and not Timaeus of Locris.

2 He speaks frequently in the first person plural and refers back on occasion to the speech as a whole, e.g., 40d7, 48e1, 69a6-b2, 90e1-3, and so forth.

3 Cf. κατὰ λόγον τὸν εἰκότα at 30b7, κατὰ τὸν . . . εἰκότα λόγον at 53d5-6, κατὰ τὸν εἰκότα λόγον at 55d5, τὸν εἰκότα λόγον at 56a1, κατὰ τὸν . . . λόγον . . . εἰκότα at 56b4, εἰκότι λόγῳ at 57d6.

4 59c5-d3: τἆλλα δὲ τῶν τοιούτων οὐδὲν ποικίλον ἔτι διαλογίσασθαι τὴν τῶν εἰκότων μύθων μεταδιώκοντα ἰδέαν· ἣν ὅταν τις ἀναπαύσεως ἕνεκα τοὺς περὶ τῶν ὄντων ἀεὶ καταθέμενος λόγους, τοὺς γενέσεως πέρι διαθεώμενος εἰκότας ἀμεταμέλητον ἡδονὴν κτᾶται, μέτριον ἂν ἐν τῷ βίῳ παιδιὰν καὶ φρόνιμον ποιοῖτο. ταύτῃ δὴ καὶ τὰ νῦν ἐφέντες τὸ μετὰ τοῦτο τῶν αὐτῶν πέρι τὰ ἑξῆς εἰκότα δίιμεν τῇδε.

5 Cf. respectively 56b4, 26e4-5, 20d7, 92c4. One should note that in the *Timaeus*, no λόγος is described as καλός.

Λόγος. Therefore, since a μῦθος is not analytically 'likely,' i. e., since εἰκός is not a superfluous adjectival addition, what is meant by "likely myth"?

A μῦθος is an account of a genesis. Timaeus's account of the cosmos is emphatically an account of a genesis. As such, Timaeus's account of the cosmos illustrates the definition of μῦθος on a grand scale.[1] Therefore, insofar as Timaeus's account is genetic, it is a myth.

Why is it likely? It is likely because it presents the cosmos as made. Insofar as it does so, its likeliness is falseness, i. e., it is "a tool of understanding" or a "blueprint."[2] In other words, Timaeus's account is as much a construct as is the cosmos of which his account is an account. Insofar as it is a construct, a πλασθείς,[3] it is merely likely, but it is not likely insofar as it is a myth.

The difference between μῦθος and λόγος is made clearer by the ways in which accounts in general and the accounts of Socrates, Timaeus, and Critias in particular are designated.

In Timaeus's account (27b7 to the end of the dialogue), there are usages of Λόγος in the sense of any verbal utterance,[4] of λόγος in the sense of classificatory description or delimiting or dividing or reckoning,[5] and of μῦθος in the sense of a synagogic genetic account.[6] This is a categorization of which the interlocutors seem well aware. Critias's story is referred to exclusively as a λόγος,[7] and in the *Critias* itself, the word μῦθος occurs nowhere.[8] In addition, in the introductory section of the *Timaeus* (to 27b6), we find the same variety of usages: Λόγος,[9] λόγος,[10] ἀκοή as equivalent to λόγος,[11] and μῦθος.[12]

---

1 The word γένεσις occurs in the *Timaeus* at 27a6, d6, 28b6, 29c3, 5, d7, e4, 34c4, 37e3, 38a2, 6, c4, 39e3, 40e4, 41e3, 42c1, 3, 48a1, b4, 6, 49c7, e7, 52b1, 53e3, 54b7-8, d3, 58a2, c3, 59c8, 61c7, d4, 62a2, 73b3, 75b8, 76e4, 77c3, 90a8, 90d2, 91a1, d5.

2 Seth Benardete, "On Plato's *Timaeus* and Timaeus' Science Fiction," *interpretation; a journal of political philosophy*, vol. 2, no. 1, Summer 1971, pp. 22, 32, 40.

3 Cf. *Timaeus* 26e4-5, which contains a double opposition, of πλασθέντα to ἀληθινὸν and of μῦθον to λόγον. This does not mean that one could not have an ἀληθινὸς μῦθος or a πλασθεὶς λόγος. We have examined above the ἀληθινὸς μῦθος in the seventh epistle. In addition, one may fashion a λόγος (cf. πλάττοντι λόγους at *Apol. Socr.* 17c5).

4 Cf. 27b8, 29b8, c6, 46d4, 47c5, 6, 49a4, 51c5, 53c1, 62a6, 69a7, 70a4-5 (bis), b3, 71a3, 5, d4, 75e3, 87b1, 91b1, 92c4.

5 Cf. 28a1, 29a6, b4, 30b7, 32b5, 37e6-38a1, 48d2, 49a3, b5, 51b6, c7, e3, 52c6, d3, 53d5-6, 54b1, 55d5, 7, 56a1, b4, 57d6, 59c7-8, 67d2, 68b7, 70d5, 74e4, 76e4-5, 77b4, 80d1, 83c4, 87c4, 88e4, 89e3, 90e5, 8, 91b6. One should add the phrase ἀνὰ λόγον at 29c2, 53e4, 56c7, 69b5, 82b3-4.

6 Cf. 29d2, 59c6, 68d2.

7 Cf. 19c3, 20b3, d1, 7, 21a7, c5, d3, 6-7, 26a5, d7, e5 (explicitly in opposition to μῦθος, e4).

8 Therefore, it is puzzling that there is such widespread agreement among commentators—cf. Frutiger's list, pp. 129-130; Cornford's allusion to it as "romance" and "legend," *Cosmology*, pp. 4 and 18; Taylor, note ad *Tim.* 25a1; Archer-Hind, p. 78; Stewart's list, pp. 100-101; Friedländer, pp. 200-203; Martin's description of it as "fable," I. p. 258; and Couturat, *De platonicis mythis* (Paris, 1896), pp. 28 ff.—that the account of Atlantis is a μῦθος when it is emphatically treated as a λόγος. In other words, the account of the war between Athens and Atlantis is not a genetic account of either Athens or Atlantis, but a descriptive account of the best city (ancient Athens) in motion (cf. *Tim.* 19b8), i. e., engaged in the biggest of its big and wondrous deeds (cf. *Tim.* 20e4-6). In the *Critias*, the word μυθολογία occurs once, but only in a general remark, and it does not refer specifically to the account of Atlantis: "For mythology and the re-seeking of the ancient things come upon cities simultaneously with leisure, when they [i. e., mythology and re-seeking] see the compulsory things already having been prepared for them [i. e., for the cities] for a lifetime, but not before." (110a3-6: μυθολογία γὰρ ἀναζήτησίς τε τῶν παλαιῶν μετὰ σχολῆς ἅμ' ἐπὶ τὰς πόλεις ἔρχεσθον, ὅταν ἴδητόν τισιν ἤδη τοῦ βίου τἀναγκαῖα κατεσκευασμένα, πρὶν δὲ οὔ.) And if μυθολογία and ἀναζήτησις τῶν παλαιῶν are identical, then when the natural compulsions have been met, i. e., when the so-called useful arts have come to be, searching out the originary things arises, i. e., philosophy arises.

9 Cf. 17c1-2 (about the *Republic*), 19c7 (about interpreting), 19e1 (opp. ἔργον), 7 (opp. ἔργον), 20c1, 21e6 (about the way the Hellenes talk), 26e7 (about the *Republic*), 27a8. In addition, the generic use of Λόγος at 22a5 is then specified as μῦθος by the equation between γενεαλογεῖν and μυθολογεῖν (b1-2), between a particular kind of genetic account and genetic accounts as a whole (cf. 23b3-5).

10 Cf. 27b1, 6.

11 Cf. 20d1, 21a6, 22b8 (about originary accounts), 23a2 (about accounts of big deeds), 25e1.

12 Cf. 22c7 (about genetic accounts), 23b5 (about genealogies that are childlike), 26e4 (opp. λόγος), 26c8 (about the account of the genesis of the best city and its citizens in the *Republic*).

One occurrence of μῦθος needs to be singled out, namely the description of the *Republic* as a μῦθος, because it completes a suggested classification of the whole tetralogy:

Republic:	μῦθος τῆς ἀρίστης πόλεως[1]
Timaeus:	μῦθος τοῦ ἀρίστου κόσμου
Critias:	λόγος τῆς ἀρίστης πόλεως
[Hermocrates]:	λόγος τοῦ ἀρίστου κόσμου

One must fill in the missing fourth and designate it in accordance with what seems to be required to complete the pattern:[2] (1) a genetic account of the best city; (2) a genetic account of the best cosmos; (3) a descriptive account of the best city (in motion); (4) a descriptive account of the best cosmos (in motion).

In order descriptively to bring the best city, so to speak, to life (cf. *Tim.* 19b3 ff.), Socrates asks that it be set in motion, which means sent to war (cf. *Tim.* 19b8, c4-5). Presumably, then, Hermocrates's task would have been to set the cosmos in motion, to send the cosmos to war. For the cosmos, this would mean a Herakleiteanism, in which the following assertions would be the basis for the account:

> War is the father of all things, and king of all things.[3]
>
> It is useful to have envisioned [i.e., understood] war [as] being the [i.e., that which is] with [everything], and strife being the right way [of everything], and all things coming to be in accordance with strife and use.[4]
>
> Somewhere Herakleitos speaks that all things advance [i.e., move] and nothing remains [still], and likening forth the beings to the flow of a river, he speaks how one would not step twice into the same river.[5]

To show an embodiment of such a view in action, as it were, seems impossible.

Perhaps Socrates was wrong in asking for the city to be transformed from peace or rest (ἡσυχία: cf. *Tim.* 19b7) to war or motion. Not only is ἡσυχία equivalent to εἰρήνη and opposed to πόλεμος (cf. *Rep.* 9. 575b2-3), which is equivalent to κίνησις (cf. *Laws* 7. 790d6-7), but also it is opposed to seriousness (σπουδή: cf. Xenophon, *Hellenica* 6. 2. 28).

Perhaps, then, Socrates should have asked for the playful Timaean cosmos to be transformed into the serious cosmos, but that is forbidden by the prescriptions of the seventh epistle.

The dilemma that is adumbrated here may suggest why the *Critias* is incomplete and the *Hermocrates* is missing. Beings at war behave unaccountably (ἀλόγως), as Tolstoy saw so clearly:

---

1 Cf. Couturat, p. 48.

2 In this connection, let it be said that Seth Benardete is on the right track when he says: "Timaeus' speech is an attempt to give the cosmological equivalent to the *Phaedrus* myth." ("Plato's *Timaeus*," p. 51) However, he seems to mean by "the *Phaedrus* myth" Socrates's palinode, and hence he goes off the track. The correct parallel, I believe, is between Socrates's Lysian speech (a myth) with its combination of calculation and compulsion and Timaeus's speech with its combination of intellect and compulsion, and between Socrates's mythic palinode (the motion of the soul) and the missing *Hermocrates* (the cosmos in motion).

3 Herakleitos, DK5 53B: Πόλεμος πάντων μὲν πατήρ ἐστι, πάντων δὲ βασιλεύς.

4 Herakleitos, DK5 80B: εἰδέναι δὲ χρὴ τὸν πόλεμον ἐόντα ξυνόν, καὶ δίκην ἔριν, καὶ γινόμενα πάντα κατ' ἔριν καὶ χρεών.

5 *Cratylus* 402a8-10: λέγει που Ἡράκλειτος ὅτι πάντα χωρεῖ καὶ οὐδὲν μένει, καὶ ποταμοῦ ῥοῇ ἀπεικάζων τὰ ὄντα λέγει ὡς δὶς ἐς τὸν αὐτὸν ποταμὸν οὐκ ἂν ἐμβαίης. (I have deleted the quotation marks from Burnet's text as unnecessary.)

> The actors of 1812 have long since left the stage, their personal interests have vanished leaving no trace, and nothing remains of that time but its historic results . . . .
>
> The cause of the destruction of the French army in 1812 is clear to us now. No one will deny [what] that cause was . . . . But no one at that time foresaw (what now seems so evident) that this was the only way an army of eight hundred thousand men—the best in the world and led by the best general—could be destroyed in conflict with a raw army of half its numerical strength, and led by inexperienced commanders as the Russian army was. *Not only did no one see this*, but *on the Russian side* every effort was made to hinder the only thing that could save Russia, while *on the French side*, despite Napoleon's experience and so-called military genius, every effort was directed . . . to doing the very thing that was bound to lead to destruction . . . .
>
> [It] was not the result of any plan, for no one believed it to be possible; it resulted from a most complex interplay of intrigues, aims, and wishes among those who took part in the war and had no perception whatever of the inevitable, or of the one way of saving Russia. Everything came about fortuitously.[1]

War and chance, then, go hand in hand.

It would seem as though no true likeness of chance is possible. Only a universal motion picture camera could reproduce such motion. Hence, Seth Benardete is correct when he says that Socrates's "desire to see a living animal move does not differ from the desire to see a picture of an animal move,"[2] although he seems not wholly correct in emphasizing that "the clearest example of two-dimensional kinematics is geometrical construction,"[3] rather than motion pictures, the theoretical possibility of which is implicit in the projected images on the wall in the image of the cave. The making of a motion picture is, in a literal sense, a λόγος, a διαίρεσις, a breaking down of a one into a many, but not simply, since a three-dimensional moving one is broken down into a two-dimensional motionless many that is then projected to produce a two-dimensional apparently moving one:

> Therefore, the nature of the living thing chanced to be eternal, and indeed it was not possible altogether perfectly to fasten this to what is generated; and he was of a mind to make a certain movable likeness of the eternal, and simultaneously with thoroughly ordering heaven, he makes an eternal likeness hurtling in accordance with number of the eternal which remains in what is one, this [eternal likeness] which indeed we have named "time" . . . and the was and the will be are time's looks which have come to be, bearing which indeed upon the eternal beingness, we do not escape our own notice correctly [i.e., we incorrectly do not notice our error in applying it to eternal beingness] . . . but these have come to be [as] looks of time] imitating the eternal and circling in accordance with number.[4]

---

1 Leo Tolstoy, *War and Peace*, tr. Louise and Aylmer Maude (NY, Norton Critical Ed., 1966), Book 10, ch. 1, pp. 761-763.

2 Benardete, "On Plato's *Timaeus*," p. 26. Cf. *Republic* 10. 596d8-e4 to *Timaeus* 19b4-c1. Also cf. *Rep.* 10. 598b8-c4.

3 Benardete, "On Plato's *Timaeus*," p. 26.

4 *Timaeus* 37d3-7, e3-5, 38a7-8: ἡ μὲν οὖν τοῦ ζῴου φύσις ἐτύγχανεν οὖσα αἰώνιος, καὶ τοῦτο μὲν δὴ τῷ γεννητῷ παντελῶς προσάπτειν οὐκ ἦν δυνατόν· εἰκὼ δ' ἐπενόει κινητόν τινα αἰῶνος ποιῆσαι, καὶ διακοσμῶν ἅμα οὐρανὸν ποιεῖ μένοντος αἰῶνος ἐν ἑνὶ κατ' ἀριθμὸν ἰοῦσαν αἰώνιον εἰκόνα, τοῦτον ὃν δὴ χρόνον ὠνομάκαμεν . . . καὶ τό τ' ἦν τό τ' ἔσται χρόνου γεγονότα εἴδη, ἃ δὴ φέροντες λανθάνομεν ἐπὶ τὴν ἀίδιον οὐσίαν οὐκ ὀρθῶς . . . ἀλλὰ χρόνου ταῦτα αἰῶνα μιμουμένου καὶ κατ' ἀριθμὸν κυκλουμένου γέγονεν εἴδη.

The *Republic* and the *Timaeus* are the film script for a motion picture (a movable likeness) that it is impossible ever to film, i. e., the substitution of artificial wholeness for true wholeness renders precision of speech impossible. Therefore, it is no accident that the *Critias* breaks off at precisely that moment when direct speech is about to be articulated, while the *Hermocrates* cannot even begin.

It is time to turn now to the *Republic* which is suggested to be, as a whole, a myth.[1] Certainly the entire account, at least from Book 2 through Book 10, is a genetic account of political life from its origin in human needs through the construction of the best city to the degeneration of that best city. In addition, insofar as the city is a big individual human (cf. *Rep.* 2. 368c7-369b4), it is a genetic account of the individual human lifetime. Consequently, the *Republic* as a whole can be taken as a myth of both the city and the individual. Not only is the *Republic* as a whole a myth, but also some of its parts are myths of whose parts in turn some are myths too. For example:

(1) Glaucon's account of Gyges's ancestor is a myth.[2]
(2) The account of the education of the guardians is a myth.[3]
(3) The guardians' education consists of myths.[4]
(4) The well-born (gennaic) falsehood is a myth.[5]
(5) The genesis of soul types is a myth.[6]
(6) Er's account is a myth.[7]

---

1 Socrates says (2. 376d9-10): "Come therefore, let us, as persons mythologizing in a myth and having leisure, educate the men in speech." ("Ἴθι οὖν, ὥσπερ ἐν μύθῳ μυθολογοῦντές τε καὶ σχολὴν ἄγοντες λόγῳ παιδεύωμεν τοὺς ἄνδρας.) The mythologizing is the giving an account of the guardians' education. The myth in which that mythologizing occurs is meant to be the *Republic* as a whole. In addition, consider Socrates's reference to "the regime which we mythologize in speech" (ἡ πολιτεία ἣν μυθολογοῦμεν λόγῳ, 6. 501e4). As a whole, then, the *Republic* corresponds to Phaedrus's remark (*Phaedrus* 276e1-3): "Oh Socrates, you bespeak an althogether beautiful . . . childlike-playing . . . in speeches, [namely] mythologizing aboout both justice and the other things of which you speak" (Παγκάλην λέγεις . . . παιδιάν, ὦ Σώκρατες, . . . ἐν λόγοις . . . δικαιοσύνης τε καὶ ἄλλων ὧν λέγεις πέρι μυθολογοῦντα).

2 Cf. μυθολογοῦσιν at *Rep.* 2. 359d6.

3 Cf. *Rep.* 2. 376d9-10.

4 Cf. μῦθον at 2. 377c1; μῦθοι at 2. 378e5; μύθων at 3. 386b8-9; μύθοις at 2. 377a6, c4, 7; μύθους at 2. 377a4, b6, d5, 379a4, 381e3, 3. 391e12; μυθολογοῦντα at 2. 380c2; μυθολογεῖν at 2. 379a2, 3. 392b6; μυθολογητέον at 2. 378e3; at 2. 378c4; μυθοποιοῖς at 2. 377b11; μυθολογίας at 3. 394b9-c1; μυθολόγῳ at 2. 382d1; at3. 398b1; μυθολόγων at 3. 392d2. The myths of the best city will be based on and will perfect a θεολογία (cf. 2. 379a5-6), a λόγος or classificatory description of the gods (that is formulated, in outline at least, into two laws, *Rep.* 2. 379a5-383c7, and then elaborated in Book 3). In other words, the best city will educate, not through a groundless θεογονία, but rather through a θεογονία grounded in a θεολογία. Although the myths of the best city still may be falsehoods, they are falsehoods grounded in truth, and they are useful or beneficial falsehoods (cf. χρήσιμον at 2. 382c6-7, d3; ὠφελίᾳ at 3. 389b8). One can falsify in such a way as to adumbrate the truth that is being falsified. Cf. Rep. 2. 382b9-c1: "since the [falsehood] in speeches at any rate is a certain imitation of the affection in the soul and [it is] a look-alike which has come to be later, it is not an altogether unmixed falsehood [i. e., it is a falsehood mixed with truth]" (ἐπεὶ τό γε ἐν τοῖς λόγοις μίμημά τι τοῦ ἐν τῇ ψυχῇ ἐστὶν παθήματος καὶ ὕστερον γεγονὸς εἴδωλον, οὐ πάνυ ἄκρατον ψεῦδος).

5 Cf. μύθου at 3. 415a2, μυθολογοῦντες at 3. 415a3, and μῦθον at 3. 415c7.

6 Cf. μυθολογοῦνται at 9. 588c2.

7 Cf. μῦθος at 10. 621b8.

The Republic is composed of myths within myths within myths.[1] It culminates in the γένεσις of all γενέσεις, the good, "the beginning of the all" or "the beginning which is the all."[2]

Since Glaucon is concerned with origins, insofar as the *Republic* treats justice largely through its genesis, Glaucon is responsible. This is evident in the myth with which he illustrates his objections to Socrates's procedure in the first book, a myth that he takes from Herodotus (I. 8-13) and alters to suit his purposes. In Herodotus, the protagonist is Gyges himself, but in Glaucon's version, the protagonist is one of Gyges's ancestors. This change is consistent with Glaucon's tendency to go back to the origins, to see things genetically.

According to Glaucon's hypothetical account,[3] no one is just voluntarily, but only by convention: justice is that which is agreed upon—after they have entered into a compact with each other (*Rep.* 2. 358e5-359a5)—by those who are incapable of avoiding suffering injustice and electing to do injustice. Justice is the established advantage of the weak, even though everyone who could, would elect to do injustice with impunity (*Rep.* 2. 359a5-b4). The story of Gyges's ancestor shows that justice has its genesis in the fear of being visible at, i. e., being punishable for, doing injustice. The story shows that anyone who is given invisibility, i. e., impunity, will do injustice.[4] The desire for injustice is all-pervasive.

Gyges's ancestor acquires the ring of invisibility by stealing it from a corpse before he knows its special power: he is a simple thief, a tomb robber.[5] Prior to the earthquake, as a rule, fear kept him from doing injustice. However, as soon as the opportunity arose to do injustice unseen,[6] he seized it without hesitation. The ring simply gives him the power to do all the time what he did only occasionally before, and what he would have done all the time, if he had had the power to do so.[7]

This account has its analogue in the myth of Er. When the first lot falls to the person of habitual virtue from an ordered regime, he chooses the biggest tyranny (cf. *Rep.* 10. 619b6-d1). In the myth of Er, it is strongly suggested that what Glaucon had presented as merely hypothetical is the case in actuality and is not at all hypothetical. The only qualification is that the assertion that no one is voluntarily just is refined into the assertion that no one is voluntarily just, except the philosopher.[8]

---

1 Cf. Eva Brann, "The Music of the *Republic*," *ΑΓΩΝ*, vol. 1, April 1967, pp. 1-2, esp. the diagrammatic representation of the structure of the *Republic* (p. 2) as a series of concentric circles, except that the circles that she labels "Logos" and "Ergon" should be labeled as deepening layers of "Myth."

2 *Republic* 6. 511b7: τὴν τοῦ παντὸς ἀρχήν. The genitive here can be taken as either a genitive of contents/material or an objective genitive or both simultaneously: cf. Smyth, *Greek Grammar* (Cambridge, MA, 1973), sections 1323, 1328, 1331-1334.

3 That this is purely hypothetical is indicated by Glaucon's assertion that the position that he takes does not represent his own opinion: cf. *Rep.* 2. 358b7-d6, esp. c6, ἔμοιγε . . . οὔ τι δοκεῖ οὕτως. In a sense, then, insofar as the rest of the *Republic* is a response to Glaucon's interruption here, it too is purely hypothetical.

4 The sophist's version of invisibility is the chameleon-like shifting from city to city: cf. *Tim.* 19e2-8.

5 If Gyges's ancestor—and not Leontios himself (cf. *Rep.* 4. 439e6-440a3)—had come upon the corpses outside the wall of Athens, he would have stripped them of all their valuables instead of debating within himself whether to look or not.

6 The opportunity is provided by a natural event. Nature—through an upheaval—cooperates in giving him the means to act invisibly in accordance with his previously invisible nature.

7 Without a doubt, his fellow shepherds would have done the same, as their behavior at the conference, when Gyges's ancestor vanishes, indicates: no sooner is he "gone" than they begin to converse about him as though he is gone. One can assume that their remarks were not filled with praise but rather, in all likelihood, were filled with low backbiting.

8 Socrates is the living embodiment of Glaucon's construct, i. e., he is the perfectly just man who has the biggest reputation for injustice (cf. *Rep.* 2. 361b5-d1). However, it should not be forgotten that the philosopher—at least, the philosopher who has learned from Socrates's fate—must employ a protective ring of invisibility too, either by sequestering himself in a school or by writing invisibly or by both, as Plato did.

The account of the education of the guardians is a myth because it shows the genesis of habitual virtue through an education based on a θεολογία from which a θεογονία is generated. So, the account of the education of the guardians is doubly genetic: it shows the genesis of habitual virtue, and it shows the genesis of the proper theogony, which—as a genetic or genealogic account—is itself also to be regarded as consisting of myths.

The founding falsehood of the best city (2. 414b8-415d8) is a myth, a genetic account, that is both γενναῖον and a ψεῦδος. Its being a μῦθος does not make it—as seen before—a ψεῦδος. Therefore, its mythical character must have something to do with its being γενναῖον. In what sense?

The adjective γενναῖος has an enormous range of meaning. In the *Republic* alone, it is used to describe: the type of naiveté that Thrasymachus regards justice to be (1. 348c12); the perfect, simple just person whom Glaucon constructs (2. 361b7); Homer and Hesiod (2. 363a8); loaves of barley and wheat (2. 372b4); bred dogs (2. 375e1-2); the good judge (3. 409c2); comportment in the face of adversity (4. 440d1); the power of the contradicting art (5. 454a1); bred birds (5. 459a3); the big and vigorous, but inept, shipowner (6. 488c4); the philosophic nature in its imminent corruption (6. 494c6); tyranny (8. 544c6); and democracy (8. 558c2).

What unifies this range of meanings of γενναῖος is its fundamental meaning: "reflective of its genesis or birth" (cf. LSJ). In that sense, every μῦθος is γενναῖος, a designation that implies nothing either way about its truth or falsity. The γενναῖον ψεῦδος is both true and false.[1]

Finally, there are the big soul myths that conclude the *Republic*, Book 9. 588b1-592b6 and Book 10. 614a5-621d3, the first of which is meant to be the mythical prologue to the second. Nettleship has observed:

> The first half of Book X is disconnected from the rest of the *Republic*, and the transition to the subject of art and poetry . . . is sudden and unnatural . . . . It does not bear in any way on the last section of Book X, in which the immortality of the soul is treated, and which would naturally follow at the end of Book IX, forming a fitting conclusion to the whole work.[2]

Although Nettleship is correct in emphasizing the direct connection between the end of Book 9 and the second half of Book 10, and in emphasizing the abruptness of the re-introduction of the subject of poetry, he is incorrect in saying that the discussion of poetry does not bear on the last section of Book 10. To show that it does bear on the last section of Book 10, it is necessary briefly to review the overall context.

The initial discussion of poetry was carried on in a politico-educational context, in the context of the founding of the city, which leads through false myths (of which the foundation is the gennaic falsehood), for the purpose of inculcating habitual virtue,[3] and through a partitive political psychology in the service of habitual virtue (cf. *Rep.* 4. 430c2-3), to a discussion of the institutions of the best city that culminates in philosophy.

1 Cf. Leo Strauss, *CM*, pp. 102-103; Eva Brann, pp. 10-11.

2 Richard Lewis Nettleship, *Lectures on the* Republic *of Plato* (NY, 1968), pp. 340-341.

3 That the education of the guardians was directed to habitual virtue alone is made especially clear at *Rep.* 7. 522a3-b1.

The introduction of philosophy impels a refining of what had been discussed previously, beginning at the image of the cave with a new discussion of education, of philosophic education, going through a recompletion of the founding of the city (7. 540d1-541b5), a new psychology in terms of a manifold of soul types and their genesis, a new discussion of poetry (this time from the perspective of the ancient quarrel between philosophy and poetry[1]), a non-partitive psychology, and culminating in a true myth, a transpolitical philosophic myth.

Consider now the final myths themselves, beginning with Socrates's account of the genesis of soul types. Without this account, one cannot begin to penetrate the obscurities of the myth of Er. Socrates fashions an image of the soul of a human thus:[2]

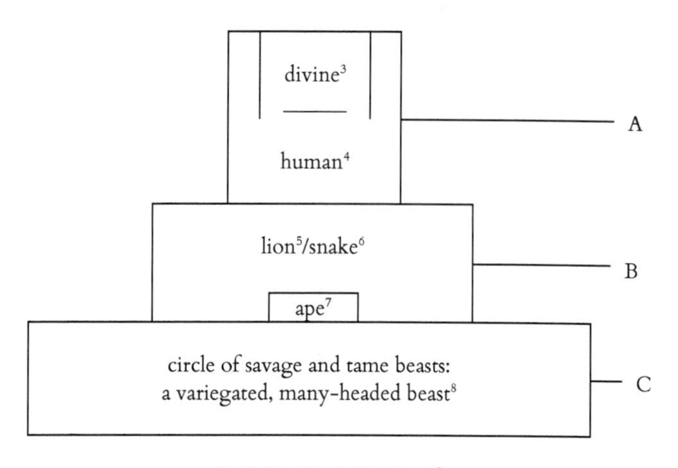

IMAGE OF A HUMAN[9]

On the basis of this schema, Socrates enumerates the following natural[10] types of soul:

(1) **A dominant:**

(a) Ah or Ad dominating B and C: produced by τὰ καλά (cf. 589c8-d2)

(b) A dominating C and making B and C friends or allies of each other: the just soul (cf. 589a6-b7)

(c) A lulls and gentles B and Cs, thereby freeing Cτ for habituation to virtue: the unjust soul punished (cf. 591b1-8)

1 *Rep.* 10. 607b5-6: παλαιὰ μέν τις διαφορὰ φιλοσοφίᾳ τε καὶ ποιητικῇ.

2 Each part is designated by a capital letter (A, B, C) so as to simplify the summary that follows. The parts within the parts have also been specified by lower case affixes, as follows: Ad = A, divine; Ah = A, human; Bl = B, lion; Bs = B, snake; Ba = B, ape; Cς = C, savage; Cτ = C, tame.

3 Cf. 589c8-d1, e4, 590c9-d1, 3-4.

4 Cf. 588d3-4, e6-589a1, a7-b1, c8-d1.

5 Cf. 588d3, e6, 589b4, 590a9-b1, 9.

6 Cf. 590b1 and Adam, note ad loc.

7 Cf. 590b9.

8 Cf. 588c7-10, e5, 589b1-3, c8-d3, e4, 590a6-7, b6-7, c4-5, 591b2, c6.

9 Cf. 588d10-e2. For the relative sizes of the three parts, see 588d4-5.

10 Cf. τῆς φύσεως at 589d2.

(2) **B and C dominant:**

(a) B and C feast and become strong, while A starves and is weak: the unjust soul (cf. 588e3-589a5)

(i) A follows B and C anywhere

(ii) A does not habituate B and C

(iii) A fails to reconcile B and C, which battle, bite, and eat each other

(b) Bl and Bs, strengthened by stubbornness and irascibility, ally with C: the uncontrolled soul I (cf. 590a5-b2)

(c) Bl and Bs, weakened or made cowardly by luxury and softness, ally with C: the uncontrolled soul II (cf. 590a5-8, b3-5)

(3) **C dominant:**

(a) Cς dominating Cτ, B, and A: love of gold, produced by τὰ αἰσχρά (cf. 589d2-590a4)

(b) C dominating B from flattery and unfreedom: Bl metamorphoses into Ba (cf. 590b6-c1)

(c) C dominating A weakened by mechanical and manual art so as to learn only what flatters it (cf. 590c2-7)

Several things should be noted about this psychology.

First, it is not actually true—any more than that Socrates is an openable statue (cf. *Symp.* 216d2-217a2) or that souls have metal in them (cf. *Rep.* 3. 414b8-415d8) or that humans are chained in a cave (cf. *Rep.* 7. beg.) is actually true—that the human is fashioned by putting three parts together and then placing the image of a human around them.

Second, it is an attempt to give, in imaged shorthand, as it were, a matrix for understanding types of human behavior (e.g., just acts or unjust acts or stubbornness or softness or greed and so forth).

If someone asserts that a human has the look (ἰδέα) of a snake, that means not that the human is actually a snake, but rather that the human acts like a snake. Similarly, if someone asserts that the soul of a human leaves a human body and enters the body of a beast, that is not to be taken at face value as a belief in transmigration of souls, but rather it is to be taken as a way of describing an alteration in that person's behavior.

Alfarabi judiciously remarks:

> For there is no difference between seeing a man who possesses the most perfect bestiality and performs the most perfect activities thereof, and assuming that he is dead and transformed into that beast and its shape. Thus there is no difference between a man who acts like a fish, and a fish with a shape like that of a man: *his* only virtue is his human shape and the fact that he acts like a *perfect* fish, nor is there any difference between this and his shape's being like a fish, and yet calculating his actions well like a man. For in all this he does not possess humanity except insofar as the calculation, by which he performs the activity of that beast well, is the calculation of a man. He [i. e., Plato] explained that the more perfectly one performs the activity of the beast, the further he is from being human; had the activities of that beast proceeded from some animate body having the shape of that beast along with man's calculation about these activities, such activities would be nothing but the most perfect activity that can proceed

> from that beast—the more perfectly and effectively the animate body performs the activities of that beast, the further it is from being human.[1]

It is in this sense that Thrasymachus, for example, acts "as a beast"[2] or that "a misologist . . . and unmusical person . . . acts in regard to everything by violence and savageness as a beast."[3]

In accordance with this, the myth of the transformation of a person into a tyrant is the paradigm both for the regime/soul transformations down from the best city[4] and for all the other transformations in the *Republic*[5] and elsewhere in Plato[6]:

> "Therefore, what is the beginning of the change from an outstanding leader to a tyrant? Or is it clear that it is whenever the outstanding leader begins to do the same thing as the thing in the myth which is spoken in respect to the temple of Wolfian Zeus in Arcadia?"
>
> "What?" he [i. e., Adeimantus] asserted.
>
> "As then [for] the person who has tasted the human innard, which has been cut up among other [innards] of other sacred victims, indeed there is a compulsion for this person to become a wolf. . . . Then indeed, is there a compulsion after this for the suchlike person, and has he been destined either to perish at the hands of his personal enemies or to be a tyrant and to become a wolf from a human?"
>
> "There is much compulsion," he asserted. . . . .

1 Alfarabi, *Philosophy of Plato and Aristotle*, tr. Muhsin Mahdi (Glencoe, IL, 1962), p. 64. Cf. Aristotle, *Historia animalium* 8. 1. 588a15-b6: "For there are in most even of the other animals tracks of the manners in respect to the soul, which very things for humans have more apparent differences; for also tameness and savageness, and gentleness and harshness, and courage and cowardice, and fears and boldness, and spirits and roguishness and similarities of awareness in respect to thinking are in many of them [i. e., in many animals], in accordance with which very things we bespoke for the parts. For some differ [only] by the more and less in regard to a human, and the human [differs only by the more and less] in regard to many of the animals (for some of the suchlike things internally underpin the humans more, and some internally [underpin] the other animals more), and some differ by analogy; for as in a human, there are art and wisdom and awareness, thus there is a certain other suchlike natural power in some of the animals. And about the things which we bespeak, the suchlike is apparent to those who have gazed upon the age of children; for in them [i. e., in children], one is to see tracks and seeds of the aptitudes/attitudes which will be later, and the soul in accordance with this time-of-life [i. e., childhood] differs in no way from the soul of beasts, so that it is not unaccountable if some things the same underpin the other animals, and some things nearly so and some things by analogy. And thus nature crosses over from the unsouled things to the animals in accordance with a little, so that their dividing-line escapes notice by [their] contiguity and is the middle of the ones before [them]." ("Ενεστι γὰρ ἐν τοῖς πλείστοις καὶ τῶν ἄλλων ζῴων ἴχνη τῶν περὶ τὴν ψυχὴν τρόπων, ἅπερ ἐπὶ τῶν ἀνθρώπων ἔχει φανερωτέρας τὰς διαφορας· καὶ γὰρ ἡμερότης καὶ ἀγριότης, καὶ πραότης καὶ χαλεπότης, καὶ ἀνδρεία καὶ δειλία, καὶ φόβοι καὶ θάρρη, καὶ θυμοὶ καὶ πανουργίαι καὶ τῆς περὶ τὴν διάνοιαν συνέσεως ἔνεισιν ἐν πολλοῖς αὐτῶν ὁμοιότητες, καθάπερ ἐπὶ τῶν μερῶν ἐλέγομεν. Τὰ μὲν γὰρ τῷ μᾶλλον καὶ ἧττον διαφέρει πρὸς τὸν ἄνθρωπον, καὶ ὁ ἄνθρωπος πρὸς πολλὰ τῶν ζῴων (ἔνια γὰρ τῶν τοιούτων ὑπάρχει μᾶλλον ἐν ἀνθρώποις, ἔνια δ' ἐν τοῖς ἄλλοις ζῴοις μᾶλλον), τὰ δὲ τῷ ἀνάλογον διαφέρει· ὥσπερ ἐν ἀνθρώπῳ τέχνη καὶ σοφία καὶ σύνεσις, οὕτως ἐνίοις τῶν ζῴων ἐστί τις τοιαύτη ἑτέρα φυσικὴ δύναμις. Φανερὸν δὲ περὶ ὧν λέγομεν ἐστὶν τὸ τοιοῦτον ἐπὶ τὴν τῶν παίδων ἡλικίαν βλέψασιν· ἐν τούτοις γὰρ τῶν μὲν ὕστερον ἕξεων ἐσομένων ἔστιν ἰδεῖν οἷον ἴχνη καὶ σπέρματα, διαφέρει δ' οὐθὲν ἡ ψυχὴ τῆς τῶν θηρίων ψυχῆς κατὰ τὸν χρόνον τοῦτον, ὥστ' οὐδὲν ἄλογον εἰ τὰ μὲν ταὐτὰ τὰ δὲ παραπλήσια τὰ δ' ἀνάλογον ὑπάρχει τοῖς ἄλλοις ζῴοις. Οὕτω δ' ἐκ τῶν ἀψύχων εἰς τὰ ζῷα μεταβαίνει κατὰ μικρὸν ἡ φύσις, ὥστε τῇ συνεχείᾳ λανθάνει τὸ μεθόριον αὐτῶν καὶ τὸ μέσον προτέρων ἐστίν.) [I have adopted in most instances, against Bekker (see apparatus criticus ad loc.), the readngs of ms. Aa].

2 *Republic* 1. 336b5: ὥσπερ θηρίον.

3 *Republic* 3. 411d7-e1: Μισόλογος . . . καὶ ἄμουσος . . . βίᾳ . . . καὶ ἀγριότητι ὥσπερ θηρίον πρὸς πάντα διαπράττεται.

4 This would also suggest that if the transformation of the democrat into the tyrant is a myth, then the entire account of regime/soul transformations may be a myth too.

5 For example, the transformation of the guardians from dogs into wolves.

6 For example, the transformation of the philosopher into a dead man in the *Phaedo*. Cf. Alfarabi, pp. 63-64.

"And let us again bespeak that armed camp which the tyrant is, [an armed camp] which is beautiful and big and variegated and never the same, [and bespeak] whence it will be nurtured." . . .

"By Zeus, then, already then," he said, "such a populace will recognize the sort of nurtured-creature which it, generating, has welcomed and caused to increase."[1]

The wolf that is the tyrant is one of the savage heads of the many-headed beastlike part of the human soul (cf. *Rep.* 9. 571c5). Therefore, whenever, in a Platonic dialogue, there is an ostensible transformation from a human into a beast, or from a beast into a human, or even from a beast into another beast, that transformation must not be taken at face value, but rather it must be taken as an imaged way of delineating an internal transformation within a human from one type of behavior to another.[2]

The same rule must apply to every account of transmigration of souls, such as the account that is found within the myth of Er.

The myth has the following outline:

(1) 614a5-616b1: Introduction
  (a) 614a5-b1: The theme adumbrated
  (b) 614b2-8: Whose it is and the circumstances
  (c) 614b8-615a4: : Er's account of the souls
  (d) 615a4-c4: Socrates's interruption and summary
  (e) 615c5-616b1: Er's account of Ardiaios (dialogue)
(2) 616b1-617d1: Er's account: cosmography
  (a) 616b1-c4: Pillar of light
  (b) 616c4-617b4: Spindle of compulsion and the whorls
  (c) 617b4-7: Sirens
  (d) 617b7-d1: Moirai
(3) 617d1-618b6: Er's account: the lottery of lifetimes
(4) 618b6-619b1: Socrates's second interruption
(5) 619b2-620d5: Er's account: the electings
(6) 620d6-621b7: Er's account: the return
  (a) 620d6-e1: Daimons
  (b) 620e1-4: Klotho
  (c) 620e4-6: Atropos
  (d) 620e6-621a1: Compulsion
  (e) 621a2-b1: Plain of Forgetfulness and the River Uncaringness
  (f) 621b1-7: Return to earth
(7) 621b8-d3: Conclusion (Socrates directly discoursing to Glaucon)

1 *Republic* 8. 565d4-e1, 566a2-5, 568d4-6, 569a8-b1: Τίς ἀρχὴ οὖν μεταβολῆς ἐκ προστάτου ἐπὶ τύραννον; ἢ δῆλον ὅτι ἐπειδὰν ταὐτὸν ἄρξηται ὁρᾶν ὁ προστάτης τῷ ἐν τῷ μύθῳ ὃς περὶ τὸ ἐν Ἀρκαδίᾳ τὸ τοῦ Διὸς τοῦ Λυκαίου ἱερὸν λέγεται; Τίς; ἔφη. Ὡς ἄρα ὁ γευσάμενος τοῦ ἀνθρωπίνου σπλάγχνου, ἐν ἄλλοις ἄλλων ἱερείων ἑνὸς ἐγκατατετμημένου, ἀνάγκη δὴ τούτῳ λύκῳ γενέσθαι . . . . ἆρα τῷ τοιούτῳ ἀνάγκη δὴ τὸ μετὰ τοῦτο καὶ εἵμαρται ἢ ἀπολωλέναι ὑπὸ τῶν ἐχθρῶν ἢ τυραννεῖν καὶ λύκῳ ἐξ ἀνθρώπου γενέσθαι; Πολλὴ ἀνάγκη, ἔφη . . . . λέγωμεν δὲ πάλιν ἐκεῖνο τὸ τοῦ τυράννου στρατόπεδον, τὸ καλόν τε καὶ πολὺ καὶ ποικίλον καὶ οὐδέποτε ταὐτόν, πόθεν θρέψεται . . . . Γνώσεταί γε, νὴ Δία, ἦ δ' ὅς, τοτ' ἤδη ὁ δῆμος οἷος οἷον θρέμμα γεννῶν ἠσπάζετό τε καὶ ηὖξεν.

2 To work this out systematically throughout the Platonic corpus—which is beyond the scope of this work—one would have to catalogue all the references to beasts in that corpus in order to compile a precise set of human equivalencies for all such references.

First (614a5-b1), Socrates adumbrates the theme of the myth in an apparently straightforward manner. However, it is not as straightforward as it seems. He says that his account will detail the "prizes and wages and gifts" (614a1) of justice for a person who has come to the end of life, as opposed to the previous account of the wages[1] of a person who is living. The stress is to be on rewards for justice. However, the myth as recounted belies this: the emphasis is rather on punishments for injustice, and there is comparatively little about rewards for justice.[2]

Socrates gives this account because it is owed by the speech.[3] Thus, it is a paying back to speech, in speech, what is owed by speech to speech. It is an act of justice in the Cephalean sense, and it brings to bear the entire conventional apparatus[4] of the underworld and afterlife. The model for the philosophic undersanding of that conventional apparatus is not pious acceptance, which would be the salutary model for the many, but rather it is the onomatology that Socrates practices in the *Cratylus* with regard to the conventional apparatus of names and naming.

In addition, it is important that the repayment of debt is internal to speech: it is self-repayment. By analogy, the elections of lifetimes and the so-called transmigration of souls too will need to be understood internally as an imaged way of describing internal transformations of a human in this lifetime.[5]

The distinction that Socrates makes between the living and the ended appears to be—and is imaged as—a distinction between the living and the dead. Furthermore, Socrates's use of the participle τελευτήσαντα,[6] the person who has come to the end, for what is usually regarded as the person who is dead instead of the participle ἀποθανόντα or τεθνηκότα, the person who has died, suggests another distinction, the distinction between the person in potentiality and the person in actuality or ἐντελέχεια. The person in actuality or ἐντελέχεια is the person in the state of having reached that for which that person would strive by nature, namely the τέλος, even if the state of having reached the τέλος and the desire that would initiate movement toward it are belied by habitual actions. As though to emphasize the connection between τελευτήσαντα and τέλος, Socrates uses the adverb τελέως in the very next phrase.

Then Socrates describes whose account it is. As in the palinode in the *Phaedrus*, the description is composed of punning names:

---

1 It should be noted that at 614a1, wages are central.

2 For example, at 615a4-616b1, the remarks have to do with punishment for injustice, while there is only a perfunctory remark (616b1) that "doings of good works are in turn antistrophes to these" (αὖ τὰς εὐεργεσίας ταύταις ἀντιστρόφους). This emphasis on injustice continues through the myth.

3 Cf. 614a7-8: τὰ ὑπὸ τοῦ λόγου ὀφειλόμενα.

4 There is an analogy here between μῦθος and λόγος, and a difference. With λόγος, which is a descriptive classification of the things that are, one either simply confronts τὰ ὄντα or one confronts speeches (the conventional apparatus) about τὰ ὄντα. With μῦθος, which is a genetic account, an account of origins (in a double sense, the from which and the to which, on the basis of which one can see why things which are, are what they are), one cannot confront the phenomena involved simply, and therefore, one must confront speeches about them. The speeches about them are, to a large extent, the prevailing codified theology. Therefore, to investigate the origins, one must go through the conventional apparatus. However, this going through the conventional apparatus does not entail compulsorily a belief in that apparatus. When one is faced with it in a Platonic dialogue, one must act as Socrates did with respect to the Delphic oracle's pronouncement that no one was wiser than he, namely one must investigate whether it is to be taken at face value or not. For the myths in Plato, this involves an act of mental translation of the conventional apparatus into a non-conventional language.

5 Cf. *Gorgias* 492e8-493a1: "For I would not wonder if Euripides speaks truly in these things, speaking—"And who has envisioned [i.e., understood], if living is dying, / and dying living?" and we beingly are dead equally." (οὐ γάρ τοι θαυμάζοιμ' ἂν εἰ Εὐριπίδης ἀληθῆ ἐν τοῖσδε λέγει, λέγων—"τίς δ' οἶδεν, εἰ τὸ ζῆν μέν ἐστι κατθανεῖν, / τὸ κατθανεῖν δὲ ζῆν;" καὶ ἡμεῖς τῷ ὄντι ἴσως τέθναμεν.)

6 Cf. 618e3-4: ζῶντί τε καὶ τελευτήσαντι.

> "But yet," I said, "I shall not say to you the account of Alkinoos, then, but that of a man with defensive strength, Er the [son] of Armenios, a Pamphylian with respect to his race."[1]

The account of Alkinoos that Socrates's myth is not, is Odysseus's narrative—in Books 9-12 of the *Odyssey* (cf. Adam, note ad loc.)—of his experiences after leaving Troy. The very denial invites a comparison of the two, especially since the soul of Odysseus himself appears in the myth (620c3-d2) as the person who has received the last lot, since we meet the Sirens in a purified form (617b4-7), and since the soul of Aias is the twentieth soul in both the *Odyssey*[2] and Er's tale.[3]

If one considers the structure of Odysseus's narrative and Er's account, one may see that Er's account is an inverted Odyssean narrative, as the following table of correspondences shows:

	Odyssey	*Republic*
(1)	Kalypso (promise of immortality and arrival at Phaiakia), 12. 447-453 (and 7. 240-297)	Introduction, 614a5-616b1
(2)	Helios's cattle, 12. 260-446	Pillar of light, 616b1-c4
(3)	Skylla and Charybdis, 12. 201-259	Spindle of compulsion and the whorls, 616c4-617b4
(4)	Sirens, 12. 144-200	Sirens, 617b4-7
(5)	Circe II, 12. 1-143	Moirai, 617b7-d1
(6)	Underworld II (men and demigods), 11. 385-640	Lottery of lifetimes, 617d1-618b6
(7)	Alkinoos's and Arete's interruption, 11. 333-384	Socrates's interruption, 618b6-619b1
(8)	Underworld I (Teiresias and women), 11. 1-332	Electings, 619b2-620d5
(9)	Circe I (enchanted beasts), 10. 133-574	Daimons, 620d6-e1
(10)	Laistrygones (cannibalism), 10. 80-132	Klotho, 620e1-4
(11)	Aiolian island (bag of winds), 10. 1-79	Atropos, 620e4-6
(12)	Cyclopes (lawless savagery), 9. 105-566	Compulsion, 620e6-621a1
(13)	Lotos eaters (drugged forgetfulness and uncaringness), 9. 67-104	Plain of forgetfulness and the River Uncaringness, 621a2-b1
(14)	Sack of the Kikonian city, 9. 39-66	Return to earth, 621b1-7
(15)	Prologue (departure from Troy), 9. 1-38	Conclusion, 621b8-d3

The more obvious connections at (1), (2), (3), (4), (7), (12), and (13) make one suspect that the less obvious connections are as parallel as the obvious ones, but to explore these correspondences fully would require a work unto itself, so let this simply be offered as a suggesstion or program for future study.

---

1 *Republic* 10, 614b2-4: Ἀλλ᾽ οὐ μέντοι σοι, ἦν δ᾽ ἐγώ, Ἀλκίνου γε ἀπόλογον ἐρῶ, ἀλλ᾽ ἀλκίμου μὲν ἀνδρός, Ἠρὸς τοῦ Ἀρμενίου, τὸ γένος Παμφύλου.

2 Except for Teiresias, to whom the prophet of Lachesis in the myth of Er corresponds, Odysseus saw the following named souls: (1) Antikleia, his mother, (2) Tyro, (3) Antiope, (4) Alkmene, (5) Megara, (6) Epikaste, (7) Chloris, (8) Leda, (9) Iphimedeia, (10) Phaidra, (11), Prokris, (12) Ariadne, (13) Maira, (14) Klymene, (15) Eriphyle, (16) Agamemnon, (17 Achilleus, (18) Patroklus, (19) Antilochus, (20) Aias, (21) Minos, (22) Orion, (23) Tityos, (24) Tantalos, (25) Sisyphos, (26) Herakles.

3 He is called εἰκοστήν explicitly at 620b1.

If one notices the paronomasia 'Αλκίνου . . . ἀλκίμου (strong intellect . . . strong), one could render Socrates's introduction thus: "I shall not say to you the account of a strong intellect, but that of a man who is [nonetheless] strong." This strong man is a man at the time of life when he has to make the choice of the lifetime that he will lead, i. e., he is a man in the spring of his lifetime, ἦρ being a contraction of ἔαρ (spring: cf. LSJ). He is of the Pamphylian race, i.e., he is of every tribe, which means that he is not a Greek, so even though Greek examples predominate, the myth is directed, not at Greeks as Greeks, but rather at humans as humans.[1]

Consider now Er's account itself, focusing upon certain key passages.

When the souls come to the daimonic place,[2] the judges place signs upon them:

> And [he asserted] judges to be seated between these [chasms], [judges] whom, since they thoroughly judged, [he asserted] to bid the just persons to proceed [in their way] to the right and upward through the heaven, having fastened around [them] signs in front, [signs] of the things which have been judged, and the unjust persons [to proceed in their way] to the left and downward, these having signs too, in back, [signs] of all the things which they acted.[3]

The signs for the just indicate only their justice, but not their actions, while the signs for the unjust indicate only their actions, but not their injustice.

Is the reason for this that a just person may act unjustly without impairing that person's justice, while an unjust person never acts except unjustly? Or is it that justice need not manifest itself in actions, while injustice necessarily eventuates in actions, all of which are unjust? Or is it that the primary behavioral manifestation of justice is in refraining from certain actions (i. e., justice is behaviorally negative, but psychically positive), while the primary behavioral manifestation of injustice is in performing certain actions (i. e., injustice is behaviorally positive, but psychically negative), a distinction that might explain the relative attractiveness of injustice, the advantages of which one wears, as it were, on one's sleeve,[4] and unattractiveness of justice, the advantages of which are hidden, as it were, in one's heart?[5]

In Socrates's interruption and summary (615a4-c4), several things should be emphasized. First, as throughout the myth, his presentation is skewed toward injustice and the wages of injustice.[6] Second, wages or salaries, μισθοί, is a neutral term and may designate rewards or punishments, i. e., it designates the appropriate remuneration for the act. Third, Socrates implies that private injustice is more reprehensible than public injustice, because killing someone by one's own hand is in the class of acts that receive bigger wages for injustice (615c2-4), while indirectly causing many to be killed politically (615b2-5) is implicitly in the class of acts that receive smaller wages for injustice. Finally, in the whole Socratic parenthesis here, there is no reference to the gods as inflicting the punishments or dispensing the rewards, i. e., the

---

1 I am unable to explain the significance of his being 'Αρμενίου, [son] of Armenios (cf. Adam, note ad loc.). The difficulty of determining the meaning of this designation, as well as the others, is exacerbated by the difficulty that each ('Αλκίνοος, ἀπόλογος, ἄλκιμος, Ἠρ, 'Αρμένιος, Πάμφυλος) is a ἅπαξ λεγόμενον in Plato.

2 614c1: τόπον τινὰ δαιμόνιον.

3 614c3-d1: δικαστὰς δὲ μεταξὺ τούτων καθῆσθαι, οὕς, ἐπειδὴ διαδικάσειαν, τοὺς μὲν δικαίους κελεύειν πορεύεσθαι τὴν εἰς δεξιάν τε καὶ ἄνω διὰ τοῦ οὐρανοῦ, σημεῖα περιάψαντας τῶν δεδικασμένων ἐν τῷ πρόσθεν, τοὺς δὲ ἀδίκους τὴν εἰς ἀριστεράν τε καὶ κάτω, ἔχοντας καὶ τούτους ἐν τῷ ὄπισθεν σημεῖα πάντων ὧν ἔπραξαν. The use of the word σημεῖα here suggests—in the light of the traditional σῶμα/σῆμα word play—that although the myth is ostensibly about disembodied souls in the afterlife, it is at bottom about embodied souls in this life. Cf. *Cratylus* 400b9-c9. Also cf. *Gorgias* 493a2-3: καὶ τὸ μὲν σῶμά ἐστιν ἡμῖν σῆμα.

4 Hence in front, so that in the judgment, to redress this, the signs are placed in back.

5 Hence in back, so that in the judgment, to redress this, the signs are placed in front.

6 In the whole fifteen line passage (615a4-c4), only two lines (b6-c1) deal with wages for justice.

philosophical version of the account would require stripping away the conventional theological causal explanation.

Er's account of Ardiaios[1] (615c5-616b1) is a dialogue between two anonymous souls at which Er was present. The inquiry of the first person, the inquiring soul, is perplexing. There are several possible explanations for his inquiry. Perhaps the first person knows only that Ardiaios was a ruler, but does not know anything about his character. However, if this were so, it would be difficult to explain his curiosity about Ardiaios, because there surely would have been others whom he would have known better, and about whom he would be curious. This seems especially unlikely since Er knows of Ardiaios even a thousand years after Ardiaios lived, and the two anonymous souls, who are just returning from having completed their thousand year sojourn, would have been contemporaries of Ardiaios (cf. 615c7-8). Perhaps, then, the first person knows that Ardiaios was a patricide and fratricide and unholy tyrant, but does not regard these necessarily as bads,[2] or is not sure whether they are bads, perhaps because he regards political crimes as somehow justifiable, which would explain the second person's emphasis on the political character (cf. 615d6-7) of these incurable, or virtually incurable, souls. Or perhaps—and this is not inconsistent with the preceding alternative—the first person knows Ardiaios's character as vicious, but is unsure whether vice is punished. In any case, presumably the first person's sojourn was in heaven, so that he would not have encountered Ardiaios. However, the second person's sojourn was under the earth (cf. 615d5), where he did encounter Ardiaios.

Er's cosmography (616b1-617d8) is perhaps the most difficult passage in the entire myth. Although it purports to be a description of ἐκεῖ, it is actually a description of ἐνθάδε:

> And [he asserted] the nature of the whorl to be suchlike; its shaped-surface
> is of the very sort as the [shaped-surface] of the [whorl] here.[3]

The description of the the things there, then, is an indirect description of the things here.[4]

Which things here? A partial answer may be contained in the hymning of the Moirai:

> And [he asserted] three others to be seated around at an equal [distance], each on a throne, daughters of Compulsion, [namely] the Fates, being clad in white, having wreaths over their heads, Lachesis and Klotho and Atropos, [—he asserted them] to hymn to the Sirens's harmony, Lachesis the things which have come to be, and Klotho the things which are, and Atropos the things which are going to be.[5]

This echoes Socrates's introduction to his discussion of narrating:

1 Cf. Adam, note ad loc.: "'Ἀρδιαῖος is a purely fictitious personage, no doubt, although verisimilitude is preserved;" also cf. Bloom, p. 471, n. 15: "Ardiaeus is apparently of Socrates' invention." The Pamphylia of which Ardiaios was tyrant is as fictitious as Ardiaios himself.

2 The theme of the attractiveness of tyranny pervades the myth.

3 616c7-d2: τὴν δὲ τοῦ σφονδύλου φύσιν εἶναι τοιάνδε· τὸ μὲν σχῆμα οἵαπερ ἡ τοῦ ἐνθάδε.

4 Socrates makes the same point in his summary at the end, 10. 621c4-d2: "we shall always hold to the upper road and pursue justice with prudence in every manner, so that we may be friends to ourselves and the gods, both remaining here and there, and when we bring in its prizes . . . both here and in the thousand year journey" (τῆς ἄνω ὁδοῦ ἀεὶ ἑξόμεθα καὶ δικαιοσύνην μετὰ φρονήσεως παντὶ τρόπῳ ἐπιτηδεύσομεν, ἵνα καὶ ἡμῖν αὑτοῖς φίλοι ὦμεν καὶ τοῖς θεοῖς, αὐτοῦ τε μένοντες ἐνθάδε, καὶ ἐπειδὰν τὰ ἆθλα αὐτῆς κομιζώμεθα . . . καὶ ἐνθάδε καὶ ἐν τῇ χιλιέτει πορείᾳ).

5 617b7-c5: ἄλλας δὲ καθημένας πέριξ δι' ἴσου τρεῖς, ἐν θρόνῳ ἑκάστην, θυγατέρας τῆς Ἀνάγκης, Μοίρας, λευχειμονούσας, στέμματα ἐπὶ τῶν κεφαλῶν ἐχούσας, Λάχεσίν τε καὶ Κλωθὼ καὶ Ἄτροπον, ὑμνεῖν πρὸς τὴν τῶν Σειρήνων ἁρμονίαν, Λάχεσιν μὲν τὰ γεγονότα, Κλωθὼ δὲ τὰ ὄντα, Ἄτροπον δὲ τὰ μέλλοντα.

> However, then, do not as many of all things as are spoken by mythologizers or poets chance to be a narrating either of things which have come to be or of things which are or of things which are about to be?[1]

This suggests that, in one sense at least, the Moirai are the deities who preside over narrating. If so, the 'Ἀνάγκη who is the mother of the Moirai could be understood as the logographic compulsion to which Socrates refers in the *Phaedrus* (264b7). Hence, what is presented as a cosmography actually would be a logography.[2]

A properly constructed writing, then, would be like a series of concentric whorls, presenting different colors at different levels, and moving at different speeds, to different persons. A properly constructed writing would be written so that one person might hear the one sound or tone of one Siren, and another the sound or tone of another Siren, and still another perhaps the harmony that all the Sirens produce together. That harmony is the unity behind the variegated structure of the writing. That unity is adumbrated here especially by the pillar of light, whose function as co-bond is analogous to the function as co-bond of being seen and seeing, or of being and knowing, of the sun and the good in the analogy between them. If the *Timaeus* establishes that the cosmos is a ζῷον, and the *Phaedrus* that a writing is a ζῷον, then the *Republic* suggests that a writing is a cosmos.[3]

In the lottery of lifetimes (617d1 ff.), there is a turn—rather a return—to the problem of soul types. Since Lachesis, the fate of the past, presides over the lottery—which includes all lifetimes, the lifetimes of all beasts and all humans (cf. 618a3-4)—the implication is that all lifetimes that are have been already, and that no new lifetimes will arise. The zoic γένη, then, are fixed in number—however large that number may be—for all time.

In addition, there is a significant shift in emphasis here from the bulk of the *Republic.*[4] Throughout the *Republic,* it had been assumed that there were a small, finite number of human natures that fitted some humans for one thing and others for other things, and that these natures were predetermined for each person. In terms of responsibility for one's lifetime, this would have meant—although this was not stated explicitly—that one is not responsible for oneself. If one were not perfectly just, one could not be blamed, because one simply had a nature of which perfect justice was not a part.[5]

However, here (617e1-5), each person, each soul, elects both its daimon and its lifetime—with whatever degree of virtue that lifetime contains. Hence, a person is the cause of, bears the responsibility for, that person's own nature. While the bulk of the *Republic* depends on the assumption that one simply is what one is, according to the myth of Er, one is what one chooses to be.[6]

This shift produces a perplexity. If one is to choose *freely,* one's soul must be without a τάξις (618b2-4), i. e., it must be empty. Yet if one is to *choose* freely, one's soul must contain all possibilities, at least as possibilities (618b4-6), i. e., it must be full.

This problem is the problem of learning. Consequently, when Socrates interrupts the narrative at precisely this point (618b6), he takes up the question of learning:

---

1 *Republic* 3. 392d2-3: ἆρ' οὐ πάντα ὅσα ὑπὸ μυθολόγων ἢ ποιητῶν λέγεται διήγησις οὖσα τυγχάνει ἢ γεγονότων ἢ ὄντων ἢ μελλόντων;

2 This may account partially for the conclusion that "this conception of close-fitting concentric whorls . . . appears to be unique in ancient astronomy." (Adam, note ad 616D, E)

3 One should not assert that this is the only thing that Er's cosmography suggests, although one should assert that it is not meant to be taken as a 'scientific' cosmography.

4 The myth is filled with such shifts.

5 One could even say that the entire program of eugenics of the best city was designed to insure that such natures would be bred out of the citizenry.

6 In a way, the emphasis on punishment in the myth reflects this shift too.

> Indeed, as is likely, oh friend Glaucon, all risk for a human is there, and because of these things, one must take care especially, so that—being uncaring of [i.e., necessarily neglecting] other learnings, each of us will be both a seeker and a learner of this learning, if somewhere he is such as to learn and to find out who will make him [to be] thoroughly recognizing both the useful and the vicious lifetime [and] capable and knowledgeable of always everywhere electing the better [lifetime] from [among] the possible [lifetimes].[1]

The learning is the learning and seeking of the learning and finding out[2] who will make one an infallible elector of the better possible lifetimes by enabling one to recognize the criteria for distinguishing useful lifetimes from vicious lifetimes. In other words, *the* learning is a learning of a learning about a teacher, i. e., *the* learning is a learning of who is the best teacher of decency.

Presumably Plato himself has engaged in such a learning and has determined that the best such teacher is Socrates. Therefore, his dialogues revivify Socrates, so that others may learn through writings about Socrates what Plato himself learned through direct being together with Socrates. The Socratic assertion that to acquire such a learning is to equip oneself to elect a good lifetime forms the prologue to Er's account of the electings, an account that, to a large extent, shows what can happen when one lacks this learning.

Er begins his account of the electings with the prophet's speech that outlines the terms of the electings. According to the prophet (619b2-6), the electing of one's nature takes the form of choosing a lot that does nothing more than establish the numerical order in which lifetimes are chosen. Apparently, one's numerical position—whether one is first or n^{th}—is in no way decisive, because somehow there are enough lifetimes: in principle, everyone could choose a good lifetime. Hence, no one would be prevented by numerical order from choosing a good lifetime.

The description of the person who received the first lot—the one who is numerically first to elect—is especially important:

> He asserted the person who had obtained the first lot having gone up straightway to elect the biggest tyranny . . . and [he asserted] him to be of the persons having come from heaven, having spent his lifetime in his earlier lifetime in an ordered regime, having partaken of virtue by habit without philosophy.[3]

The first lot and electing fell to someone who had only habitual (demotic) virtue before, and who resided in an ordered regime. This person chooses the worst tyranny. That he chose in haste is no excuse (619b8-c6). This suggests that there can be no adequate solution to the problem of virtue on the political plane, on the plane of habituation to virtue.

---

1 618b6-c6: ἔνθα δή, ὡς ἔοικεν, ὦ φίλε Γλαύκων, ὁ πᾶς κίνδυνος ἀνθρώπῳ, καὶ διὰ ταῦτα μάλιστα ἐπιμελητέον ὅπως ἕκαστος ἡμῶν των ἄλλων μαθημάτων ἀμελήσας τούτου τοῦ μαθήματος καὶ ζητητὴς καὶ μαθητὴς ἔσται, ἐάν ποθεν οἷος τ᾽ ᾖ μαθεῖν καὶ ἐξευρεῖν τίς αὐτὸν ποιήσει δυνατὸν καὶ ἐπιστήμονα, βίον καὶ χρηστὸν καὶ πονηρὸν διαγιγνώσκοντα, τὸν βελτίω ἐκ τῶν δυνατῶν ἀεὶ πανταχοῦ αἱρεῖσθαι.

2 The two yoke pairs καὶ ζητητὴς καὶ μαθητὴς and μαθεῖν καὶ ἐξευρεῖν, indicate that one must not only be guided to this by another, but also that one must, and to an equal degree, exert one's own efforts.

3 619b7-8, c6-d1: τὸν πρῶτον λαχόντα ἔφη εὐθυς ἐπιόντα τὴν μεγίστην τυραννίδα ἑλέσθαι . . . εἶναι δὲ αὐτὸν τῶν ἐκ τοῦ οὐρανοῦ ἡκόντων, ἐν τεταγμένῃ πολιτείᾳ ἐν τῷ προτέρῳ βίῳ βεβιωκότα, ἔθει ἄνευ φιλοσοφίας ἀρετῆς μετειληφότα.

Insofar as the person of exclusively habitual virtue represents virtually everyone but the philosopher, the lesson of Glaucon's account of Gyges's progenitor's ring—that all humans by nature desire to do injustice with impunity—prevails. That means that in actual political life, in political life in deed, there will be no cessation of bads.

The myth asserts that the city in speech is only in speech. This brings to the surface the anti-utopianism that has been the pervasive subsurface aspect of the surface utopianism of the bulk of the *Republic*. In other words—and all the discussions in the *Republic* would have to be read with an eye to this—the *Republic* is, at one and the same time, a utopian book and an anti-utopian book.

The first lot makes the choice that he does because, as a reward for virtue, he went to heaven. This seems paradoxical, so Er interrupts his narrative to discuss (619d1-7) the two paths, the heavenly and the subearthly.

The path of heaven is too easy, and those who travel to heaven are not exercised in toils. Hence, the majority of them made senseless and gluttonous choices in haste. On the other hand, the subearthly path is filled with toils. Hence, the majority of those who traveled that path made better and less hasty choices.

The first soul chooses as he does because, without true virtue, he was corrupted by the easy life in heaven, and he did not have philosophy as an antidote to heaven. The very radical and paradoxical teaching of the *Republic* is that without philosophy, there is no true virtue, or—to put it inversely—knowledge is virtue.

In the choosings, as a rule, the bad souls from the subearthly path choose good lifetimes, while the good souls from heaven choose bad lifetimes.[1] The reasons for this are the path from which they came and the lot that they happened to pick. The latter reason is odd because the lottery was presented initially as little more than a convenience, yet now it is suggested that it plays a role. Such an assertion calls for interpretation.

Socrates interrupts, in direct discourse, to answer that call:

> Since, if someone always, when he should come to his lifetime here, should philosophize healthily, and [if] the lot of his electing should not fall among the ones at the end, on the basis of the things which are messaged from there, he runs the risk not only of being happy here, but also of proceeding, not [along] the subterranean and rough journey from here to there and here again, but [along] the smooth and heavenly [journey].[2]

Socrates repeats the second factor in the electing, but only with respect to the philosophers.

As Socrates interprets this, a certain exhaustion of lifetimes occurs that is not decisive for non-philosophers (whose choices are grossly irrational), but that is decisive for philosophers. What is the meaning of this qualification? At the least, in the choices enumerated here, since there is available at the very end the lifetime of the just person as defined earlier in the *Republic* (cf. 620c6-7), one can infer that the life of such a just person is not what the philosopher would choose. The philosopher, whose lot is at the end, then, would wish to choose a lifetime that is not available at the end.

1 Cf. 619d5-7: "Because of which indeed also [he asserted] there to come to be a change of bads and goods for many of the souls, and because of the luck of the lot." (διὸ δὴ καὶ μεταβολὴν τῶν κακῶν καὶ τῶν ἀγαθῶν ταῖς πολλαῖς τῶν ψυχῶν γίγνεσθαι καὶ διὰ τὴν τοῦ κλήρου τύχην.)

2 619d7-e5: ἐπεὶ εἴ τις ἀεί, ὁπότε εἰς τὸν ἐνθάδε βίον ἀφικνοῖτο, ὑγιῶς φιλοσοφοῖ καὶ ὁ κλῆρος αὐτῷ τῆς αἱρέσεως μὴ ἐν τελευταίοις πίπτοι, κινδυνεύει ἐκ τῶν ἐκεῖθεν ἀπαγγελλομένων οὐ μόνον ἐνθάδε εὐδαιμονεῖν ἄν, ἀλλὰ καὶ τὴν ἐνθένδε ἐκεῖσε καὶ δεῦρο πάλιν πορείαν οὐκ ἂν χθονίαν καὶ τραχεῖαν πορεύεσθαι, ἀλλὰ λείαν τε καὶ οὐρανίαν.

Which one? If we stick strictly to the myth as presented, it would have to be one of the possibilities that have been selected before Odysseus's turn comes:[1]

(1) swan (κύκνος), chosen by a musical man who hates women (Orpheus: 620a3-6)

(2) nightingale (ἀηδών), chosen by a musical man who lost his voice and memory because he rivaled the Muses (Thamyros: 620a6-7; cf. *Iliad* 2. 594-600)

(3) lion, chosen by a disgruntled warrior (Aias: 620b1-3)

(4) eagle, chosen by a king turned misanthrope (Agamemnon: 620b3-5)

(5) athlete, chosen by an athlete from love of honors (Atalanta: 620b5-7)

(6) artisan woman, chosen by a boxer and builder (Epeios: 620b7-c2)

(7) ape, chosen by a laughmaker (Thersites: 620c2-3)

Since Socrates is the philosopher par excellence in the Platonic corpus, one could re-ask the question thus: "Which lifetime would Socrates choose?"

First, one should eliminate which ones he would not choose. He would not choose any of the lifetimes in which θυμός is a dominant factor. Those would be the lifetimes characterized by, or elected out of, anger and hatred and indignation and love of honors, namely lifetimes (1) (hatred), (2) (love of honors), (3) (anger: the lion is *the* thymoeidetic beast, cf. *Rep.* 9. 588b1-592b6, esp. 588d3, e6, 589b4, 590a9-b1, b9), (4) (hatred) (5) (love of honors), (7) (indignation: the ape is an auxiliary thymoeidetic beast, cf. *Rep.* 9. 590b9, *Iliad* 2. 212 ff.).

Therefore, the lifetime that Socrates would choose, if he could, would be (6) an artisan woman. From the points of view of both the lifetime elected and the elector, this choice is appropriate to the Socrates of the *Republic* for the following reasons: it is the lifetime of an artisan elected by an artisan;[2] the electing of a woman's lifetime assumes the equality of the sexes (i. e., man[-artisan] = woman[-artisan]); the elector is the progeny of comprehensiveness of vision;[3] and this is the only instance in which the electing soul elects a nature.[4]

Finally, after the preceding denigration of the heavenly way, Socrates restores the desirability of that way, but within very severe limits, the limits of healthy philosophizing: the heavenly path should be restricted to healthy philosophers alone, which means that only healthy philosophy is true justice.

When Er's account resumes, he indirectly reemphasizes what Socrates has said:

> For [he asserted them] to elect the many things in accordance with the habituation of their earlier lifetime.[5]

Their vision,[6] then, is dimmed by habituation, from which only the philosopher is free. The operation of vision dimmed by habituation can be seen throughout the electings.

1 Tyranny is excluded here because it is presented as the electing of a person without philosophy. The human lifetimes of unspecified type chosen by musical animals are also left out, because they are unspecified, and because Socrates is neither musical nor a beast. Only those that are specified are retained.

2 Epeios was the builder of the Trojan horse: *Odyssey* 8.493.

3 Epeios is the son of Panopeus, υἱὸς Πανοπῆος (*Iliad* 23. 665); cf. *Rep.* 10. 620c1, τοῦ Πανοπέως.

4 Cf. *Republic* 10. 620c2: φύσιν.

5 *Republic* 10. 620a2-3: κατὰ συνήθειαν γὰρ τοῦ προτέρου βίου τὰ πολλὰ αἱρεῖσθαι.

6 In the account of the soul's electings, the emphasis is on vision: cf. τὴν θέαν at 619e6; ἰδεῖν at 619e6, 620a3, 6, 7, c1, 2; ἰδοῦσαν at 620d1; κατιδοῦσαν at 620b6.

For example, with Orpheus (620a3-6), his misogyny eventuates in his unwillingness to be a human again, and his musical skill eventuates in his election of a musical beast, the swan (cf. *Phaedo* 84e3-85b7). In addition, the phrasing ψυχὴν . . . τήν ποτε 'Ορφέως γενομένην, "the soul which once came to be Orpheus" is striking for several reasons. First, it mirrors the continuity of the cycle: the soul was once Orpheus's soul, but before that, it was the soul of another, and another. In addition, it could mean 'the soul when it came to be Orpheus's,', i. e., when Orpheus made it his own, as it were, a sense that does not require transmigration. Furthermore, it could mean that it is not now Orpheus's soul, although its present possessor is unidentified,[1] which would suggest how strong the persistence of habituation is, namely that habituation is virtually ineradicable. Finally, the foolishness of the choice is suggested by the subsequent assertion that a swan and musical beasts generally elect the lifetimes of humans, which means that Orpheus's desire not to be human again will, in all likelihood, be thwarted.

For Aias (620b1-3), his misanthropy eventuates in his avoidance of being human, while his habituation as a warrior eventuates in his electing the lifetime of a lion, the lifetime of θυμός incarnate.

With Atalanta, an athlete elects to be an athlete.

With Epeios—as has been seen—an artisan elects to be an artisan.

Finally, with Thersites, his becoming an ape culminates the pattern of habituation-compelled metamorphoses, so much so that his passage into an ape is the only metamorphosis that is not called an electing: "and [he asserted himself] to see far among the last, the [soul] of laughter-making Thersites sinking into an ape."[2]

In the addendum (620d2-5), the emphasis that the choices are determined by habit, and not made freely, surfaces. It is asserted that the unjust changed into wild beasts, the just into tame beasts. The so-called freedom is merely an illusion.

The last to elect is Odysseus. Having toiled and freed himself from love of honor, he makes a considered choice of a lifetime that had been neglected by the others, i. e., the choice of a lifetime that οὖτις (no one) wants.[3] The toils that enable him to make such a choice must be the toils that he has experienced on the subearthly path,[4] rather than any experiences that he underwent while he was alive.[5] This would mean that the Odysseus who elects is an unjust person[6] who has been converted to justice.

The account opened with an incurably unjust person (Ardiaios), and it ends with a curably—indeed cured—unjust person. However, the cure eventuates in abstention from politics. This drives home the point that there can be no solution to the problem of human virtue and happiness on the political plane.

---

1 The situation would be this: {soul of Orpheus}→{soul of x}→{soul of swan}. However, this is merely a suggestive undertone.

2 *Republic* 10. 620c2-3: πόρρω δ' ἐν ὑστάτοις ἰδεῖν τὴν τοῦ γελωτοποιοῦ Θερσίτου πίθηκον ἐνδυομένην. This also stresses the diminishing degree of freedom of choice as one nears the end.

3 Cf. *Odyssey* 9. 366-367: "'No one' is my name; and my mother and father and all my other comrades call me 'No one.'" (Οὖτις ἐμοί γ' ὄνομα· Οὖτιν δέ με κικλήσκουσι / μήτηρ ἠδὲ πατὴρ ἠδ' ἄλλοι πάντες ἑταῖροι.)

4 Cf. τῶν . . . πόνων at 620c5 to πόνων at 619d3 and πεπονηκότας at 619d4.

5 If the reference were to be made strongly to the experiences of the *Odyssey*, the word would not have been οἱ πόνοι, but rather τὰ πάθη, as in the case of Agamemnon (620b5).

6 Cf. Graves, vol. 2, 161. o. ff., pp. 299-300.

VII. A NON-MYTH AND MYTHS: *Gorgias, Protagoras, Phaedo, Theaetetus*

Since the scope of the present work makes an exhaustive analysis of all Platonic myths unfeasible, a brief sketch of the remaining ones will have to suffice.

However, before giving this sketch, it is necessary to examine a non-myth that almost always is referred to as a myth,[1] namely the λόγος at the end of the *Gorgias* (522e1-527e7). The virtually universal tendency to call it a myth persists despite Socrats's explicit and emphatic statement that it is not a μῦθος but a λόγος (*Gorgias* 523a1-2; cited in Chapter II above). Socrates reiterates the statement at the end of the first section of his account (italics mine):

> These things, oh Callicles, are things which—having heard—I trust to be true; and on the basis of these *speeches, I reckon* something suchlike to come along.[2]

Why does Socrates make these remarks? This question must be faced, on the one hand, because Socrates casually calls those accounts myths to which the *Gorgias* account most frequently is compared, namely the accounts at the end of the *Republic* and toward the end of the *Phaedo*, and, on the other hand, because his designation of them as such is accepted just as casually by his interlocutors.

However, the *Gorgias* is different. How does it differ? In externals alone, it differs in that while the final underworld myths of the *Republic* and the *Phaedo* contain cosmographies, the final underworld λόγος of the *Gorgias* does not. However, the difference goes beyond externals. While the final myths of the *Republic* (as has been seen) and the *Phaedo* (as will be seen) are genetic accounts, the final λόγος of the *Gorgias* is a descriptive account. It is no less a descriptive account because it uses personages and trappings that one's prejudgments would lead one to label as mythical.

If it is a descriptive account, what does it describe? It describes—appropriately in the Platonic dialogue that deals most exclusively with forensic rhetoric[3]—the defects of forensic rhetoric and its practitioners.

---

1 Cf. Søren Kierkegaard, *The Concept of Irony*, tr. Lee M. Capel (NY, 1965), p. 130, note: "there are in Plato three νεκυιαν [*sic*], i. e., myths about the underworld: in the *Phaedo, Gorgias*, and *Republic*." It was reading this note that initially propelled me on the journey toward Platonic myth. Also cf. E. R. Dodds, note ad *Gorgias* 523a2-3: "the *Gorgias* myth is called a λόγος because it expresses in imaginative terms a 'truth of religion'": it is remarkable that Dodds's prejudgment is so deeply imbedded that he explains away its explicit designation as a λόγος, in order to declare it to be a myth. Further cf. Friedländer, pp. 181, 184-185, 186; Frutiger, pp. 29-30; Stewart, pp. 100-101; Robin, *Platon*, pp. 126, 142, 148; Voegelin, pp. 39 ff.

2 *Gorgias* 524a8-b2 (italics mine): Ταῦτ' ἔστιν, ὦ Καλλίκλεις, ἃ ἐγὼ ἀκηκοὼς πιστεύω ἀληθῆ εἶναι· καὶ ἐκ τούτων *τῶν λόγων* τοιόνδε τι *λογίζομαι* συμβαίνειν.

3 In the early stages of the dialogue, Gorgias is led gradually by Socrates to reduce his definition of rhetoric to forensic rhetoric: compare 452e1-4 to 454b5-6. In the former, Gorgias describes rhetoric as "persuading . . . by speeches judges in a court of justice and councillors in a council and assemblymen in an assembly and in every other convocation which becomes a political convocation" (Τὸ πείθειν . . . τοῖς λόγοις καὶ ἐν δικαστηρίῳ δικαστὰς καὶ ἐν βουλευτηρίῳ βουλευτὰς καὶ ἐν ἐκκλησίᾳ ἐκκλησιαστὰς καὶ ἐν ἄλλῳ συλλόγῳ παντί, ὅστις ἂν πολιτικὸς σύλλογος γίγνηται). In the latter, he describes it as "persuasion . . . in courts of justice and in the other mobs" (τῆς πειθοῦς . . . τῆς ἐν τοῖς δικαστηρίοις καὶ ἐν τοῖς ἄλλοις ὄχλοις).

In particular, the figures of Minos, Rhadamanthus, and Aiakos are representative of Gorgias, Polus, and Callicles. Gorgias and Polus are described as teacher and pupil in a way analogous to the way in which Minos and Rhadamanthus are described as teacher and pupil in the *Minos*.[1] Callicles is identified strongly with Alcibiades,[2] whose ancestry could be traced back to Aiakos (cf. *Alcibiades I* 121a1-2, b1-4).

Socrates enjoins upon them that they become dead to the allure of the body, which is the clothing of the soul,[3] so as to substitute for their own cosmetic rhetoric a true rhetoric spoken from soul to soul. Although Socrates's kolastic reprimand is through images, it is remarkably direct,[4] and it is not a myth.

However, there is a myth in the *Gorgias*, the myth of the soul as a sieve and wine jar:

> *Socrates.* But indeed also, according to what you speak, a lifetime is a formidable thing. For I would not wonder if Euripides speaks truly in these things, speaking—"and who has envisioned [i.e., understood] if living is dying, / and dying living?" And equally we are beingly dead; for already I at least also heard a certain one of the wise [speaking] how we now are dead and the body is our tomb/sign, and [how] this [part] of the soul, in which there are desires, chances to be such as to be persuaded repeatedly and to teeter upward and downward, and [how] then some elegant mythologizing man, perhaps some Sicilian or Italian, bringing this along [i.e., punning] by the name, named [it] "wine jar," because of its being both persuadable and persuasive, and [he named] the mindless "uninitiates," and this [part] of the soul of the mindless, [the part] in which there are desires, the uncontrollable and not watertight [part] of it, having likened it forth because of its unfillableness, [he spoke] how it would be a perforated wine jar. Indeed, this shows the contrary to [what] you [speak], oh Callicles, how of those in [the domain] of Hades—bespeaking indeed the unseeable—these uninitiates would be most wretched and would bear water into the perforated wine jar by another suchlike perforated sieve. And then, as the person speaking to me asserted, [the mythologizer] speaks the sieve to be the soul; and he likened forth the soul of the mindless—because it is perforated—to a sieve, since it is not capable of being watertight, because of untrustingness and forgetfulness. Likelily these

1 Cf. *Minos* 318c4-321d10, esp. 320b8-c3: "And Rhadamanthus was a good man; for he was educated by Minos. Yet he was educated not in the whole basilic [i.e., kingly] art, but in an underling to the basilic [art], as much as [is needed] to oversee in the courts of justice; whence also he was spoken to be a good judge." (Ῥαδάμανθυς δὲ ἀγαθὸς μὲν ἦν ἀνήρ· ἐπεπαίδευτο γὰρ ὑπὸ τοῦ Μίνω. ἐπεπαίδευτο μέντοι οὐχ ὅλην τὴν βασιλικὴν τέχνην, ἀλλ' ὑπηρεσίαν τῇ βασιλικῇ, ὅσον ἐπιστατεῖν ἐν τοῖς δικαστηρίοις· ὅθεν καὶ δικαστὴς ἀγαθὸς ἐλέχθη εἶναι.)

2 *Gorgias* 519a7-b2: "And perhaps they will take hold of you, if you do not take good hold of yourself [i. e., if you are not careful], and of my comrade Alcibiades, when they destroy both their originary things and the things which they have acquired, [although your both] are not causes of [their] bads, but perhaps co-causes." (σοῦ δὲ· ἴσως ἐπιλήψονται, ἐὰν μὴ εὐλαβῇ, καὶ τοῦ ἐμοῦ ἑταίρου Ἀλκιβιάδου, ὅταν καὶ τὰ ἀρχαῖα προσαπολλύωσι πρὸς οἷς ἐκτήσαντο, οὐκ αἰτίων ὄντων τῶν κακῶν ἀλλ' ἴσως συναιτίων.)

3 Cf. *Cratylus* 403b5-6: ἡ ψυχὴ γυμνὴ τοῦ σώματος.

4 Since Socrates speaking to Gorgias, Polus, and Callicles here is analogous to Zeus speaking to Minos, Rhadamanthus, and Aiakos, there is a suggestion that in the more august triad—the *Gorgias* is pervaded by triads—of Zeus, Poseidon, and Pluto, Socrates corresponds to Zeus. It is also possible to construe—this is highly speculative—Poseidon as Alcibiades (cf. Alcibiades's oath to Poseidon at *Symposium* 214d6) and Pluto as Homer (compare the description of Pluto as "a perfect sophist" at *Cratylus* 403e4 and its context to *Republic* 10. 596d1, where the pan-mimic is called "an altogether wondrous sophist" and its context, which focuses especially on Homer, e.g., at 595b10, 597e6, 598d7-8, 599b9-c1 ff., 600b6-c1, c2 ff., e4, 605c10-11, 606e1-607a3, d1). Also cf. *Iliad* 15. 184-199. Let me add that Diotima too is referred to as a perfect sophist (cf. *Symp.* 208c1). Since her name means 'honored by Zeus,' then insofar as Socrates is identified with Zeus, and insofar as Diotima is a poeticized philosopher (a Homerized philosopher), Socrates (Zeus) may be regarded as honoring Homer.

things are in some way under [the category of] eccentric things, yet it should clarify what I wish to show to you, if somehow I am able, [so as] to persuade [you] to change, to elect the lifetime which is orderly and sufficient by means of the things which are always present to it instead of the lifetime which is unfillable and uncontrollable. But do I persuade you in any way to change over to the orderly [as] being happier than the uncontrollable, or will you rather not change in any way, [even] if I mythologize many other suchlike things?

Callicles. You have spoken this [latter] more truly, oh Socrates [i. e., I shall not change].[1]

Socrates presents three accounts: the account of a poet (492e7-493a1); the account of a wise man (493a1-5); and the account—related by the wise man—of a mythologizer (493a5-b3, b7-c3). Socrates—a mythologizer too (493d3)—interrupts the third account (493b3-7) and appends his own conclusion (493c3-d3). The accounts of the poet and the wise man describe the human condition, while the mythologizer provides an account of the origin of the human condition in a bipartite account of soul.

The soul is a sieve, fundamentally a perforated receptacle. What does a sieve do? A sieve discriminates (separates and refines). Different souls have different capacities for discrimination. As children, humans all begin with a perforated sieve. The mindless remain in this condition, and hence, they are at the mercy of their desires, i. e., they are unsatisfied and unfilled. Presumably, as a soul becomes mind-full, it blocks the perforations: its capacity for fine discriminations increases, and it can be satisfied and filled.

However, for persons in whom this does not happen, the result is the uncontrollable desire that is the preferred auditor of rhetoric. As such, these persons may be either led astray (by sham rhetoric) or led aright (by true rhetoric). The uncontrollable desire for power is—in terms of the image—no different from the uncontrollable desire for punishment, a motif that resurfaces in the final λόγος.

Socrates tries here—as he will in the final λόγος too—to admonish Callicles and those who are like him, but Callicles is unfillable, as the sequel in which Socrates somewhat elaborates the myth indicates by reemphasizing Socrates's goal of persuading:

[*Socrates.*] Speaking these things, do I persuade you in any way to concede the orderly lifetime to be better than the uncontrollable [lifetime], or do I not persuade [you]?

Callicles. You do not persuade [me], oh Socrates.[2]

---

1 *Gorgias* 492e7-493d4: ΣΩ. Ἀλλὰ μὲν δὴ καὶ ὥς γε σὺ λέγεις δεινὸς ὁ βίος. οὐ γάρ τοι θαυμάζοιμ' ἂν εἰ Εὐριπίδης ἀληθῆ ἐν τοῖσδε λέγει, λέγων—"τίς δ' οἶδεν, εἰ τὸ ζῆν μέν ἐστι κατθανεῖν, / τὸ κατθανεῖν δὲ ζῆν;" καὶ ἡμεῖς τῷ ὄντι ἴσως τέθναμεν· ἤδη γάρ του ἔγωγε καὶ ἤκουσα τῶν σοφῶν ὡς νῦν ἡμεῖς τέθναμεν καὶ τὸ μὲν σῶμά ἐστιν ἡμῖν σῆμα, τῆς δὲ ψυχῆς τοῦτο ἐν ᾧ ἐπιθυμίαι εἰσὶ τυγχάνει ὂν οἷον ἀναπείθεσθαι καὶ μεταπίπτειν ἄνω κάτω, καὶ τοῦτο ἄρα τις μυθολογῶν κομψὸς ἀνήρ, ἴσως Σικελός τις ἢ Ἰταλικός, παράγων τῷ ὀνόματι διὰ τὸ πιθανόν τε καὶ πειστικὸν ὠνόμασε πίθον, τοὺς δὲ ἀνοήτους ἀμυήτους, τῶν δ' ἀνοήτων τοῦτο τῆς ψυχῆς οὗ αἱ ἐπιθυμίαι εἰσί, τὸ ἀκόλαστον αὐτοῦ καὶ οὐ στεγανόν, ὡς τετρημένος εἴη πίθος, διὰ τὴν ἀπληστίαν ἀπεικάσας. Τοὐναντίον δὴ οὗτος σοί, ὦ Καλλίκλεις, ἐνδείκνυται ὡς τῶν ἐν Ἅιδου—τὸ αἰδὲς δὴ λέγων—οὗτοι ἀθλιώτατοι ἂν εἶεν, οἱ ἀμύητοι, καὶ φοροῖεν εἰς τὸν τετρημένον πίθον ὕδωρ ἑτέρῳ τοιούτῳ τετρημένῳ κοσκίνῳ. τὸ δὲ κόσκινον ἄρα λέγει, ὡς ἔφη ὁ πρὸς ἐμὲ λέγων, τὴν ψυχὴν εἶναι· τὴν δὲ ψυχὴν κοσκίνῳ ἀπῄκασεν τὴν τῶν ἀνοήτων ὡς τετρημένην, ἅτε οὐ δυναμένην στέγειν δι' ἀπιστίανῴ τε καὶ λήθην, ταῦτ' ἐπιεκῶς μέν ἐστιν ὑπό τι ἄτοπα, δηλοῖ μὴν ὃ ἐγὼ βούλομαί σοι ἐνδειξάμενος, ἐάν πως οἷός τε ὦ, πεῖσαι μεταθέσθαι, ἀντὶ τοῦ ἀπλήστως καὶ ἀκολάστως ἔχοντος βίου τὸν κοσμίως καὶ τοῖς ἀεὶ παροῦσιν ἱκανῶς καὶ ἐξαρκούντως ἔχοντα βίον ἑλέσθαι. ἀλλὰ πότερον πείθω τί σε καὶ μετατίθεσθαι εὐδαιμονεστέρους εἶναι τοὺς κοσμίους τῶν ἀκολάστων, ἢ οὐδ' ἂν ἄλλα πολλὰ τοιαῦτα μυθολογῶ, οὐδέν τι μᾶλλον μεταθήσῃ; ΚΑΛ. Τοῦτ' ἀληθέστερον εἴρηκας, ὦ Σώκρατες.

2 494a3-6: [ΣΩ.] πείθω τί σε ταῦτα λέγων συγχωρῆσαι τὸν κόσμιον βίον τοῦ ἀκολάστου ἀμείνω εἶναι, ἢ οὐ πείθω; ΚΑΛ. Οὐ πείθεις, ὦ Σώκρατες.

Socrates fails in his use of the correct rhetoric, which—as mythology—is the gymnastic of the soul:

> *Socrates.* Indeed, bear with me, let me speak to you another image from the same gymnasium as the [image] now.[1]

The final λόγος, that calls for soul stripping by speaker and auditor, must be supplemented by the gymnastic art of mythmaking.

In the *Protagoras*, there is a clear case of a μῦθος (320c8-324d1) juxtaposed to a λόγος (324d1-328d4): an account of the genesis[2] of virtue precedes a descriptive account of virtue and its teachability in cities. Throughout his account, Protagoras[3] equates virtue with justice, which arose out of the interaction of nature (Epimetheus and the subterranean gods), art (Prometheus), and convention (Zeus and Hermes).[4]

According to Protagoras, nature (Epimetheus in particular) is both thoughtless and persuasive of its own thoughtfulness (320d3-8):

> And when [the gods] were about to lead [the mortal races] to light, they ordered Prometheus and Epimetheus[5] to adorn and to apportion powers to each severally as is proper. And Epimetheus asks Prometheus for he himself [to be the one] to apportion [the powers], "and when I have apportioned [them]," he asserted, "you inspect;"[6] and so [Epimetheus], having persuaded [Prometheus], apportions.[7]

Yet Epimetheus provides well for the beasts, balancing their powers appropriately, but using up all powers in the process. Thus, the only mortals to suffer from his (nature's) thoughtlessness are humans, who are left physically naked and defenseless (γυμνόν . . . καὶ ἄοπλον: 321c5-6). Yet they, at least implicitly, have speech,[8] although it must have been inarticulate speech, atomistic

---

1 493d5-6: ΣΩ. Φέρε δή, ἄλλην σοι εἰκόνα λέγω ἐκ τοῦ αὐτοῦ γυμνασίου τῇ νῦν.

2 Cf. αἰτία at *Protagoras* 323a4.

3 The name "Protagoras" means "first of the marketplace."

4 Cf. Leo Strauss, *Natural right and history* (Chicago, 1953), p. 117: "As regards the most famous sophist, Protagoras, Plato imputes to him a myth which adumbrates the conventionalist thesis. The myth of the *Protagoras* is based on the distinction between nature, art, and convention. Nature is represented by the subterraneous work of certain gods and by the work of Epimetheus. Epimetheus, the being in whom thought follows production, represents nature in the sense of materialism, according to which thought comes later than thoughtless bodies and their thoughtless motions. The subterraneous work of the gods is work without light, without understanding, and has therefore fundamentally the same meaning as the work of Epimetheus. Art is represented by Prometheus, by Prometheus' theft, by his rebellion against the will of the gods above. Convention is represented by Zeus' gift of justice to "all": that "gift" becomes effective only through the punitive activity of civil society, and its requirements are perfectly fulfilled by the mere semblance of justice."

5 The meanings of the names "Prometheus" and "Epimetheus" are respectively "prospect" and "retrospect." In this account, neither one of them lives up to his name very well.

6 The word here is "*ἐπί*σκεψαι," which has the same prepositional prefix as the name "*Epi*metheus," and hence signals a potentially dangerous role reversal.

7 ἐπειδὴ δ' ἄγειν αὐτὰ πρὸς φῶς ἔμελλον, προσέταξαν Προμηθεῖ καὶ Ἐπιμηθεῖ κοσμῆσαί τε καὶ νειμαῖ δυνάμεις ἑκάστοις ὡς πρέπει. Προμηθέα δὲ παραιτεῖται Ἐπιμηθεὺς αὐτὸς νειμαῖ, "Νείμαντος δέ μου," ἔφη, "ἐπίσκεψαι" καὶ οὕτω πείσας νέμει.

8 Cf. 321b6-c3, where humans are contrasted with τὰ ἄλογα (c1).

speech.[1] Only the intervention of art (Prometheus) can alter their situation, yet it can only alter it from hopeless to merely precarious, because although art enables them to provide for themselves, it still leaves them unable to defend themselves against the stronger beasts and against their own propensity to injure each other (322a8-b8). In other words, the natural condition of living things is a battle of every living thing against every living thing, but with no war, for there is no polemics without politics.[2]

Only convention (Zeus and Hermes) can secure humans by imposing cities and bonds of friendship on all humans and by making available to all—but not imposing on all[3]—modesty and justice (αἰδῶ τε καὶ δίκην: 322c2) in the form of law, convention, νόμος (cf. 322c1-d5, esp. d4). Without justice and moderation, there would be no cities, no political virtue; and without cities and political virtue, the human condition would be precarious at best (cf. 323a1-4). However, the justice that binds humans together and saves them from destruction is merely a pretense, a facade, that one must employ whether one possesses it or not (cf. 323a5-c2).

At this point in his μῦθος, Protagoras begins to move toward his λόγος that virtue is teachable.[4] However, since justice is nothing more than a conditioned set of behavioral responses, teaching is equated with punishment.[5] Instead, then, of the natural battle of all against all, politics produces a conventional punishment of all by all (cf. 324a2, 325a6-7). If this is what teaching virtue means, then clearly virtue is teachable, because virtue is an offer that no one can refuse, and cities are gangsterism incarnate.[6] This is Protagoras's μῦθος.

The λόγος that follows[7] is fundamentally a description of the punishing toward virtue that is the teaching of virtue.

---

1 Only later do they develop articulate speech: "then quickly [the human] articulated sound and names by art" (322a5-6).

2 Cf. 322b4-6: "and in regard to their war against the beasts, [the demiurgic art] was lacking—for they did not yet have the political art, of which war-skill is a part."

3 Cf. 322d4-5: anyone who is not capable of partaking of modesty and justice will be killed as a disease of the city.

4 Cf. λόγου at 324b1, and κατὰ τοῦτον τὸν λόγον at 324c3-4.

5 Cf. 323d1-2 (οὐδεὶς θυμοῦται ουδὲ νουθετεῖ ουδὲ διδάσκει ουδὲ κολάζει), e2-3 (οἵ τε θυμοὶ . . . καὶ αἱ κολάσεις καὶ αἱ νουθετήσεις), 324a2 (θυμοῦται καὶ νουθετεῖ), 3-4 (τὸ κολάζειν), 6 (κολάζει), b1 (τιμωρεῖται), 2 (κολάζειν), 3 (τιμωρεῖται), 5 (κολασθέντα), 7 (κολάζει), c1 (τιμωροῦνται), c1-2 (τιμωροῦνται . . . καὶ κολάζονται), 325a5-6 (διδάσκειν καὶ κολάζειν), 7 (κολαζόμενος), 8 (κολαζόμενος καὶ διδασκόμενος), c5-6 (καὶ διδάσκουσι καὶ νουθετοῦσιν), d5-7 (καὶ ἐὰν μὲν ἑκὼν πείθηται· εἰ δὲ μή, ὥσπερ ξύλον διαστρεφόμενον καὶ καμπτόμενον εὐθύνουσιν ἀπειλαῖς καὶ πληγαῖς), 8 (ἐντέλλονται), e5-326a1 (ἐκμανθάνειν ἀναγκάζουσιν . . . νουθετήσεις), b2 (ἀναγκάζουσιν), c1 (ἀναγκάζωνται), 7-8 (ἀναγκάζει μανθάνειν), d4 (ἀναγκάζουσι γράφειν), 7 (ἀναγκάζει), 8-e1 (κολάζει· καὶ ὄνομα τῇ κολάσει ταύτῃ . . . ὡς εὐθυνούσης τῆς δίκης, εὐθῦναι), 327a6-7 (καὶ ἐδίδασκε καὶ ἐπέπληττε), d2 (ἀνάγκη . . . ἀναγκάζουσα).

6 Cf. Mario Puzo, *The Godfather* (New York, 1969), Book I, p. 39: "'He's a businessman,' the Don said blandly, 'I'll make him an offer he can't refuse.'" The offer is described in detail on pp. 41-42, but its core is this (p. 42): "With no other witnesses Don Corleone persuaded Les Halley to sign a document . . . . Don Corleone did this by putting a pistol to [his] forehead . . . and assuring him with the utmost seriousness that either his signature or his brains would rest on that document in exactly one minute. Les Halley signed." Also cf. Book V, p. 294: "The other Dons in the room applauded and rose to shake hands with everybody in sight and to congratulate Don Corleone and Don Tattaglia on their new friendship. It was not perhaps the warmest friendship in the world, they would not send each other Christmas gift greetings, but they would not murder each other. That was friendship enough in this world, all that was needed." Finally, cf. Book VII, p. 385: "Michael [Corleone, the Don's son,] said quietly, "I'll make him an offer he can't refuse.'" This is a striking example of the Protagorean notion of justice and the teachability of virtue.

7 Cf. 324d2, 6-7: "there is indeed still a perplexity.... Indeed about this, oh Socrates, I shall say to you no longer a myth but a speech." (Ἔτι δὴ λοιπὴ ἀπορία ἐστίν,.... τουύτον δὴ πέρι, ὦ Σώκρατες, ουκετι μῦθόν σοι ἐρῶ ἀλλὰ λόγον.)

By the time that Protagoras concludes, "I have spoken to you, oh Socrates, the suchlike myth and speech, how virtue is teachable,"[1] one can see that his usage of the terms μῦθος and λόγος is consistent with the general Socratic-Platonic usage of those terms.[2]

In the *Phaedo*, there are two myths, the myth of the genesis of the concomitance of the pleasant and the painful (60b1-c7), which has been discussed already (see Chapter V), and the myth of the beautiful earth (110a8-111e5), which will be considered now.

First, one must see precisely what in Socrates's final account (*Phaedo* 107c1-114c6) is myth and what is not. Socrates is very careful in drawing the dividing lines, beginning with the remark prefatory to the account:

> Socrates asserted, "Well, oh Simmias, you bespeak well, not only these things, but also our first hypotheses, and [even] if they are trustable to you, nevertheless they must be considered more distinctly; and if you divide [i.e., analyse] them sufficiently, as I believe, you will follow the speech, in accordance with as much as it is possible especially for a human to follow; and if this very thing becomes distinct, you will seek in no way beyond it." "You speak truly," [Simmias] asserted.[3]

Socrates, then, will begin his further consideration with a λόγος,[4] a διαίρεσις,[5] a classificatory description of souls and of the forms of the true earth's places.

Having concluded this initial λόγος (at 110a7), Socrates remarks, and Simmias replies:

> "And those things in turn would appear still much more to differ from the things among us; for if indeed it is beautiful to speak a myth also, it is worth hearing, oh Simmias, of what sorts of things chance to be on the earth under the heaven." "But, oh Socrates," Simmias asserted, "we would hear this myth pleasantly."[6]

The myth consists only of the account of the things *on* the earth, not of the things under the earth. Since it is a myth, it is synagogic or synoptic, i. e., it presents "the earth itself [as seen] if someone should behold it from above,"[7] and it is genetic, causal.[8]

When Socrates has concluded the myth proper, which began and was governed throughout by λέγεται (110b5), he signals his return to a λόγος by shifting (at 111e5) from

---

1 *Protagoras* 328c3-4: Τοιοῦτόν σοι . . . ὦ Σώκρατες, ἐγὼ καὶ μῦθον καὶ λόγον εἴρηκα, ὡς διδακτὸν ἀρετή. Cf. Protagoras's opening remark in this section, 320c2-4: "'But, oh Socrates,' he asserted, 'I shall not begrudge [you this]; but am I, as an older person to younger persons, to show off to you either [by] speaking a myth or [by] narrating a speech?'" ('Αλλ', ὦ Σώκρατες, ἔφη, οὐ φθονήσω· ἀλλὰ πότερον ὑμῖν, ὡς πρεσβύτερος νεωτέροις, μῦθον λέγων ἐπιδείξω ἢ λόγῳ διεξελθών;)

2 It is perhaps to emphasize this consistency that there is, in this segment of the dialogue, an extraordinary density of the vocative ὦ Σώκρατες in Protagoras's account: cf. 320c2, 322d6, 323a4, 324c8, 325c4, 326e3.

3 *Phaedo* 107b4-10: Οὐ μόνον γ', ἔφη ὦ Σιμμία, ὁ Σωκράτης, ἀλλὰ ταῦτά τε εὖ λέγεις καὶ τάς γε ὑποθέσεις τὰς πρώτας, καὶ εἰ πισταὶ ὑμῖν εἰσιν, ὅμως ἐπισκεπτέαι σαφέστερον· καὶ ἐὰν αὐτὰς ἱκανῶς διέλητε, ὡς ἐγῷμαι, ἀκολουθήσετε τῷ λόγῳ, καθ' ὅσον δυνατὸν μάλιστ' ἀνθρώπῳ ἐπακολουθῆσαι· κἂν τοῦτο αὐτὸ σαφὲς γένηται, οὐδὲν ζητήσετε περαιτέρω. 'Αληθῆ, ἔφη, λέγεις.

4 Cf. τῷ λόγῳ at 107b7.

5 Cf. διέλητε at 107b7.

6 *Phaedo* 110a8-b4: ἐκεῖνα δὲ αὖ τῶν παρ' ἡμῖν πολὺ ἂν ἔτι πλέον φανείη διαφέρειν· εἰ γὰρ δὴ καὶ μῦθον λέγειν καλόν, ἄξιον ἀκοῦσαι, ὦ Σιμμία, οἷα τυγχάνει τὰ ἐπὶ τῆς γῆς ὑπὸ τῷ οὐρανῷ ὄντα. 'Αλλὰ μήν, ἔφη ὁ Σιμμίας, ὦ Σώκρατες, ἡμεῖς γε τούτου τοῦ μύθου ἡδέως ἂν ἀκούσαιμεν.

7 110b6: ἡ γῆ αὐτὴ . . . εἴ τις ἄνωθεν θεῷτο.

8 Cf. αἴτιον at 110e2.

indirect discourse to direct discourse. Although the λόγος that follows (111e5-114c6) promises itself as a causal account,[1] the promise is unfulfilled, and no cause ever is given for the continual oscillation. Instead, the account—as one expects for a λόγος—is a classificatory description of the subterranean streams (Ocean, Acheron, Pyriphlegethon, and Cocytus) and of human types (persons with neutral lives, incurable criminals, curable criminals, persons with holy lives, and philosophers).

Finally, although the *Phaedo* account cannot be examined in detail here, this much should be remarked: there is a descent from the heavenly account in the first λόγος, through the account of the earth's surface in the μῦθος, to the subterranean account in the second λόγος, a descent into body as such,[2] however beautified. Therefore, it stands as an encomium to body that should serve as a warning to those readers of the *Phaedo* who would take at face value the apparent denigration of the body that the *Phaedo*, perhaps more than any other Platonic dialogue, ostensibly presents.

In the *Theaetetus*, the Protagorean conventionalist epistemological position is presented in a way that is analogous to the presentation of the Protagorean conventionalist political position in the *Protagoras*, namely a Protagorean μῦθος (*Theaetetus* 155e3-164e4) followed by a Protagorean λόγος (*Theaetetus* 164e4-168c2). The μῦθος of which Protagoras is the father (cf. 164e2-3) describes the genesis of the Protagorean account of the sensing that is exact knowledge out of the Herakleitean ἀρχή (cf. 156a3, 152e2-4, 160d5-e2) that "the all was moving and nothing other besides this,"[3] i. e., it is about the generation of sensing out of motion (cf. 156a3-c3).

Since the μῦθος is, in a way, a genetic account of genesis, a generative account of generation, it not only contains, but also is imbedded among, discussions of generation: Socrates's earlier discussion of his midwifery (148e6-151d6; cf. 187a8-b2, 210b4-d1), the immediately preceding genealogy of philosophy and of Iris (155d2-5), the internal reference back to Socratic midwifery (157c7-d3), and the subsequent description of the account as a generated infant (160e5-161a4, 164d8-e6) and as susceptible of perishing (164d8-9; cf. *Republic* 10.621b8). So, not only does motion generate sensing, but also humans generate accounts, and indeed the whole question of generation, preservation, and perishing of λόγοι is an undertone of the *Theaetetus* from the introductory conversation between Euclides and Terpsion.[4]

The *Theaetetus*, then, is concerned with the generation of accounts (λόγοι),[5] i. e., it is as concerned with accounts as it is with the phenomena of which the accounts are accounts. Hence, it ends with a λόγος that is a classificatory διαίρεσις of Λόγος (206c7-210b3).

---

1 Cf. αἰτία at 112b1.

2 As Seth Benardete correctly remarked, in lectures that he gave at the Graduate Faculty of the New School in the Spring of 1971, and which I was fortunate enough to attend, the subterranean account uses language and describes functions as though the inside of the earth were the inside of the human body.

3 *Theaetetus* 156a5: τὸ πᾶν κίνησις ἦν καὶ ἄλλο παρὰ τοῦτο οὐδέν.

4 One could even conjecture that if there is any notion of the literal transmigration of souls in the Platonic corpus, it would be the transmigration not of the souls of humans or beasts but of account souls (cf. *Phaedo* 89a9-c4).

5 This also entails the problem of the security, as it were, of Λόγος and philosophy, a problem that is forced upon one by the setting of the dialogue. The brief description of Theaetetus's behavior at the battle of Corinth (*Theaetetus* 142a6-c1) is reminiscent of the lengthy description of Socrates's behavior at the battle of Potidaea (*Symposium* 219e5-221c1). Since Theaetetus and Socrates are look-alikes (*Theaet.* 143e7-144a1), and since Theaetetus is at least potentially philosophical (*Theaet.* 144a1-b7; cf. 155c8-d5), the question arises as to how Socrates could emerge from battle unscathed, while a potential alternative Socrates (i. e., Theaetetus) did not. It is not a question of courage. Wherein does the difference lie? Perhaps (cf. *Laws* 3. 690a1-c9, esp. c5-8) the difference is luck, namely Socrates was luckier than Theaetetus. The role of luck or chance points to the precariousness of the perpetuation of philosophy. In this regard, it seems no accident that in the frame dialogue, Theaetetus is presented at the point in his lifetime at which his luck has run out, while in the inner dialogue, Socrates is presented at the point in his lifetime at which his luck has run out (cf. *Apol. Socr.* 32d7-8).

Three types of Λόγος are divided off as different from one another. The first (206d1-e3) is that Λόγος means any verbal utterance: this is what one may call Λόγος in the broad or generic signification. The second (206e4-208b12) is the technical[1] division of something itself into its parts. The third (208b12-210a9) is the division by its differentness[2] of something from other things. The second and third together constitute λόγος in its narrow signification as a διαίρεσις.

The possibility of a λόγος as a genetic account is not even considered. However, this is intelligible in the light of the consistent usage throughout the Platonic corpus, by both Socrates and others, of the term μῦθος to designate a genetic account. Perhaps if Theaetetus (at 201c9-d1) had defined knowledge as ἡ μετὰ λόγου τε καὶ μύθου ἀληθὴς δόξα (true opinion with a speech and a myth), he would have been closer to the mark.

The *Statesman* myth already has been considered sufficiently for the purposes of this work (see Chapter V above).

As for the *Laws*, its length precludes a full examination, and it supports the conclusions reached thus far. Therefore, a brief survey of it will suffice.

In Book 1, through a brief reference to the myth of Ganymede that the Cretans feigned to justify their practice of homosexuality (636b7-e4), one sees that myths can be false in that persons may invent false genetic accounts in order, say, to make behavior respectable, to justify behavior, that otherwise would be neither respectable nor justifiable.

In the myth-image of animals as divine puppets or marionettes (1. 644b6-645c3), the strings are pleasure and pain, hope (= the opinion of pleasure to come) and fear (= the opinion of pain to come), reckoning or law (= the common opinion of a city), and so forth. In this image, the genesis is adumbrated of virtue (= law-abidingness) and badness out of the interaction of the strings as controlled, presumably by the puppeteer-lawgiver through education.

In Book 3 (682a1-683d5, but esp. 682a1-b1, e4-6, 683c8-d5), the account of the genesis (the founding) of cities is called a myth (cf. 4. 711d6-712a7, 712e9-714b2; 6. 751d7-752a4).

In Book 4 (719a7-720a2), a contrast is drawn between poets and law-positers. The origin of the contradictions or equivocations of poets is traced to their being inspired so as to be out of their senses. On the other hand, law-positers must be univocal.

One perhaps should add here that if this mythical account of poetry were a true account—and it is not—Plato's dialogues would have been produced when he was out of his senses (cf. 7. 811c6-10).

In Book 6 (771a5-d1, esp. c5-d1), it is asserted that the λόγος (division/classification/description/cuttings) of the apportionment of the city into twelve would require an extensive myth (πολὺς . . . μῦθος: c6-7), i. e., a genetic account, for the showing that these are true apportionments.

The myth governing marriage (6. 773b4-6 ff.) declares that the origin of marriage should be serviceability to the city, and not pleasure.

---

1 Cf. *Theaetetus* 207c2: τεχνικόν.

2 Cf. *Theaetetus* 209a5: διαφορότητος.

In Book 7, it is asserted that ancient myths have persuaded the Athenian Stranger that one could found or generate institutions based on equality of the sexes (804d6-805b4).

Then, as in the *Republic*, the program of education (*Laws* 7. 809b3-812b1) is called a myth (812a1-2)[1]

This concludes the survey of myth as such in the Platonic corpus. There is one type of account, however, that is left to consider, because it is connected, at least etymologically, with myth, namely the paramyth.

1 Also consider *Laws* 9. 865d3-866a2, 872c7-873b1; 11. 926e9-928a2; 12. 941b2-c4.

VIII. PARAMYTHS: *Republic, Laws, Phaedo*

In the course of cataloguing all the occurrences of the word μῦθος and its derivatives in the Platonic corpus, a hitherto unremarked category of account emerged with sufficient clarity as to merit separate consideration. That new category is the consolation or paramyth (ἡ παραμυθία or τὸ παραμύθιον).

What are the characteristics that the various interlocutors in the Platonic dialogues attribute to paramyths? They are persuasions[1] of citizens to tractability,[2] i. e., to lawful behavior.[3] In addition, they are playful[4] teaching devices that are rough but not harsh.[5] They tame the spirited,[6] make the reticent eager,[7] and are a form of speechmaking to crowds.[8] They can be compulsions from oneself to love and to praise one's own.[9] They are trusts (πίστεις)[10] that are preparations for initiation[11] and that bring ease.[12] Above all, although they are not incorrect,[13] nevertheless they are lies[14] that mitigate fears.[15]

What, then, is a paramyth? It is a preparatory, soothing, trustable lie.

The following accounts in the dialogues are paramyths:

(1) *Republic* 5. 450d3-451b1: the safe audience;
(2) *Republic* 5. 476e1-480a13: the "theory of looks;"
(3) *Republic* 6. 499d10-501a1: the philosopher's pursuit;
(4) *Laws* 10. 885a6 ff.: warnings against atheism;
(5) *Laws* 11. 922e1-923c4: the city is the true owner of all possessions.
(6) *Phaedo* 70a6-b4: persistence of soul after death;[16]
(7) *Phaedo* 82b10-84b8: separation of soul from senses;

Since this list contains assertions and accounts of things that would appear routinely in summaries of Platonic philosophy as among Plato's central teachings, and since these are described as lies (paramyths), one must seek precisely what the status of these accounts is.

1 Cf. *Euthydemus* 288b3-c5; *Critias* 108b8-d8; *Laws* 10. 899d4-6.
2 Cf. *Laws* 9. 880a6-b1 (= proemia to laws). Also cf. *Laws* 11. 922e1-923c4 (esp. 923c2-4), 928a1-2.
3 Cf. *Laws* 6. 773e5-774a3.
4 Cf. *Sophist* 224a1-5, 229e1 ff.; *Statesman* 267e7-268b7.
5 Cf. *Sophist* 224a1-5, 229e1 ff..
6 Cf. *Republic* 4. 441e4-442a7.
7 Cf. *Laws* 2. 666a2-3 (= wine) and context.
8 Cf. *Euthydemus* 289d8-290a6.
9 Cf. *Protagoras* 346b1-5; also cf. 361a3 ff.
10 Cf. *Phaedo* 70a6-b4, esp. πίστεως at 70b2.
11 Cf. *Euthydemus* 277d1-8.
12 Cf. *Republic* 1. 329d7-e6 (= wealth); *Critias* 115a3-b6; *Menexenus* 247c5-7 (cf. 236e1-237a4); *Laws* 1.625b1-7, 632d9-633a4, 4. 704d3-705a8, 9. 853e10-854b1.
13 Cf. *Epinomis* 976a5-b1 and context.
14 Cf. *Laws* 10. 885a6 ff. (cf. 888c6-7).
15 Cf. *Epistles* 7. 329d1-e1 (cf. 345e4-5).
16 Socrates's response to Cebes here (*Phaedo* 70b5-7) indicates that a paramyth is not a myth.

In seeking this, two factors must be considered with respect to the paramyth. First, their being lies does not make them simply or necessarily incorrect: they may be lies and still be correct in some sense. Second, the meaning of παρά in composition[1] is 'by' (as in 'byproduct,' e.g., πάρεργον) or 'beside' (as in 'alongside,' e.g., πάρειμι) or 'beyond' (as in 'overstep,' e.g., παραβαίνω) or 'aside' (as in 'turn-aside,' e.g., παρατρέπω) or 'over' (as in 'overlook,' e.g., παροράω).

If one puts all this together, one can see that the Platonic usage of paramyth is the closest to what we ordinarily mean by our usage of myth as an account that lacks evidence because it deals with things in regard to which knowledge is either impossible or virtually impossible to achieve. In other words, it is an account that lacks evidence because it deals with things that are somehow outside or beyond rational certitude or one's capacity for rational certitude, and which hence must be adumbrated through an imaginative, largely hypothetical account.

Since the designation of an account as a paramyth depends upon its addressee, that which is a paramyth for the many (e.g., some of the proemia to the laws in the *Laws*) may be a μῦθος or a λόγος for the philosopher, although that which is a paramyth for the philosopher would be a paramyth for everyone.

For example, the account of the philosopher's pursuit (*Rep.* 6. 499d10-501a1) is a paramyth for the many as an antidote to their antipathy toward philosophy and philosophers,[2] an antipathy grounded in the many's perception that philosophy is destructive of the city, destructive of demotic virtue (cf. *Rep.* 6. 497d6-498c4). That antidote consists in showing them how philosophers may become craftspersons of demotic virtue.[3]

The paramyth about the safe audience (*Rep.* 5. 450d3-451b1) shows how different persons need different paramyths. When Glaucon directly consoles Socrates, he describes the safe audience by inversion as discerning and trustable and benevolent,[4] but when Socrates reformulates the consolation, so that it truly does console him, he describes the safe audience as composed of prudent friends.[5] Whereas for Glaucon, they need not be friends, for Socrates, they need not be benevolent.

The "theory of looks" is first presented in the *Republic* as an antidote, for the person of opinion without knowledge, to an antipathy toward philosophers. It is a drug that must be administered to the person without revealing the person's unhealthiness:

> "Therefore, what if this person, whom we assert to opine but not to know, be harsh to us and dispute as though we do not speak truly? Will we have something to console and gently persuade him, [while we are] hiding [from him] that he is not healthy?" "It is indeed obligatory," he [i. e.,

---

1 See Smyth 1692. 4.

2 Cf. *Republic* 6. 500d10-e5: "'But if indeed the many sense that we speak truly about it, will they indeed be harsh to the philosophers, and will they distrust us when we speak how a city would not ever otherwise be happy, unless the painters using the divine paradigm should thoroughly sketch it?' 'They will not be harsh,' he [i. e., Adeimantus] said, 'if indeed they sense [this].'" ('Αλλ' ἐὰν δὴ αἴσθωνται οἱ πολλοὶ ὅτι ἀληθῆ περὶ αὐτοῦ λέγομεν, χαλεπανοῦσι δὴ τοῖς φιλοσόφοις καὶ ἀπιστήσουσιν ἡμῖν λέγουσιν ὡς οὐκ ἄν ποτε ἄλλως εὐδαιμονήσειε πόλις, εἰ μὴ αὐτὴν διαγράψειαν οἱ τῷ θείῳ παραδείγματι χρώμενοι ζωγράφοι; Οὐ χαλεπανοῦσιν, ἦ δ' ὅς, ἐάνπερ αἴσθωνται.)

3 Cf. *Republic* 6. 500d4-9: "'Therefore,' I spoke, 'if some compulsion comes to be for him to be concerned to put the things which he sees there into the habits of humans both privately and publicly, and to fashion not only himself, then do you believe he will come to be a bad craftsperson of moderation and justice and public virtue all together?' 'Least so,' he [i. e., Adeimantus] said." ("Αν οὖν τις, εἶπον, αὐτῷ ἀνάγκη γένηται ἃ ἐκεῖ ὁρᾷ μελετῆσαι εἰς ἀνθρώπων ἤθη καὶ ἰδίᾳ καὶ δημοσίᾳ τιθέναι καὶ μὴ μόνον ἑαυτὸν πλάττειν, ἆρα κακὸν δημιουργὸν αὐτὸν οἴει γενήσεσθαι σωφροσύνης τε καὶ δικαιοσύνης καὶ συμπάσης τῆς δημοτικῆς ἀρετῆς; Ἥκιστά γε, ἦ δ' ὅς.)

4 Cf. 6. 450d3-4: οὔτε . . . ἀγνώμονες οὔτε ἄπιστοι οὔτε δύσνοι.

5 Cf. 6. 450d10: φρονίμοις τε καὶ φίλοις.

> Glaucon] asserted. "Indeed, come, consider what we shall say to him. Or do you wish us thus to inquire from him, [we] speaking how if he has envisioned [i.e., understood] something, there is no envy of him, but we would be pleased to see [him] having envisioned [i.e., understood] something. But [we would say,] 'Speak this to us.'"[1]

In the sense of paramyth as it is developed briefly here, a Platonic dialogue is, in one sense, a paramyth, namely a gently persuasive and salutary dialogic lie that prepares the transformation from the disease of opinion to the health of knowledge, without revealing that opinion is a disease.

The paramythic proemia of the *Laws* function analogously, except that their preparatory persuasion is not so gentle and is meant to effect a transformation from one level of opinion to the level of opinion that the founded colony requires. These proemia too are antidotes, on the one hand, against atheism and, on the other, against private accumulation.

Finally, the paramyths of the *Phaedo* are antidotes to the fear of death, although the death whose fear they counter is not the death with which the philosopher would be concerned. The philosopher is concerned, not with the death of the body or soul in any personal sense, but rather with the death of the Λόγος:

> *Phaedo*. I shall say. For I chanced to be sitting beside the couch on a certain low stool on his right, and he was much loftier than I. Therefore, having stroked my head and having squeezed the hairs on my neck—for he was accustomed, whenever he should chance to, to play with my hairs—he asserted, "Indeed, perhaps tomorrow, oh Phaedo, you may cut off these beautiful locks." "It is likely, oh Socrates," I said. "Not if you are persuaded by me." "But what?", I said. "Today," he asserted, "both I [may cut off] my [hairs] and you these, if then our speech comes to its end [i.e., dies], and we are not capable of reviving it. And I then, if I would swear to do as the Argives [do], [namely] not to let my hair grow earlier than until, rebattling, I shall be victorious over Simmias's and Cebes's speech."[2]

It is the Λόγος that must not come to an end, and the death to be feared is the death of the Λόγος. In this sense too, the Platonic dialogues serve as a paramythic antidote to the fear that the Λόγος, and philosophy with it, will die. Writing, then, does generate immortality, not primarily one's own immortality, but rather the immortality of Λόγος.

---

1 *Republic* 5. 476d8-e7: Τί οὖν ἐὰν ἡμῖν χαλεπαίνῃ οὗτος, ὅν φαμεν δοξάζειν ἀλλ' οὐ γιγνώσκειν, καὶ ἀμφισβητῇ ὡς οὐκ ἀληθῆ λέγομεν; ἕξομεν τι παραμυθεῖσθαι αὐτὸν καὶ πείθεν ἠρέμα, ἐπικρυπτόμενοι ὅτι οὐχ ὑγιαίνει; Δεῖ γέ τοι δή, ἔφη. Ἴθι δή, σκόπει τί ἐροῦμεν πρὸς αὐτόν. ἢ βούλει ὧδε πυνθανώμεθα παρ' αὐτοῦ, λέγοντες ὡς εἴ τι οἶδεν οὐδεὶς αὐτῷ φθόνος, ἀλλ' ἄσμενοι ἂν ἴδοιμεν εἰδότα τι. ἀλλ' ἡμῖν εἰπὲ τόδε.

2 *Phaedo* 89a9-c4: ΦΑΙΔ. Ἐγὼ ἐρῶ. ἔτυχον γὰρ ἐν δεξιᾷ αὐτοῦ καθήμενος παρὰ τὴν κλίνην ἐπὶ χαμαιζήλου τινός, ὁ δὲ ἐπὶ πολὺ ὑψηλοτέρου ἢ ἐγώ. καταψήσας οὖν μου τὴν κεπαλὴν καὶ συμπιέσας τὰς ἐπὶ τῷ αὐχένι τρίχας—εἰώθει γάρ, ὁπότε τύχοι, παίζειν μου εἰς τὰς τρίχας—Αὔριον δή, ἔφη, ἴσως, ὦ Φαίδων, τὰς καλὰς ταύτας κόμας ἀποκερῇ. Ἔοικεν, ἦν δ' ἐγώ, ὦ Σώκρατες. Οὔκ, ἄν γε ἐμοὶ πείθῃ. Ἀλλὰ τί; ἦν δ' ἐγώ. Τήμερον, ἔφη, κἀγὼ τὰς ἐμὰς καὶ σὺ ταύτας, ἐάνπερ γε ἡμῖν ὁ λόγος τελευτήσῃ καὶ μὴ δυνώμεθα αὐτὸν ἀναβιώσασθαι. καὶ ἔγωγ' ἄν, εἰ σὺ εἴην καί με διαφεύγοι ὁ λόγος, ἔνορκον ἂν ποιησαίμην ὥσπερ Ἀργεῖοι, μὴ πρότερον κομήσειν, πρὶν ἂν νικήσω ἀναμαχόμενος τὸν Σιμμίου τε καὶ Κέβητος λόγον.

> Finally: it was stated at the outset, that this system would not be here, and at once, perfected. You cannot but plainly see that I have kept my word. But I now leave my cetological System unfinished, even as the great Cathedral of Cologne was left, with the crane still standing upon the top of the uncompleted tower . . . . This whole book is but a draught—nay, but the draught of a draught. Oh, Time, Strength, Cash, and Patience!
>
> —Herman Melville, *Moby Dick* (NY, Norton Crit. Ed., 1967), ch. 32, pp. 127-128.

IX. CONCLUSION

In the enterprise of understanding Plato's writings in themselves, one can never claim—to use Coleridge's phrase—that one understands Plato's ignorance:

> In the perusal of philosophical works I have been greatly benefited by a resolve, which, in the antithetic form and with the allowed quaintness of an adage or maxim, I have been accustomed to word thus: *Until you understand a writer's ignorance, presume yourself ignorant of his understanding* . . . . I have now before me a treatise of a religious fanatic, full of dreams and supernatural experiences. I see clearly the writer's grounds, and their hollowness. I have a complete insight into the causes, which through the medium of his body has acted on his mind; and by application of received and ascertained laws I can satisfactorily explain to my own reason all the strange incidents, which the writer records of himself . . . . *I understand his ignorance.*
>
> On the other hand, I have been re-perusing with the best energies of my mind the *Timaeus* of Plato. Whatever I comprehend impresses me with a reverential sense of the author's genius; but there is a considerable portion of the work, to which I can attach no consistent meaning. In other treatises of the same philosopher, . . . I have been delighted with the masterly good sense, with the perspicuity of the language, and the aptness of the inductions. I recollect likewise that numerous passages in this author, which I thoroughly comprehend, were formerly no less unintelligible to me, than the passages now in question. It would, I am aware, be quite fashionable to dismiss them at once as Platonic jargon. But this I cannot do with satisfaction to my own mind, because I have sought in vain for causes adequate to the solution of the assumed inconsistency. I have no insight into the possibility of a man so eminently wise, using words with such half-meanings to himself as must perforce pass into no-meaning to his readers. When in addition to the motives thus suggested by my own reason, I bring into distinct remembrance the number and the series of great men, who after long and zealous study of these works had joined in honouring the name of Plato with epithets, that almost transcend humanity, I feel, that a contemptuous verdict on my part might argue

> want of modesty, but would hardly be received by the judicious, as evidence of superior penetration. Therefore, utterly baffled in all my attempts to understand the ignorance of Plato, *I conclude myself ignorant of his understanding.*[1]

Coleridge was by no means a Platonist. The example of Plato here is meant to represent how to study all writers who are one's superior in understanding.

How, then, should one study Plato?

One must begin by recognizing the most massive datum that the Platonic corpus presents, namely that Plato wrote dialogues virtually exclusively. In addition, Plato himself is not an interlocutor in any of his own dialogues.[2] Since Plato is acknowledged to be a philosopher, and since that acknowledgement is based on the dialogues, one cannot dismiss the dialogic character of the Platonic writings as somehow extraneous to the philosophical content that it adumbrates. Instead, one must regard that dialogic character to be as intrinsically a part of the philosophical import of the dialogues as any other aspect of them. In other words, the Platonic dialogues are philosophical dramas, and they are as truly dramatic as they are truly philosophical.

How, then, does this affect the reading of Plato? In the first place, Plato does not speak, but his interlocutors speak. In the second place, insofar as his interlocutors are fully drawn dramatic personages, what they speak is accompanied by what they do (which would include what they neither speak nor do), and what they speak and do (together with what they neither speak nor do) is a reflection of what and who they are. This totality of their intradialogic being, speaking, and doing for themselves is the totality of their speaking to the dialogue's auditors. One's speaking to the dialogue, on the basis of which one's speaking about (commenting upon) the dialogue is formulated, must be addressed to the totality of the dialogue's speaking to one. What Plato means by the totality of the dialogue's speaking to its auditors must be discerned, not only through that speaking to the auditors, but also through the dialogue outside the dialogue in which the auditors themselves are the expected interlocutors.

Perhaps it is this dialogue outside the dialogue that is the "longer road" to the traveling of which the Platonic Socrates sometimes invites his intradialogic interlocutors (cf. *Republic* 4. 435d3; 6. 504b1-4, c9-d3), a traveling which—since it is never performed inradialogically—must be performed extradialogically by the auditors along the lines suggested by the intradialogic conversation which the auditors have experienced.

Although these intradialogic lines are drawn clearly, they are not drawn univocally. Hence, they must be studied with an eye as much to their suggestiveness as to their literal sense.[3] This is what I have tried to do in my attempt to explore the kinds of accounts that one finds in the Platonic dialogues.

---

1 Samuel Taylor Coleridge, *Biographia Literaria* (1817), chapter 12.

2 He does appear once as a spectator: cf. *Apol. Socr.* 34a1, 38b6. Also cf. note 1 to Chapter III above.

3 Cf. St. Thomas Aquinas, *In Aristotelis librum De anima commentarium*, Liber I, lectio VIII, section 107: "Whereas it must be noted, in that more when [Aristotle] reproves the opinions of Plato, he does not reprove them so much toward the intention of Plato, but [rather he reproves them] so much toward the sound of his words [i. e., with respect to the surface meaning of his words]. In-that he does thereto, wherefore Plato has had a bad [i.e., deceptive] manner of teaching. For he says all-things figuratively, and he teaches through symbols: intending through the words [something] other than [what] the words themselves sound [i. e., other than what the words mean on the surface]; thus-as [i.e., for example] in-that he has said the soul to be a circle. And thereto, lest someone fall into error on account of the words themselves [i.e., lest someone fall into the error of taking them in their literal signification], Aristotle disputes against him [i.e., against Plato] [only] as-much [as] toward that which his words sound [i. e., that which his words mean on the surface]." (Ubi notandum est, quod plerumque quando reprobat opiniones Platonis, non reprobat eas quantum ad intentionem Platonis, sed quantum ad sonum verborum ejus. Quod ideo facit, quia Plato habuit malum modum docendi. Omnia enim figurate dicit, et per symbola docet: intendens aliud per verba, quam sonent ipsa verba; sicut quod dixit animam esse circulum. Et ideo ne aliquis propter ipsa verba incidat in errorem, Aristoteles disputat contra eum quantum ad id quod verba ejus sonant.)

The result of that exploration was to delineate four types of Λόγος in the broad sense:

> (1) λόγος in the narrow sense: a descriptive and/or classificatory and/or diairetic account;
>
> (2) μῦθος: a genetic and/or originary and/or synagogic account;
>
> (3) ἀκοή: a tale or story, either loosely 'historical' in our sense or fictional;
>
> (4) παραμυθία/παραμύθιον: a consolation, a myth in our sense of an imaginative account of what is outside or beyond one's capacity for rational certitude.

Of these four accounts, none is simply incorrect, although the fourth is false, while the first three may be either true or false.

Therefore, in the case of a λόγος or a μῦθος or an ἀκοή, the designation of the kind of account that it is does not tautologically bring along with it any determination as to its truth status. Its truth status can be determined only by studying each account itself in its context. However, one can say generally that in the Platonic corpus, there are neither any simply true nor any simply false accounts. There are only accounts that are more or less true, which means also more or less false. In addition, as accounts, they are all to be treated the same: the methodology of reading is no different for a μῦθος from what it is for a λόγος.

Finally, although this inquiry began with a survey of the lexicon senses of μῦθος and λόγος, on the basis of that inquiry, one can say that the lexicon needs revision. In particular, the assumed separation out of the meanings of λόγος and μῦθος into respectively true account and false account is not as clearcut as it seems. Rather, it may stem in many—if not in all—instances from a modern and contemporary prejudgment that such a separation out occurred, rather than from a close scrutiny of each term in its organic and contextual determination.

Therefore, what I have tried to establish with respect to Platonic usage should suggest that a similar attempt at reevaluating the respective meanings of λόγος and μῦθος in all the classical Greek authors—from Homer's use of μῦθος for Λόγος to Aristotle's use of μῦθος for the soul of a tragedy[1]—needs to be undertaken. In such an undertaking, this book is intended as a first step, as a program for a project, rather than as a completed edifice.

1 Aristotle, *Poetics* 6. 1450b1: "Therefore, the myth is the ruling-beginning and, as it were, the soul of the tragedy" (ἀρχὴ μὲν οὖν καὶ οἷον ψυχὴ ὁ μῦθος τῆς τραγῳδίας). The universal contemporary tendency to translate μῦθος in the *Poetics* by our word "plot" is very misleading (as is, I might add, the tendency to translate ἀρχή sometimes by 'principle' instead of translating it more neutrally as 'ruling-beginning' or 'origination'). The reason that μῦθος is so translated in Aristotle must be that his usage of the term—at least in the *Poetics*—is so contrary to our assumptions about its meaning that there seems to be no way in English to render it in the usual way. This is typical of the translation of μῦθος in many scattered places in both Plato and Aristotle, but the *Poetics* is a particularly dense example. However, if the rendering of the term μῦθος as a genetic or originary account is accurate, the difficulty, at least with regard to meaning, dissipates. Aristotle means by it something like the unified synoptic whole (cf. τὸ ἓν καὶ τὸ ὅλον at *Poetics* 7. 1451a1-2 et passim, and εὐσύνοπτον at 7. 1451a4) that is the origin of, or out of which are generated, the disparate speakings and actings of the unfolding drama. This is quite consistent with the meaning of μῦθος as one finds it in the Platonic corpus.

Appendix I

ΜΥΘΟΣ AND ITS DERIVATIVES IN THE PLATONIC CORPUS

This list was compiled on the basis of Ast's *Lexicon Platonicum*, which purported to be a complete concordance of the Platonic writings. However, it was not exhaustive.

I have supplemented it with Des Places's *Lexique de langue philosophique et religieuse de Platon*, which forms tome 14 of the so-called Budé edition of the *Oeuvres complètes* of Plato. However, this is rather a dictionary than a concordance, giving only as many citations as are necessary to illustrate the various meanings of a word. Nonetheless, it occasionally cites something that is missing from Ast.

Still, even the two together are not exhaustive. Therefore, I have had to supplement them by a line-by-line reading of the entire Platonic corpus, including the *Definitiones* and *Spuria*. To the best of my ability, the following list is exhaustive.

All references are to the Oxford Classical Text of the *Opera Omnia*, ed. J. Burnet, 5 volumes. The references, therefore, are presented in each group in the order in which the OCT presents the works.

[Note: In the lists that follow,
* = cited by Ast alone;
** = cited by Des Places alone;
*** = cited by both.]

μῦθος, ὁ

Theaetetus	156c4	ὁ μῦθος *
	164d9	μῦθος ***
Philebus	14a4	μῦθος **
Phaedrus	241e8	ὁ μῦθος
Gorgias	527a5	μῦθος . . . ὥσπερ γραὸς ***
Republic	10. 621b8	μῦθος ἐσώθη **
Laws	1. 645b1	ὁ μῦθος ἀρετῆς **
	4. 712a4	μῦθός τις ***
	4. 719c1	Παλαιὸς μῦθος ***
	6. 771c7	μῦθος ***
	6. 773b4	μῦθος γάμου ***
	7. 812a2	μῦθος ***
	9. 872c7-e1	ὁ. . . μῦθος ἢ λόγος ***
Epinomis	975a6	ὁ μῦθος ***
Epistles	12. 359d5	ὁ παραδεδομένος μῦθος *
Phaedo	110b4	τοῦ μύθου
Theaetetus	164e3	μύθου *
Statesman	268d9	μεγάλου μύθου
	274e1	τοῦ μύθου **
	277b5	θαυμαστὸν ὄγκον . . . τοῦ μύθου **
Phaedrus	237a9	τοῦ μύθου *
	253c7	τοῦ μύθου
Republic	3. 415a2	τοῦ μύθου *
Timaeus	22c7	μύθου ***
Laws	1. 636d4-5	τοῦ μύθου
	3. 682a8	μύθου
	3. 683d3	τοῦ μύθου
Statesman	268e4	τῷ μύθῳ *
	277b7	τῷ μύθῳ
Protagoras	361d2	ἐν τῷ μύθῳ
Republic	2. 376d9	ὥσπερ ἐν μύθῳ μυθολογοῦντες
	3. 390d4	μύθῳ (= *Odyssey* 20. 17)
	8. 565d6	τῷ μύθῳ
Timaeus	26c8	ὡς ἐν μύθῳ ***
	69b1	τῷ μύθῳ *
Laws	4. 713a6	μύθῳ
	8. 841c6	ἐν μύθῳ **
	11. 927c7-8	τῷ πρὸ τοῦ νόμου μύθῳ ***
	12. 944a2	μύθῳ ***
Epistles	7. 344d3	τῷ μύθῳ **
Phaedo	60c2	μῦθον [κατὰ Αἴσωπον] ***
	110b1	μῦθον
Sophist	242c8	Μῦθόν τινα *
Statesman	272d5	τὸν μῦθον
Alcibiades I	123a1	κατὰ τὸν Αἰσώπου μῦθον ***

Protagoras	320c3	μῦθον λέγων . . . ἢ λόγῳ διεξελθών ***
	320c7	μῦθον
	324d6	οὐκέτι μῦθον . . . ἀλλὰ λόγον ***
	328c3	καὶ μῦθον καὶ λόγον **
Gorgias	523a2	μῦθον . . . λόγον ***
Hippias Minor	365a2	τὸν μῦθον (= *Iliad* 9. 309)
Republic	2. 377c1	καλὸν μῦθον
	3. 415c7	τὸν μῦθον
Timaeus	26e4	πλασθέντα μῦθον ***
	29d2	τὸν εἰκότα μῦθον ***
	68d2	τὸν εἰκότα μῦθον *
Minos	318d11	μῦθον . . . τραγικόν
Laws	1. 636c7	τὸν περὶ Γανυμήδη μῦθον *
	1. 636d2-3	τὸν μῦθον . . . κατὰ τοῦ Διός
	4. 713b8-c1	τὸν . . . μῦθον
	6. 752a2	τὸν μῦθον ἀκέφαλον ***
Epinomis	980a5	κατὰ τὸν ἡμέτερον μῦθον ***
Demodocus	383c1	μῦθον
Cratylus	408c8	οἱ μυθοί τε καὶ τὰ ψεύδη
Republic	1. 330d7	οἱ . . . μυθοί περὶ τῶν ἐν Ἅιδου *
	2. 378e5	οἱ μυθοί
Republic	3. 386b8-9	παίδων . . . μύθων
Timaeus	23b5	τῶν εἰκότων μύθων *
	59c6	τῶν μύθων ***
Laws	7. 790c3	τῶν περὶ τὰ σώματα μύθων ***
	9. 865d5	τῶν ἀρχαίων μύθων ***
Sophist	242d6	τοῖς μύθοις
Meno	96a1	μύθοισι σαόφροσιν (= Theognis)
Republic	2.377a6	μύθοις πρὸς τὰ παιδία ἢ γυμνασίοις *
	2. 377c4	πλάττειν τὰς ψυχὰς . . .τοῖς μύθοις
	2. 377c7	Ἐν τοῖς μείζουσιν . . . μύθοις
Laws	2. 664a6	ᾠδαῖς καὶ μύθοις καὶ λόγοις ***
	8. 840c1	ἐν μύθοις τε καὶ ἐν ῥήμασιν **
	887d2	τοῖς μύθοις *
Phaedo	61b4	ποιεῖν ἀλλ' οὐ λόγους ***
	61b6	μύθους [τοῦ Αἰσώπου]
Statesman	272c7	διελέγοντο πρὸς ἀλλήλους καὶ τὰ θηρία μύθους *
Republic	1. 350e3	ὥσπερ ταῖς γραυσὶν ταῖς τοὺς μύθους λεγούσαις ***
	2. 377a4	τοῖς παιδίοις μύθους λέγομεν
	2. 377b6	μύθους πλασθέντας
	2. 377d5	μύθους . . . ψευδεῖς
	2. 379a4	μύθους
	2. 381e3	τοὺς μύθους
	2. 391e12	τοὺς τοιούτους μύθους
	2. 398b7	λόγους τε καὶ μύθους ***
Laws	7. 804e4	μύθους παλαιοὺς *

μυθολόγημα, τό

Phaedrus	229c5	σὺ τοῦτο τὸ μυθολόγημα πείθη ἀληθὲς εἶναι; ***
Laws	2. 663e5	τὸ μὲν τοῦ Σιδωνίου μυθολόγημα ***

μυθικός, -ή, -όν

Phaedrus	265c1	μυθικόν τινα ὕμνον ***

μυθώδης, ὁ or ἡ

Republic	7. 522a7	μυθώδεις ***

μυθολογέω

Phaedo	61e2	διασκοπεῖν τε καὶ μυθολογεῖν ***
Phaedrus	276e3	μυθολογοῦντα *
Gorgias	493a5	τις μυθολογῶν κομψὸς ἀνήρ ***
	493d3	μυθολογῶ ***
Hippias Maior	286a2	χρῶνται ὥσπερ ταῖς πρεσβύτισιν οἱ παῖδες πρὸς τὸ ἡδέως μυθολογῆσαι ***
Republic	2. 359d6	μυθολογοῦσιν ***
	2. 376d9	ὥσπερ ἐν μύθῳ μυθολογοῦντες ***
	2. 378c4	μυθολογητέον ***
	2. 378e3	ὅτι κάλλιστα μεμυθολογημένα ***
	2. 379a2	δεῖ μυθολογεῖν τοὺς ποιητάς ***
	2. 380c2	μυθολογοῦντα ***
	2. 392b6	ᾄδειν τε καὶ μυθολογεῖν ***
	3. 415a3	μυθολογοῦντες ***
	6. 501e4	ἡ πολιτεία ἣν μυθολογοῦμεν ***
	9. 588c2	οἷαι μυθολογοῦνται παλαιαὶ γενέσθαι φύσεις *
Timaeus	22b1	μυθολογεῖν, καὶ . . . γενεαλογεῖν ***
Laws	3. 682e5	μυθολογεῖτέ τε καὶ διαπεραίνετε***
Epistles	8. 352e1	μυθολογοῦντες

μυθολογία, ἡ

Statesman	304d1	δι μυθολογίας ἀλλὰ μὴ διὰ διδαχῆς ***
Phaedrus	243a4	μυθολογίαν *
Hippias Maior	298a4	οἱ λόγοι καὶ αἱ μυθολογίαι ταὐτὸν τοῦτο ἐργάζονται ***
Republic	2. 382d1	ταῖς μυθολογίαις ***
	3. 394b9–c1	τῆς ποιήσεως τε καὶ μυθολογίας ***
Critias	110a3	μυθολογία γὰρ ἀναζητησις τε τῶν παλαιῶν ***
Laws	3. 680d3	τὸ ἀρχαῖον αὐτων . . . διὰ μυθολογίας ***
	6. 752a1	κατὰ τὴν . . . μυθολογίαν ***

μυθοποιός, ὁ

Republic	2. 377b11	ἐπιστατητέον τοῖς μυθοποιοῖς *

μυθολόγος, ὁ

Republic	3. 392d2	ὑπὸ μυθολόγων ἢ ποιητῶν ***
	3. 398b1	ποιητῇ . . . καὶ μυθολόγῳ ***
Laws	2. 664d3	μυθολόγους περὶ τῶν αὐτῶν ἠθῶν ***
	12. 941b5	ὑπό τινων μυθολόγων πλημμελῶν ***

μυθολογικός, -ή, -όν

Phaedo	61b5	αὐτὸς οὐκ ἦ μυθολογικός *

διαμυθολογέω

Apol. Socr.	39e5	διαμυθολογῆσαι πρὸς ἀλλήλους *
Phaedo	70b6	διαμυθολογῶμεν *
Laws	1. 632e4-5	διαμυθολογοῦντες *

παραμυθία, ἡ

Phaedo	70b2	παραμυθίας . . . καὶ πίστεως ***
Sophist	224a4	παραμυθίας [opp. σπουδῆς] ***
Euthydemus	290a4	παραμυθία *
Republic	5. 450d9	ἡ παραμυθία ***
Laws	4. 720a1	παραμυθίας . . . καὶ πειθοῦς ***
Axiochus	365a4	πάνυ ἐνδεᾶ παραμυθίας *

παραμύθιον, τό

Phaedrus	240d4	παραμύθιον ***
Euthydemus	272b8	παραμύθιον τοῦ μὴ φοβεῖσθαι ***
Republic	1. 329e5	παραμύθια ***
Critias	115b4	παραμύθια ***
Laws	1. 632e5	παραμύθια ***
	4. 704d8	παραμύθιον ***
	4. 705a8	παραμύθιον ***
	6. 773e5	παραμύθια ***
	9. 880a7	παραμυθίοις ***
	10. 885b3	τὸ παραμύθιον ***
	11. 923c2	παραμύθιά τε καὶ προοίμια ***

παραμυθέομαι

Phaedo	83a3	ἡ φιλοσοφία . . . παραμυθεῖται ***
	115d5	παραμυθούμενος ***
Sophist	230a2	παραμυθούμενοι ***
Statesman	268b3	παραμυθεῖσθαι καὶ . . . πραΰνειν ***

Euthydemus	277d4	μὴ ἡμῖν ἀποδειλιάσειε, παραμυθούμενος εἶπον ***
	288c4	δεώμεθα καὶ παραμυθώμεθα καὶ προσευχώμεθα ***
Protagoras	346b4	παραμυθεῖσθαι ***
Ion	540c5	ἀγριαινουσῶν βοῶν παραμυθουμένῳ **
Menexenus	237a1	παραμυθούμενος **
	247c5-6	παραμυθεῖσθαι *
Republic	4. 442a2	παραμυθουμένη, ἡμεροῦσα ***
	5. 451b1	παραμυθῇ ***
	5. 476e1	παραμυθεῖσθαι αὐτὸν καὶ πείθειν ἠρέμα ***
	6. 499e2	μὴ φιλονικῶν ἀλλὰ παραμυθούμενος ***
Critias	108c7	παραμυθουμένῳ ***
Laws	1. 625b6	ἀλλήλους παραμυθουμένους ***
	2. 666a2	αὐτοὺς παραμυθησόμεθα προθύμους εἶναι; ***
	9. 854a6	διαλεγόμενος ἅμα καὶ παραμυθούμενος **
	10. 899d6	παραμυθητέον ***
	11. 928a1-2	παραμυθούμενός τε καὶ ἀπειλῶν ὁ νόμος **
	12. 944b3	παραμυθούμενος ***
Epinomis	976a7	παραμυθούμενος **
Epistles	7. 329d4	ἐμὲ παραμυθεῖτό τε καὶ . . . διακελεύετο καὶ ἐδεῖτο . . . μένειν ***
	7. 345e4	παραμυθεῖτό τε καὶ ἐδεῖτο μένειν **

εὐπαραμύθητος, ὁ or ἡ

Laws	10. 885b8	εὐπαραμυθήτους ***
	10. 888c6-7	εὐπαραμύθητοι ***

Appendix II

EPISTLES 7. 341b7-345c3

So much then I have to declare about all persons who have *[c]* written and who will write, as many as assert themselves to have envisioned [i.e., to understand] things about which I am serious, having heard [them] either from me or from others, or as though having found [them] themselves; it is not for these persons, in accordance with my opinion at any rate, to understand anything about the business. Therefore, there is not about these *[5]* things, nor ever will come to be, a writing of mine, for in no way must they [i.e., these things], as other learnings [may], be uttered, but from much being-together coming to be in respect to the business itself, and from living-together—such as from a fire which *[d]* leapt up, light having been touched off—it suddenly having come to be in the soul already nurtures itself. And yet I have envisioned [i.e., understood] so much at least, [namely] that these things having been written or having been spoken would be spoken best by me; and that these things having been written badly would pain me not the least. And if to me *[5]* they appeared to be both things which must be written sufficiently and uttered to the many, what more beautiful than this would have been enacted by us in our lifetime than to have written a big benefit for humans and to have led forth nature *[e]* into the light for all [persons]? But I do not regard the taking them in hand which is spoken about them to be good for humans, unless for some few, however many are themselves capable of finding out through little showing out [i.e., with little direction], and indeed of the others, it would fill the ones with a contempt [that is] incorrect, *[5]* in no way seemly, and [it would fill] the others with a high-falutin and spongy hope, as though *[342a]* they had learned significant things. And still longer things about these things have come to be in my intellect to speak; for [then] quickly the things about which I speak would be more distinct than these things which have been spoken. For there is a certain true speech, over and against the person who has dared to write of the suchlike things even *[5]* anything whatever, [a true speech] which has been uttered by me many times even before, and therefore, it is likely to be a thing which must be spoken also now.

There are to each of the beings three things, through which things there is a compulsion for exact-knowledge to come to be present, and it [i. e., exact-knowledge] is a fourth—and fifth, *[b]* it is obligatory to posit a being itself which indeed both is recognizable and truly is—[and of these things,] one is the name, and second is the speech, and the third is the look-alike, and fourth is exact-knowledge. Therefore, wishing to learn the thing being spoken now [by me], you take it in respect to one, and intellect about all things in this way. A circle is *[5]* something which is spoken [to be], [something] for which this itself which we have voiced now is the name. And the second is its speech, which is composed from names and verbs; for "the thing holding itself everywhere equal from its extremities to its middle" would be the speech of that very thing for which the name is "rounded" and *[c]* "circumferent" and "circle." And third is the [circle] which is painted and which is washed out and which is turned on the lathe and is perishing, by none of which things the circle itself—in respect to which all these things are—is affected, since it is other than these. And fourth is exact-knowledge and intellect and true *[5]* opinion in respect to these things; and this in turn must be posited as all one, since it is not in sounds or in shaped-surfaces of bodies, but in souls, by which it is clear [as] being other than both the nature of the circle itself *[d]* and the three things which have been spoken before. And of these, intellect has approached nearest to the fifth by cogenericity and similarity, but the others hold off more [i. e., are farther away]. Indeed the same is about the straight as also about circumferent shaped-surface and about surface-hue, and about good and beautiful *[5]* and just, and about both all prepared [i. e., artificial] body and [body] which has come to be in accordance with nature, [namely] fire and water and all the suchlike things, and about the living thing all together and [about] habit in souls, and in respect to makings/doings and affections all together; for if someone does not grasp *[e]* the four of these in some way, somehow at least, never will he be completely a partaker of exact-knowledge, the fifth. For in addition to these things, these things take it in hand no less to clarify the certain which-sort in respect to each thing *[343a]* than [to clarify] the being of each, because of the weakness of speeches; on account of which things no one who has an intellect will dare ever to put into it [i. e., into speech] the things which have been intellected by him, and [no one who has an intellect will dare ever to put] these things into an untransmoving thing, by which indeed the things which have been written by outlines are affected. And this thing which is spoken now again in turn *[5]* it is obligatory to learn. Each circle of those which are written in actions [i.e., in practice exercises] or also of those which are turned on the lathe is full of the contrary to the fifth—for [each of these circles] touches the straight everywhere—and the circle itself, we assert, has in itself neither anything smaller nor bigger of the contrary nature. And we assert their name to be *[b]* nothing steadfast in any way, and [we assert] nothing to prevent the things which now are called "rounded" from having been called "straight," and indeed the things [which are now called] "straight" [from having been called] "rounded," and [we assert] nothing will hold less steadfastly [even] to the persons transposing [the names] and calling [things] contrarily. And about a speech then [there is] the same speech—if from names *[5]* and verbs it is composed—[namely, the speech asserting it] in no way to be sufficiently steadfastly steadfast; and [there is] a myriad speech in turn about each of the four, how [each] is indistinct, but the biggest thing, the very thing which we bespoke a little before, is that when there are two, both the being and the certain which-sort, when the soul seeks to have envisioned [i.e., to understand] not the *[c]* certain which-sort but the what, each of the four extending out to the soul, both by speech and in accordance with deeds, the thing which is not sought, each furnishing the thing which is spoken and which is shown always to be refuted easily by sensings, fills all men, *[5]* so as to speak a word, with all perplexity and indistinctness. Therefore, in things in which we are persons who have not been habituated—because of a vicious nurture—to seek the true, and [in things in which] the thing which has been extended out from the look-alikes is sufficient [for us], we do not become laughable to each other, the ones [of us] who are asked by *[d]* the ones asking and who are capable of both throwing around [i.e., examining] and refuting the four things; but in things in which we compel answering and clarifying the fifth, of those who are capable of turning [things] upside down, the person wishing [to turn things upside down] has mastery and makes the person interpreting [the fifth thing] in speeches or written *[5]* things or answerings to seem to many of those who hear to recognize nothing of the things which [that person] takes it in hand to write or to speak, [those who hear] sometimes failing to recognize how the soul of the person who has written or who has spoken is not refuted, but the nature of each of the four [is refuted], since [that nature] has natured *[e]* meanly [i.e., is defective in its nature]. But the leading-through all these things—the going over, upward and downward for each, with difficulty—brings to birth exact-knowledge of a thing which has natured well [i.e., which has a good nature] in a person who has natured wel [i.e., who has a good nature]; and if he natures badly [i.e., has a bad nature]—as the aptitude/attitude of the soul of the many has natured both unto learning and unto the things which are spoken to be *[344a]* habits—and [if] they [i. e., the habits] are corrupted, not even Lynkeus would make suchlike persons to see. But, in one speech, neither learning-well nor memory ever would make the person [who is] not cogeneric of the business [to see]—for with respect to the ruling-beginning, it does not come to be in other sorts of aptitudes/attitudes—so that *[5]* as many persons as are not natured toward, and cogeneric of, both the just things and as many of the other things as are beautiful, but some of whom are well-learning and memoried of some things and others of other things, and as many persons as are cogeneric of them, but are learning-resistant and unmemoried, of these persons, none ever yet may learn the truth of virtue *[b]* and badness unto that which is possible. For with respect to these things, there is a compulsion to learn simultaneously the false and true of the whole [of] beingness, with all diligence and much time, which very thing in the beginnings I bespoke; and each of them being rubbed against each other [i.e., being compared] with difficulty, names and speeches *[5]* and seeings and sensings, [they all] being refuted in kindly refutations and by persons using askings and answerings without envies, in respect to each thing, prudence and intellect shone out, [intellect] stretching out *[c]* unto the most human power [i.e., unto the most of what is possible for humans]. Because of which indeed, every man who is serious about the serious things is under much obligation, lest having written, he ever throws down [his writings] unto envy and perplexity among humans. Indeed, in one speech, from these things, it is obligatory to recognize—whenever anyone sees someone's writings *[5]* which have been written either in the laws of a legislator or in any other things with respect to anything whatever—how these things were not the most serious things for this person, if he himself is serious, but they lie somewhere in the most beautiful spot of this person's [spots]; and if these things—beingly having been serious for him—were put in *[d]* writings, not "gods," but mortals "themselves then indeed surely therefore destroyed his senses."

Indeed, the person who has co-followed this myth and wandering will have envisioned [i.e., understood] well, if therefore Dionysius or someone smaller or bigger wrote any of the highest and first things about nature, how he had, in accordance with my speech, neither heard nor learned anything healthy of the things of which he wrote; for similarly [if he had heard or learned anything healthy of these things], he would have reverenced them as I do, and he would not have dared to throw them out unto unharmoniousness and improperness. For he did not even write for the sake of reminders—for it is nothing *[e]* formidable [that] someone may forget it, if once he grasps around it by his soul; for it lies among the briefest of all things [to re-remember]—but [he wrote] for the sake of shameful ambition, whether as positing it to be his own or as indeed being a partaker of an education, of which he was not worthy, he cherishing [i.e., desiring himself to gain] the opinion *[345a]* of [i.e., reputation for] his partaking of it having come to be. Therefore, if, from the one being-together, this has come to be to Dionysius, perhaps it would be so, but therefore, in what way it has come to be, the Theban asserts, "Zeus kens;" for, as I spoke, I narrated it only once, but later still not ever yet. Indeed, it is obligatory *[5]* to intellect the thing after this, [namely, for the person] to whom it is a care to find the thing which has come to be in respect to them, in whatever way it has come to be, [to intellect] for what cause, then, we did not go through it the second and the third and more times; does Dionysius, who has heard only *[b]* once, thus both believe himself to have envisioned [i.e., to understand], and has he envisioned [i.e., understood] sufficiently, either he himself having found it or also having learned it before from others, or [does he believe] the things which have been spoken [by me] to be mean, or thirdly, [does he believe them to be] not in accordance with himself but bigger [i.e., beyond and too much for himself], and [does he believe himself] beingly not to be capable of living [while] being caring of both prudence *[5]* and virtue. For if [he believes them to be] mean, he battles with many witnesses speaking the contrary things, who would be altogether much more authoritative judges about the such-like things than Dionysius; and if [he believes himself] to have found or to have learned [them], and therefore [believes them] to be worthy in regard to the education of a free *[c]* soul, how would he, if he is not a wondrous human, ever have dishonored the leader and authority of thes things so recklessly? And how he dishonored, I would declare.

BIBLIOGRAPHY

[OCT = Oxford Classical Text; LCL = Loeb Classical Library; B = Budé; T = Teubner]

Aesopus, *Fables*, texte établi et tr. par Émile Chambry (Paris, 1927), "Notice," pp. xxi-xxv

Alfarabi, *Philosophy of Plato and Aristotle*, tr. Muhsin Mahdi (Glencoe, IL, 1962)

Anastaplo, George, "Human Being and Citizen: a beginning to the study of Plato's *Apology of Socrates*," in *Ancients and Moderns* (see below), pp. 16-49

Ancients and Moderns: essays on the tradition of political philosophy in honor of Leo Strauss, ed. Joseph Cropsey (NY, 1964)

Aristophanes, *Aristophanes*, with English translation by Benjamin Bickley Rogers (London, LCL, 1930-), 3 volumes

Aristophanes, *Clouds*, ed. with intro. and commentary by K.J. Dover (Oxford, 1968)

Aristoteles, *Aristotle's Metaphysics*, a revised text with intro. and commentary by W.D. Ross (Oxford, 1924), 2 volumes

Aristoteles, *De anima*, ed. W.D. Ross (Oxford, OCT, 1956)

Aristoteles, *De animalibus historia*, in *Aristotelis opera*, ed. I. Bekker (Oxford, 1837), vol. 4, *Historia animalium*

Aristoteles, *De arte poetica*, ed. W. Crist (Leipzig, T, 1882)

Aristoteles, *De generatione animalium*, ed. H.J.D. Lulofs (Oxford, OCT, 1965)

Ast, Friedrich, *Lexicon Platonicum* (Leipzig, 1835), 3 volumes in 2

Bacon, Francis, *Selected Writings of Francis Bacon* (NY, Modern Library, 1955)

Benardete, Seth, "ΧΡΗ and ΔΕΙ in Plato and others," *Glotta*, 43 (1965), pp. 285-298

Benardete, Seth, "Eidos and Diairesis in Plato's *Statesman*," *Philologus*, 107 (1963), pp. 193-226

Benardete, Seth, "On Plato's *Timaeus* and Timaeus' Science Fiction," *interpretation; a journal of political philosophy*, 2, no. 1 (Summer 1971), pp. 21-63

Benardete, Seth, "The Right, the True, and the Beautiful," *Glotta*, 41 (1963), pp. 54-62

Blake, William, *The Complete Writings of William Blake with all the variant readings*, ed. Geoffrey Keynes (NY, 1957)

Bluck, R.S., "The Second Platonic Epistle," *Phronesis*, 5 (1960), pp. 140-151

Boeder, Heribert, "Der frühgriechische Wortgebrauch von Logos und Aletheia," *Archiv für Begriffsgeschichte*, 4 (1959), pp. 82-112

Brann, Eva, "The Music of the *Republic*," *ΑΓΩΝ*, 1, no. 1 (April 1967), pp. i-vi, 1-117

Brochard, V., "Les mythes dans la philosophie de Platon," *L'année philosophique*, 11 (1900), pp. 1-13

Buck, Carl D., "Words of Speaking and Saying in the Indo-European Languages," *American Journal of Philology*, 36, nos. 1 & 2, pp. 1-18 & 125-154

Buffiere, Félix, *Les mythes d'Homère et la pensée grecque* (Paris, 1956)

Cohen, Percy S., "Theories of Myth," *Man*, n.s. 4 (1969), pp. 337-353

Coleridge, Samuel Taylor, *Selected Poetry and Prose of Coleridge*, ed. Donald Stauffer (NY, 1951)

Couturat, L., *De platonicis mythis* (Paris, 1896)

Denniston, J.D., *The Greek Particles* (Oxford, 1970)

De Santillana, Giorgio, *Hamlet's Mill: an essay on myth and the frame of time*, by Giorgio de Santillana and Hertha von Dechend (Boston, 1969)

Descartes, René, *The Philosophical Works of Descartes*, tr. E.S. Haldane and G.R.T. Ross (Cambridge, Eng., 1968), 2 volumes

Des Places, Édouard, *Lexique de la langue philosophique et religieuse de Platon* (Paris, B, 1964), in *Oeuvres complètes* (see below), tome XIV, parts 1 & 2

Dickinson, Emily, *The Poems of Emily Dickinson, including variant readings critically compared with all known manuscripts*, ed. Thomas H. Johnson (Cambridge, MA, 1955), 3 volumes

Diogenes Laertius, *Lives of the Eminent Philosophers*, with English tr. by R.D. Hicks (Cambridge, MA, LCL, 1950), 2 volumes

Dorter, Kenneth, "Imagery and Philosophy in Plato's *Phaedrus*," *Journal of the History of Philosophy*, 9 (July 1971), pp. 279-288

Edelstein, Ludwig, "The Function of Myth in Plato's Philosophy," *Journal of the History of Philosophy*, 10 (Oct. 1949), pp. 463-481

Else, Gerald F., *Aristotle's Poetics: the argument* (Cambridge, MA, 1957)

Euclidis, *Elementa*, text of I.L. Heiberg, ed. E.S. Stamatis (Leipzig, T, 1969), volume 1

Euclidis, *The Thirteen Books of Euclid's Elements*, tr. with intro, and commentary by Sir Thomas Heath, 2d ed. rev. (NY, 1956)

Euripides, *Fabulae*, ed. Gilbert Murray (Oxford, OCT, 1902)

Fournier, H., *Les verbs "dire" en Grec ancien* (Paris, 1946)

Die fragmente der Vorsokratiker . . . 5. Aufl. Herausgegeben von Walther Kranz, ed. Hermann Diels (Berlin, 1934-1937)

Friedländer, Paul, *Plato: an introduction*, tr. Hans Meyerhoff (NY, 1958)

Frutiger, Perceval, *Les mythes de Platon; étude philosophique et littéraire* (Paris, 1930)

Gaffney, Susan K., "Dialectic, the Myths of Plato, Metaphor and the Transcendent in the World," *American Catholic Philosophical Association. Proceedings*, 45 (1971), pp. 77-85

Geddes, James, *An Essay on the Composition and Manner of Writing of the Antients, particularly Plato*, Glasgow, 1748 (NY, 1970 facsimile reprint)

Goldschmidt, Victor, *Essai sur le "Cratyle": contribution à l'histoire de la pensée de Platon* (Paris, 1947)

Goldschmidt, Victor, *Le paradigme dans la dialectique platonicienne* (Paris, 1947)

Graves, Robert, *The Greek Myths* (Baltimore, 1955), 2 volumes

Grene, David, *Greek Political Theory: the image of man in Thucydides and Plato* [originally published as *Man in his Pride*] (Chicago, 1965)

Grimm, Jakob Ludwig Karl, *Grimm's Fairy Tales*. Complete edition, tr. Margaret Hunt, rev. James Stern, with illustrations by Josef Scharl (NY, Pantheon, 1944)

Guthrie, W.K.C., *History of Greek Philosophy* (Cambridge, Eng., 1962-)

Hegel, Georg Wilhelm Friedrich, *The Philosophy of History*, with prefaces by Charles Hegel and the translator J. Sibree, rev. ed. (NY, 1956)

Heidegger, Martin, *Being and Time*, tr. John Macquarrie and Edward Robinson (NY, 1962)

Heidegger, Martin, *Discourse on Thinking*, tr. John M. Anderson and E. Hans Freund (NY, 1966)

Herodotus, *Historiae*, ed. C. Hude (Oxford, OCT, 1927)

Hesiodus, *Carmina*, ed. A. Rzach (Leipzig, T, 1913)

Hesiodus, *Hesiod, the Homeric Hymns and Homerica*, with English tr. by Hugh G. Evelyn-White (Cambridge, MA, LCL, 1936)

Hirsch, E.D., *Validity in Interpretation* (New Haven, 1967)

The History of Political Philosophy, edd. Leo Strauss and Joseph Cropsey, 2d ed. (Chicago, 1972)

Homerus, *Ilias*, ed. W. Dindorf Ileipzig, T, 1855)

Homerus, *Odyssea*, ed. T.W. Allen, in *Opera* (Oxford, OCT, 1917), volumes 3 & 4

Hyland, Drew A., "Why Plato Wrote Dialogues," *Philosophy and Rhetoric*, 1, no. 1 (Jan. 1968), pp. 38-50

Jonas, Hans, *The Phenomenon of Life* (NY, 1966)

Kafka, Franz, *The Penal Colony: stories and short pieces*, tr. Willa and Edwin Muir (NY, 1961)

Kierkegaard, . Søren, *The Concept of Irony*, tr. Lee M. Capel (NY, 1965)

Kirk, G.S., *Myth: its meaning and functions in ancient and other cultures* (Berkeley, 1970)
Kirk, G.S., *The Nature of Greek Myths* (Woodstock, NY, 1975)
Klein, Jacob, "Aristotle, an introduction," in *Ancients and Moderns* (see above), pp. 50-69
Klein, Jacob, *A Commentary on Plato's Meno* (Chapel Hill, 1965)
Klein, Jacob, *Greek Mathematical Thought and the Origin of Algebra*, tr. Eva Brann (Cambridge, MA, 1968)
Klein, Jacob, *Plato's Trilogy* (Chicago, 1977)
Koyré, Alexandre, *Discovering Plato*, tr. Leonora Cohen Rosenfield (NY, 1960)
Leibniz, Gottfried Wilhelm, Freiherr von, *Discours de métaphysique et correspondance avec Arnauld*, intro., texte, et comm. par Georges Le Roy, deuxième éd. (Paris, 1966)
Liddell, Henry George, *A Greek-English Lexicon*, comp. by Henry George Liddell and Robert Scott. A new [i. e., 9th] ed. rev. and augm. By Sir Henry Stuart Jones with Roderick McKenzie (Oxford, 1968) [Usually cited as LSJ.]
Louis, Pierre, *Les metaphores de Platon* (Paris, 1945)
Lysias, *Selected Speeches*, ed. C.D. Adams (Norman, OK, 1970)
Machiavelli, Niccoló, *The Chief Works and others*, tr. Allan Gilbert (Curham, NC, 1965), 3 volumes
McClain, Ernest, "Plato's Musical Cosmology," *Main Currents in Modern Thought*, 30, no. 1 (1974), pp. 34-42
Mara, Gerald, *Political Wisdom: politics and philosophy in Plato's Statesman and Republic* (Unpublished Ph.D. dissertation, Bryn Mawr College, 1974)
Martin, Henri, *Études sur le Timée de Platon* (Paris, 1841), 2 volumes in 1
Marx, Werner, *The Meaning of Aristotle's Ontology* (The Hague, 1954)
Melville, Herman, *Moby Dick*, ed. Harrison Hayford and Hershel Parker (NY, Norton Critical Edition, 1967)
Merlan, Philip, "Form and Content in Plato's Philosophy," *Journal of the History of Ideas*, 8, no. 4 (Oct. 1947), pp. 406-430
Milton, John, *Milton's Lycidas; the tradition and the poem*, ed. C.A. Patrides (NY, 1961)
Mulhern, John J., "Treatises, Dialogues, and Interpretation," *Monist*, 53 (1969), pp. 631-641
Nettleship, Richard Lewis, *Lectures on the Republic of Plato* (NY, 1968)
Nietzsche, Friedrich Wilhelm, *Beyond Good and Evil*, tr. Walter Kaufmann (NY, 1966)
Parmenides, *Parmenides: a text with tr., commentary, and critical essays* by Leonardo Tarán (Princeton, 1965)
Pépin, Jean, *Mythe et allegorie* (Aubier, 1958)
Pieper, Josef, *Enthusiasm and Divine Madness*, tr. Richard and Clara Winston (NY, 1964)
Pindarus, *Pindari Carmina cum fragmentis*, ed. C.M. Bowra (Oxford, OCT, 1935)
Plato, *Opera omnia*, ed. John Burnet (Oxford, OCT, 1967), 5 volumes
Plato, *Plato*, with English tr. (Cambridge, MA, LCL, 1914-1964), 12 volumes
Plato, *Oeuvres complètes* (Paris, B, 1920-1964), 14 volumes
Plato, *The Works of Plato*. A new and literal version chiefly from the text of Stallbaum by George Burges (London, 1854-1865), 6 volumes
Plato, *The Epinomis of Plato*, tr. with intro. and notes by J. Harward (Oxford, 1928)
Plato, *Plato's Epistles*, tr. with critical essays and notes by Glenn R. Morrow (Indianapolis, 1962)
Plato, *Plato's Euthyphro, Apology of Socrates, and Crito*, ed. with notes by John Burnet (Oxford, 1970)
Plato, *Gorgias*, a revised text with intro. and commentary by E.R. Dodds (Oxford, 1959)
Plato, *Plato and Parmenides: Parmenides' Way of Truth and Plato's Parmenides*, tr. with intro. and commentary by Francis MacDonald Cornford (Indianapolis, n.d.)
Plato, *Plato's Phaedo*, ed. with intro. and notes by John Burnet (Oxford, 1972)
Plato, *Phédon*, tr. Léon Robin (Paris, B, 1926), in *Oeuvres complètes* (see above), tome IV, pt. 1
Plato, *Plato's Phaedo*, tr. with intro., notes and appendices by R.S. Bluck (NY, 1955)

Plato, *Plato's Phaedo*, tr. with intro. and commentary by R. Hackforth (Cambridge, Eng., 1972)
Plato, *Phaedrus, and, the Seventh and Eighth Letters*, tr. Walter Hamilton (Harmondsworth, Eng., 1973)
Plato, *The Phaedrus of Plato*, with English notes and dissertations by W.H. Thompson (NY, 1973)
Plato, Phèdre, tr. Léon Robin (Paris, B, 1933), in *Oeuvres complètes* (see above), tome IV, pt. 3
Plato, *Plato's Cosmology: the Timaeus of Plato*, tr. with commentary by Francis MacDonald Cornford (Indianapolis, n.d.)
Plato, *Plato's Examination of Pleasure (*The Philebus*)*, tr. with intro. and commentary by R. Hackforth (Indianapolis, 1945)
Plato, *Plato's Phaedrus*, tr. with intro. and commentary by R. Hackforth (Indianapolis, 1952)
Plato, *Plato's Theory of Knowledge: the Theaetetus and the Sophist of Plato*, tr. with a running commentary by Francis MacDonald Cornford (London, 1967)
Plato, *ΠΛΑΤΩΝΟΣ ΤΙΜΑΙΟΣ: the Timaeus of Plato*, ed. with intro. and notes by R.D. Archer-Hind (London, 1888)
Plato, *The Republic of Plato*, ed. with critical notes, commentary, and appendices by James Adam (Cambridge, Eng., 1926), 2 volumes
Plato, *The Republic of Plato*, tr. with notes and an interpretive essay by Allan Bloom (NY, 1968)
Plato, *The Symposium of Plato*, ed. with intro. and commentary by R.G. Bury, 2d ed. (Cambridge, Eng., 1973)
Riddell, James, *A Digest of Platonic Idioms*, in Plato, *The Apology of Plato*, with a revised text and English notes (Oxford, 1877)
Riezler, Kurt, *Man, Mutable and Immutable* (Chicago, 1950)
Robin, Léon, *Études sur la signification et la place de la physique dans la philosophie de Platon* (Paris, 1919)
Robin, Léon, *Platon* (Paris, 1968)
Rose, H.J., *Handbook of Greek Mythology* (NY, 1959)
Rosen, Stanley, "The Non-lover in Plato's *Phaedrus*," *Man and World*, 2, no. 3 (August 1969), pp. 423-437
Rosen, Stanley, *Plato's Symposium* (New Haven, 1968)
Sallis, John, *Being and Logos: the way of Platonic dialogue* (Pittsburgh, 1975)
Schaerer, René, *La question platonicienne* (Neuchatel, 1938)
Schuhl, Pierre-Maxime, *Essai sur la formation de la pensée grecque: introduction historique à une étude de la philosophie platonicienne* (Paris, 1934)
Schuhl, Pierre-Maxime, *La fabulation platonicienne* (Paris, 1968)
Shakespeare, William, *All's Well That Ends Well*, ed. G.K. Hunter (London, Arden Ed., 1967)
Shakespeare, William, *King Lear*, a new variorum edition, ed. Horace Howard Furness (NY, 1963)
Shakespeare, William, *Othello*, a new variorum edition, ed. Horace Howard Furness (NY, 1963)
Shorey, Paul, *What Plato Said* (Chicago, 1933)
Sinaiko, Herman L., *Love, Knowledge, and Discourse in Plato* (Chicago, 1965)
Smyth, Herbert Weir, *Greek Grammar* (Cambridge, MA, 1973)
Stewart, J.A., *The Myths of Plato* (Carbondale, IL, 1960)
Stormer, Gerald D., "Plato's Theory of Myth," *Personalist*, 55, no. 3 (Summer 1974), pp. 216-223
Strauss, Leo, *The Argument and Action of Plato's* Laws (Chicago, 1975)
Strauss, Leo, *The City and Man* (Chicago, 1964)
Strauss, Leo, *Liberalism, Ancient and Modern* (NY, 1968)
Strauss, Leo, *Natural Right and History* (Chicago, 1953)

Strauss, Leo, *Persecution and the Art of Writing* (Glencoe, IL, 1952)
Strauss, Leo, *The Political Philosophy of Hobbes*, tr. Elsa M. Sinclair (Chicago, 1963)
Strauss, Leo, *Thoughts on Machiavelli* (Glencoe, IL, 1958)
Strauss, Leo, *What is Political Philosophy? and other studies* (Glencoe, IL, 1959)
Swift, Jonathan, *The Writings of Jonathan Swift*, edd. Robert A. Greenberg and William B. Piper (NY, Norton Critical Ed., 1973)
Tarán, Leonardo, *Academica: Plato, Philip of Opus, and the Pseudo-Platonic Epinomis* (Philadelphai, 1975)
Tarrant, Dorothy, "Colloquialisms, Semi-Proverbs and Word-Play in Plato," *Classical Quarterly*, 40 (1946), pp. 101-117
Tarrant, Dorothy, "More colloquialisms, Semi-Proverbs and Word-Play in Plato," *Classical Quarterly*, n.s. 8 (1958), pp. 158-160
Tarrant, Dorothy, "Plato as Dramatist," *Journal of Hellenic Studies*, 75 (1955), pp. 82-89
Taylor, Alfred Edward, *A Commentary on Plato's Timaeus* (Oxford, 1928)
Thomas Aquinas, Saint, *In Aristotelis librum De anima commentarium*. Editio secunda cura ac studio P.F. Angeli M. Pirotta (Taurini, Italia, 1936)
Thompson, D'Arcy Wentworth, *Science and the Classics* (London, 1940)
Thucydides, *Historiae*, ed. H.S. Jones (Oxford, OCT, 1942), 2 volumes
Tolstoy, Leo, *War and Peace*, tr. Louise and Aylmer Maude (NY, Norton Critical Ed., 1966)
Verdenius, W.J., "Notes on Plato's *Phaedrus*," *Mnemosyne*, s. 4, 8 (1955), pp. 265-289
Vernant, Jean-Pierre, *Mythe et pensée chez les Grecs* (Paris, 1971), 2 volumes
Vlastos, Gregory, *Plato's Universe* (Seattle, 1975)
Voegelin, Eric, *Order and History*, volume 3, *Plato and Aristotle* (Baton Rouge, 1957)
Vries, Gerrit Jacob de, *A Commentary on the* Phaedrus *of Plato* (Amsterdam, 1969)
Westcott, Brooke F., "The Myths of Plato," *Contemporary Review*, 2 (1866), pp. 199-211, 469-481
Writers at Work: the Paris Review *interviews*, ed. Malcolm Cowley (NY, 1959)
Xenophon, *Opera omnia*, ed. E.C. Marchant (Oxford, OCT, 1901-1920), 5 volumes
Zaner, Richard, *The Way of Phenomenology* (NY, 1970)
Zaslavsky, Robert, "A Hitherto Unremarked Pun in the *Phaedrus*," *Apeiron*, vol. 15, no. 2, 1981, pp. 115-116
Zaslavsky, Robert, "The Platonic Godfather: a note on the *Protagoras* myth," *Journal of Value Inquiry*, vol. 16, no. 1, 1982, pp. 79-82
Zaslavsky, "A Note on Translating an Aristotelian Dative and τὸ τί ἦν εἶναι," *New Scholasticism*, 58 (2), Spring 1984
Zaslavsky, Robert, "On Recovering Homer," in *Approaches to Teaching Homer's* Iliad *and* Odyssey, ed. Kostas Myrsiades (NY, MLA, 1987)
Zürcher, Josef, *Lexicon Academicum* (Paderborn, 1954)

INDEX

English

account, vii, 5, 6, 7, 8, 13, 16, 25, 26, 28, 31, 32, 33, 40, 49, 54, 56, 59, 61, 62, 66, 67, 68, 69, 71, 72, 73, 74, 76, 77, 78, 79, 80, 81, 82, 83, 84, 85, 86, 87, 89, 90, 92, 93, 94, 95, 97, 98, 102, 103, 114
Acheron, 93
ad hominem, 10, 15
Adeimantus, 9, 63, 76, 98
Aesop, 55, 56
Agathon, 49
Aiakos, 88
Alcibiades, 35, 88, 107
Alfarabi, 75, 76
All's Well That Ends Well, vii, 120
Ammon, 59, 60
Anastaplo, 28
anonymity, 15, 23
Aphrodite, 49, 51
Apollo, 40, 41, 42, 43, 51, 54
Apollodorus, 15
Apollonian, 40, 42, 43
Apology of Socrates, 13, 19, 28, 33, 40, 60, 68, 94, 102, 110
aporetic, 16, 22
Arcadia, 76
archery, 42
Ardiaios, 77, 81, 86
Aristophanes, 29, 32, 33, 54
Aristotle, vii, 9, 12, 14, 15, 16, 20, 26, 47, 76, 102, 103
art, 28, 42, 51, 57, 58, 60, 73, 75, 76, 88, 90, 91
Athena, 64
Athenian Stranger, 95
Athens, 61, 63, 68, 72
Atlantis, 65, 68
Atreus, 55

basilic, 88
beast, 74, 75, 76, 77, 85, 86
being, 11, 14, 16, 17, 18, 19, 20, 26, 27, 31, 32, 34, 35, 37, 38, 41, 44, 45, 47, 48, 49, 50, 51, 52, 53, 54, 59, 60, 64, 67, 69, 71, 72, 73, 75, 80, 81, 82, 83, 84, 86, 88, 90, 94, 98, 102, 113, 115
beingness, 21, 36, 45, 46, 47, 48, 49, 57, 58, 64, 70, 115
Benardete, vii, 55, 68, 69, 70, 93
Bendidea, 64
Blake, 54
Bloom, 65, 81, 120
body, 6, 18, 30, 32, 40, 44, 46, 53, 54, 58, 63, 65, 66, 75, 88, 93, 99, 101, 114
Brann, 11, 72, 73
Burnet, 37, 45, 46, 49, 52, 53, 69, 105
butcher, 53, 54

Callicles, 6, 87, 88, 89
Cartesian, 1

cave, 42, 50, 65, 70, 74, 75
Cebes, 56, 97, 99
Cephalus, 63, 65
chance, 23, 35, 70, 82, 92, 93, 99
Charmides, 2, 35, 57
cicadas, 25, 30, 31, 32, 33, 34, 39
circle, 17, 18, 74, 102, 113
city, 12, 22, 27, 29, 40, 41, 49, 64, 65, 66, 68, 69, 71, 72, 73, 74, 76, 79, 82, 84, 91, 94, 97, 98
Cocytus, 93
Coleridge, 101, 102
convention, 16, 72, 90, 91
Cornford, 63, 64, 65, 67, 68
cosmography, 77, 81, 82
cosmos, 7, 8, 30, 40, 46, 65, 66, 68, 69, 82
Cratylus, 18, 19, 34, 37, 40, 41, 42, 43, 44, 48, 49, 50, 61, 69, 78, 80, 88, 108
craziness, 8, 27, 39, 41, 42, 43, 51, 53, 54, 57, 61
crazy quilt, 8, 11
Critias, 7, 25, 40, 63, 64, 68, 69, 71, 97, 109, 110, 111
Crito, 16, 40, 64

Darius, 29
De Anima, 14, 47
deed, 7, 28, 84
democracy, 3, 27, 28, 73
Denniston, 34
desire, 23, 25, 32, 35, 40, 41, 49, 54, 65, 66, 70, 72, 78, 84, 86, 89
diairesis, 55, 57
dialogue, 7, 9, 10, 11, 15, 19, 22, 23, 24, 25, 26, 28, 30, 34, 38, 59, 60, 61, 63, 64, 66, 67, 68, 77, 78, 81, 87, 92, 93, 99, 102
Dickinson, 42
Diogenes Laertius, 25, 61
Dionysius, 15, 22, 23, 24, 115
Dionysus, 51
Diotima, 35, 40, 54, 65, 88

earth, 6, 32, 33, 55, 66, 77, 79, 81, 92, 93
education, 2, 6, 23, 24, 71, 73, 74, 94, 95, 115
eidos, 55
Elean Stranger, 55
Epeios, 85, 86
Epimetheus, 7, 90
Epinomis, 7, 11, 14, 25, 97, 107, 108, 111
episteme, 6
Epistles, 7, 8, 14, 16, 26, 29, 60, 97, 107, 109, 111
epithymia, 49, 51
equality of the sexes, 65, 85, 95
Er, 6, 71, 72, 74, 77, 79, 80, 81, 82, 83, 84, 85
Erato, 34, 35, 36, 39
eros, 6, 22, 25, 35, 40, 42, 49, 51, 52, 53
esoteric, 22
Euclid, 17
Euclides, 15, 93
Euripides, 42, 78, 88
Euthydemus, 64, 97, 110, 111
Euthyphro, 7, 19, 40, 49

exact-knowledge, 13, 16, 113
existentialism, 3

Faulkner, 30
force, 2, 10, 65
Friedländer, 63, 67, 68, 87
Frutiger, 25, 63, 65, 67, 68, 87

Ganymede, 94
Generation of Animals, 20
genesis, 6, 7, 11, 12, 13, 16, 24, 25, 26, 40, 46, 47, 56, 58, 66, 67, 68, 71, 72, 73, 74, 90, 92, 93, 94
genetic, 6, 7, 21, 26, 40, 55, 56, 61, 68, 69, 71, 73, 78, 87, 92, 93, 94, 103
gennaic falsehood, 6, 73
Glaucon, 30, 38, 49, 63, 71, 72, 73, 77, 83, 84, 98, 99
god, 22, 29, 30, 35, 41, 46, 49, 52, 55, 56, 57
Gorgias, 6, 7, 22, 78, 80, 87, 88, 89, 107, 108, 109
Graves, 41, 86
Gyges, 6, 71, 72, 84
gymnastic, 6, 90

habit, 83, 86, 114
heaven, 36, 37, 39, 46, 70, 80, 81, 83, 84, 92
Hegel, 2
Heidegger, 53, 118
Helen, 39, 41
Hera, 66
Herakleitos, 48, 69
Hermes, 90, 91
Hermocrates, 40, 63, 69, 71
Hermogenes, 37, 44, 48, 49
Herodotus, 72
Hesiod, 30, 40, 73
Hestia, 47, 48, 49
heterogeneity, 59
Hippias maior, 7
Historia animalium, 76
Homer, 9, 5, 9, 11, 40, 41, 73, 88, 103
homogeneity, 59
honor, 12, 23, 24, 27, 34, 39, 64, 86
hybris, 29
hymn, 26, 27, 39, 81

Iliad, 5, 11, 22, 40, 85, 88, 108
image, 3, 33, 42, 70, 74, 75, 89, 90, 94
injustice, 49, 50, 72, 78, 80, 84
intellect, 18, 20, 21, 37, 44, 47, 48, 49, 52, 61, 69, 80, 113, 115
invisibility, 6, 72
irony, 6

Jonas, vii, 3
judge, 1, 52, 73, 88
justice, 2, 6, 7, 28, 53, 59, 71, 72, 73, 78, 80, 81, 82, 85, 86, 87, 88, 90, 91, 98

Kafka, 32
Kalliope, 34, 36, 37, 39

Kierkegaard, 87
king, 7, 29, 37, 69, 85
Klein, 11, 12, 26, 27
Kronos, 37, 49, 55, 66

law, 5, 6, 48, 51, 52, 66, 91, 94
law-abidingness, 94
Laws, 6, 7, 16, 22, 25, 26, 36, 47, 51, 69, 93, 94, 95, 97, 98, 99, 107, 108, 109, 110, 111
learning, 8, 11, 14, 21, 35, 82, 83, 114
legislator, 21, 22, 115
Leibniz, 1
Leontios, 72
life, 12, 41, 43, 44, 65, 69, 71, 76, 78, 80, 84
likeness of the eternal, 70
Locris, 64, 67
logographic compulsion, 18, 29, 82
logography, 82
logos, 1, 6, 7
look, 11, 16, 17, 18, 19, 20, 21, 31, 33, 34, 37, 42, 50, 52, 53, 54, 58, 67, 71, 72, 75, 93, 113
look-alike, 16, 17, 18, 20, 21, 50, 71, 113
luck, 43, 51, 84, 93
Lycurgus, 29
Lynceus, 21
Lysias, 25, 27, 28, 40, 41, 42, 51
Lysis, 35

Mahdi, 76, 117
marriage, 6, 94
Martin, 53, 63, 64, 65, 68
Meletus, 49
Melville, vii, 8, 101
Menexenus, 97, 111
Meno, 1, 7, 8, 16, 26, 27, 108
Metaphysics, 16
methodology, 3, 11, 57, 59, 103
midwifery, 93
Milton, 57
Minos, 6, 79, 88, 108
Mnemosyne, 26, 30, 31
Moirai, 77, 79, 81, 82
monster, 11, 32, 57, 59
monsters, 57
motion, 6, 19, 43, 44, 67, 68, 69, 70, 71, 93
Muses, 30, 31, 33, 34, 36, 37, 39, 40, 51, 85
Music, 72
myth, 1, 2, 3, 6, 7, 8, 11, 12, 13, 16, 21, 22, 23, 24, 25, 26, 38, 39, 40, 41, 47, 55, 56, 58, 59, 63, 66, 67, 68, 69, 71, 72, 73, 74, 76, 77, 78, 79, 80, 81, 82, 84, 85, 87, 88, 89, 90, 91, 92, 93, 94, 95, 97, 98, 103, 115
mythologizing, 7, 71, 88
mythos, 1, 3, 6, 7

name, 6, 11, 16, 17, 18, 19, 20, 21, 26, 30, 34, 35, 36, 37, 43, 44, 48, 52, 86, 88, 90, 101, 113
nature, 15, 16, 20, 21, 22, 26, 27, 29, 32, 33, 35, 39, 40, 43, 44, 46, 47, 49, 50, 51, 52, 53, 54, 56, 57, 58, 61, 65, 67, 70, 72, 73, 76, 78, 81, 82, 83, 84, 85, 90, 113, 115
Nettleship, 73

Nietzsche, 11, 14

Ocean, 66, 93
Odysseus, 22, 79, 85, 86
Odyssey, 5, 11, 32, 79, 85, 86, 107
onomatogenesis, 44
onomatology, 37, 78
opinion, 20, 22, 43, 64, 72, 94, 98, 99, 113, 115
orator, 29
Othello, 54, 120
Ourania, 34, 36, 37, 39
Ouranos, 37

palinode, 6, 26, 27, 29, 32, 34, 36, 39, 40, 41, 42, 47, 51, 54, 58, 59, 69, 78
Pamphylian, 79, 80
Pan, 26, 61
Panathenaea, 64
paradigm, 11, 16, 22, 55, 76, 98
paramyth, 95, 97, 98, 99
Parmenides, 7, 17, 18, 19, 25, 31, 43
pathos, 7
persuasion, 2, 87, 99
Phaedo, 6, 7, 9, 13, 15, 19, 23, 31, 32, 35, 36, 37, 38, 40, 55, 56, 76, 86, 87, 92, 93, 97, 99, 107, 108, 109, 110
Phaedrus, 6, 7, 8, 11, 14, 16, 18, 23, 25, 26, 27, 28, 29, 30, 31, 32, 33, 34, 35, 36, 37, 38, 39, 40, 41, 42, 44, 45, 46, 47, 48, 49, 50, 51, 52, 53, 54, 56, 57, 58, 59, 60, 61, 69, 71, 78, 82, 107, 109, 110
Philebus, 7, 18, 29, 30, 46, 49, 54, 55, 56, 57, 59, 60, 107
philosopher, 2, 3, 9, 22, 32, 35, 39, 49, 50, 65, 72, 76, 84, 85, 88, 97, 98, 99, 101, 102
philosophy, vii, 1, 2, 3, 8, 12, 13, 22, 27, 29, 30, 31, 32, 33, 34, 35, 36, 37, 40, 51, 64, 65, 68, 73, 74, 83, 84, 85, 93, 97, 98, 99
Phoebus, 40
Phorkys, 66
Pindar, 40, 42
Piraeus, 63
plane tree, 26
Plato, vii, 1, 2, 3, 6, 8, 9, 10, 11, 12, 13, 14, 15, 16, 17, 18, 19, 20, 21, 22, 23, 24, 25, 26, 27, 28, 29, 33, 35, 38, 40, 47, 55, 58, 59, 60, 63, 64, 65, 66, 67, 68, 69, 70, 72, 73, 75, 76, 78, 80, 83, 87, 90, 94, 97, 101, 102, 103, 105
Platonic, 1, 3, 4, 7, 8, 9, 11, 12, 13, 14, 15, 16, 17, 22, 23, 24, 25, 26, 28, 29, 32, 34, 38, 47, 54, 57, 59, 60, 61, 62, 63, 64, 65, 67, 77, 78, 85, 87, 92, 93, 94, 95, 97, 98, 99, 101, 102, 103, 105
pleasure, 6, 31, 32, 51, 67, 94
Pluto, 88
poet, 9, 10, 11, 28, 30, 39, 61, 89
Poetics, 103
Polemarchus, 32, 63
Polus, 88
Poseidon, 88
positivism, 3
Potidaea, 93
Prometheus, 7, 90, 91
Protagoras, 7, 12, 60, 61, 87, 90, 91, 92, 93, 97, 107, 108, 111
psychology, 66, 73, 74, 75
punishment, 39, 49, 78, 82, 89, 91
puppets, 6, 94
Puzo, 91

Pyriphlegethon, 93
Pythodorus, 31

reason, 1, 2, 3, 16, 24, 38, 80, 84, 101, 103
recollection, 7
regime, 6, 71, 72, 76, 83
Republic, 2, 6, 7, 9, 10, 11, 15, 16, 19, 21, 22, 28, 30, 31, 32, 33, 36, 37, 38, 40, 41, 42, 45, 47, 49, 50, 51, 52, 56, 59, 60, 63, 64, 65, 66, 68, 69, 70, 71, 72, 73, 76, 77, 79, 82, 84, 85, 86, 87, 88, 93, 95, 97, 98, 99, 102, 107, 108, 109, 110, 111
Rhadamanthus, 88
Rhea, 66
rhetoric, 57, 87, 88, 89, 90
Rival-lovers, 35
Robin, 26, 27, 36, 61, 63, 87
Rosen, 27

Sallis, 26, 27, 28, 35, 36, 41, 42, 43, 44, 47, 49, 51, 52, 53, 54
Schuhl, 63
science, 3, 67
self-knowledge, 57
sensing, 6, 20, 93
Shakespeare, vii, 54
sieve, 88, 89
Silenus, 23
Simmias, 32, 37, 92, 99
Smyth, 72, 98
Socrates, 6, 8, 9, 10, 11, 15, 16, 18, 19, 21, 22, 23, 25, 26, 27, 28, 29, 30, 31, 32, 33, 34, 35, 36, 37, 38, 39, 40, 41, 42, 43, 44, 47, 48, 49, 50, 51, 52, 53, 54, 55, 56, 57, 58, 59, 60, 61, 63, 64, 65, 66, 68, 69, 70, 71, 72, 74, 75, 77, 78, 79, 80, 81, 82, 83, 84, 85, 87, 88, 89, 90, 91, 92, 93, 94, 97, 98, 99, 102
Socratic, 1, 22, 25, 27, 28, 29, 36, 40, 41, 43, 51, 56, 59, 61, 80, 83, 92, 93
Solon, 29
Sophist, 7, 8, 17, 22, 25, 40, 52, 56, 64, 72, 88, 90, 97, 107, 108, 110
soul, 1, 6, 7, 12, 14, 19, 20, 21, 23, 26, 31, 38, 39, 42, 43, 44, 45, 46, 47, 48, 49, 50, 56, 57, 58, 59, 60, 61, 65, 66, 69, 71, 73, 74, 75, 76, 77, 79, 81, 82, 84, 85, 86, 88, 89, 90, 97, 99, 102, 103, 113, 114, 115
species, 7, 11, 61
speech, 2, 5, 6, 7, 16, 17, 18, 19, 20, 21, 22, 24, 25, 27, 28, 29, 30, 31, 34, 35, 37, 38, 39, 40, 41, 42, 43, 45, 46, 47, 48, 49, 50, 51, 52, 54, 56, 57, 59, 60, 61, 64, 65, 67, 69, 71, 78, 83, 84, 90, 91, 92, 94, 99, 113, 115
spiritedness, 49, 65, 66
Statesman, 7, 18, 22, 25, 40, 42, 52, 55, 56, 59, 94, 97, 107, 108, 109, 110
Stesichorus, 26, 40, 41
Strauss, vii, 2, 3, 12, 25, 40, 65, 73, 90
Symposium, 7, 15, 21, 22, 23, 25, 26, 27, 28, 29, 32, 33, 35, 36, 40, 41, 49, 54, 88, 93

taste, 2
Terpsichore, 34, 36, 39
Terpsion, 15, 93
Tethys, 66
Thamus, 31
Theaetetus, 6, 13, 19, 29, 40, 64, 87, 93, 94, 107
Theages, 35
Theuth, 25, 31, 59, 60
Thomas Aquinas, 102
Thrasymachus, 63, 73, 76

Thyestes, 55
thymoeidetic, 49, 51, 85
Timaeus, 6, 7, 14, 17, 19, 25, 30, 40, 42, 46, 47, 50, 52, 57, 63, 64, 65, 66, 67, 68, 69, 70, 71, 82, 101, 107, 108, 109
Tolstoy, 69, 70
transmigration, 75, 77, 78, 86, 93
transmovability, 18
transmovable, 19, 22
true opinion, 17, 20, 21, 94
truth, 1, 7, 21, 22, 39, 41, 43, 46, 47, 49, 50, 52, 58, 61, 62, 65, 67, 71, 73, 87, 103, 115
Typhon, 32
tyranny, 2, 32, 72, 73, 81, 83
tyrant, 6, 66, 76, 77, 81

underworld, 78, 87

vector, 10
virtue, 6, 7, 8, 19, 21, 72, 73, 74, 75, 82, 83, 84, 86, 90, 91, 92, 94, 98, 115
vision, 36, 40, 49, 50, 58, 61, 85

War, 69, 70
whorl, 81
wine jar, 6, 88
wolf, 76, 77
writer, 9, 14, 20, 21, 22, 23, 27, 28, 29, 30, 33, 59, 64, 101

Xenophon, 22, 29, 69

Zeus, 7, 23, 30, 32, 48, 66, 76, 77, 88, 90, 91, 115

Greek

ἀκοή, 59, 61, 68, 103
'Ανάγκη, 10, 82
ἀρχή, 45, 46, 93, 103
γένεσις, 46, 54, 66, 68, 72

διαίρεσις, 11, 42, 43, 52, 53, 54, 55, 56, 58, 61, 70, 92, 93, 94
διαλεκτική, 31, 33, 34, 50, 52
διάνοια, 33, 34, 49, 50
δόξα, 43, 94

εἴδωλον, 16, 50, 71
ἐντελέχεια, 14, 78
ἕξις, 21
ἐπίδειξις, 15, 16
ἐπιστήμη, 16
ἔργον, 52, 54, 57, 59, 65, 68
ἔρως, 25, 27, 35, 42, 43, 49, 50, 57, 65

θεογονία, 71, 73
θεολογία, 71, 73

κόσμος, 30, 46, 66

λέγω, 5, 90
λογομύθιον, 5
λογοποιέω, 5
λόγος, 3, 5, 7, 11, 16, 18, 25, 27, 28, 29, 30, 32, 35, 37, 38, 39, 47, 52, 54, 55, 56, 57, 58, 59, 61, 62, 67, 68, 69, 70, 71, 78, 87, 89, 90, 91, 92, 93, 94, 98, 99, 103, 107

μίμησις, 61
μυθέομαι, 5
μυθολογέω, 5, 109
μυθολόγος, 5, 110
μῦθος, 3, 5, 7, 25, 26, 38, 39, 55, 56, 58, 59, 61, 62, 63, 67, 68, 69, 71, 73, 78, 87, 90, 91, 92, 93, 94, 97, 98, 103, 107

νόμος, 22, 27, 52, 91, 111
νοῦς, 32, 49

οὐσία, 36, 47, 48, 49

παραμυθέομαι, 5, 110
πρᾶγμα, 57

συναγωγή, 52, 53, 54, 55, 56, 58, 61
συνουσία, 14, 21, 23

τάξις, 82
τέλος, 30, 78
τέχνη, 42, 58, 65, 76

φιλοσοφία, 23, 31, 34, 35, 36, 110
φιλοτιμία, 23, 24, 29

ψυχή, 14, 43, 44
ψυχαγωγία, 57, 59

About the Author

Dr. Robert Zaslavsky received his BA in Philosophy and English from Temple University, and his MA and Ph.D. in Philosophy from the Graduate Faculty of the New School for Social Research. In addition, he has done graduate work in English at New York University and in education at Cabrini College. At Cabrini College, he served as interim Secondary Education Advisor (observing and evaluating student teachers).

In addition to his two decades of teaching Latin and Greek in private and public middle and high schools, he has taught courses in Literature, Religion, Psychology, Philosophy, History, Film, and Art History on the university level and in secondary private and public schools.

He has made presentations to the Southwest Conference on Language Teaching, the Texas Foreign Language Association, and the Florida Foreign Language Association on methods of teaching an inflected language for today's students and on teaching students learning and translation strategies. Furthermore, he has been a guest lecturer on Greek philosophy, on poetry, on methods of textual study, and on the Bible, Maimonides, Shakespeare, and Milton.

He is the author of *An Introductory Latin Course: A First Latin Grammar for Middle Schoolers, High Schoolers, College Students, Homeschoolers, and Self-Learners*; *Answer Key to Exercises for Zaslavsky's* An Introductory Latin Course; *Cornelii Taciti, De Vita Iulii Agricolae Liber*, student text, edited with introduction, notes, and literal translation; and *Platonic Myth and Platonic* Writing. In addition, he has published scholarly essays on Plato, Aristotle, classical philology, detective fiction, Shakespeare, and Homer. He has been a guest columnist for the Fort Worth Star-Telegram and the Fort Worth Weekly. He has contributed a regular column to the Atlanta (GA) weekly The Sunday Paper, writing on politics, technology, and education.

He has been a theater judge for the Suzi Bass Awards (Atlanta, GA).

He resides in Decatur, GA (USA).

His web site is www.doczonline.com.

Made in the USA
Middletown, DE
14 October 2021

50297720R00082